Professional Planting Design

AN ARCHITECTURAL AND HORTICULTURAL APPROACH FOR CREATING MIXED BED PLANTINGS

Scott C. Scarfone, ASLA

BICENTENNIAL
1807
WILEY
2007
BICENTENNIAL

John Wiley & Sons, Inc.

This book is printed on acid-free paper. ∞

Interior design by Joel Avirom and Jason Snyder
Photography and illustrations © Scott C. Scarfone except Figures 3.24a, 4.1, 4.2, and 4.9 © Stephanie Oberle

Published by John Wiley & Sons, Inc., Hoboken, New Jersey
Published simultaneously in Canada

For general information about our other products and services, please contact our Customer Care Department within the United States at (800) 762-2974, outside the United States at (317) 572-3993 or fax (317) 572-4002.

Wiley also publishes its books in a variety of electronic formats. Some content that appears in print may not be available in electronic books. For more information about Wiley products, visit our web site at www.wiley.com.

Library of Congress Cataloging-in-Publication Data

Scarfone, Scott C.
    Professional planting design : an architectural and horticultural approach for creating mixed bed plantings / by Scott C. Scarfone.
        p. cm.
    Includes bibliographical references.
    ISBN 978-0-4717-6139-6 (pbk.)
  1. Planting design.   2. Gardens—Design.   3. Landscape design.   I. Title.
    SB472.45.S23 2007
    712'.6—dc22

                                                                          2006022534

Printed in the United States of America

10 9

Contents

Acknowledgments

Many people, places, and events—too many to fully acknowledge—have led to the production of this book. I first and foremost must thank all of my teachers, mentors, colleagues, and clients, who have taught, instructed, and guided me in my learning and provided me with the opportunities to practice my craft.

I would like to thank all of the editorial staff at John Wiley & Sons for guiding me through the process, translating my drafts into stimulating prose, and in general for helping make this project a reality. Thank you to Colleen Bathon for the illustrations that illuminate and bring to life the concepts presented in this book. In addition, I would like to thank Will Hart for the cover and book jacket design and for assisting me wih the scanning and formatting of the photographs used in this book.

Last, but certainly not least, I would like to thank my wife, Paula. She selflessly tolerated me working many long nights and weekends, reviewed and edited countless drafts, and cared for our children, Isabella and newborn Sophia, while I disappeared into these pages—for this and her endless love, I am eternally grateful.

Foreword by James A. van Sweden

Scott Scarfone is unique among American landscape architects. He has a broad interest in plants, and knows how to use them so they look their best. His knowledge of both horticulture and architecture is evident in *Professional Planting Design*. Employing both creative and practical applications, he implements his knowledge in profound ways.

This book provides a thorough discussion of a subject that I have explored throughout my professional life—the elements of good planting design. After reading the book, you will be able to experiment with nature, and use its myriad of facets to make your own original statement. You will be ready to take risks and design exciting and original gardens.

I was captivated by the author's poetic discussions and beautifully illustrated chapters. The section "The Language of Design" in Chapter 3 is especially notable. Scarfone breaks down the subject of design into scale and proportion, balance, rhythm, unity, and variety. "Assembling the Abstract Composition" in Chapter 5 includes an eloquent discussion of plant form, texture, flower type, and ornamental characteristics. Utilizing suitable plant selections for a particular location is also discussed. Chapter 9, "Understanding the Planting Environment," imparts a nitty-gritty discussion about soils, growth behavior, and plant genetics. A clear understanding of these aspects is integral to planting and appreciating a successful garden.

In addition to providing a feast for the eyes and an abundant resource of food for thought, this book supplies the technical advice needed to guide you through the creation of your dream garden. But remember, with time comes change. Gardening takes patience—to listen, to watch, to touch, and to enjoy as the garden works its peaceful magic.

James A. van Sweden, FASLA
Oehme, van Sweden & Associates, Inc.
Washington, D.C.
October 2006

Foreword by Fergus Garrett

The mixed bed will have structure and height provided by trees and shrubs. It will have a wide range of shapes, forms, and flower colors from the vast assortment of perennials available on the market. Volunteering biennials can dance through the planting linking arms with everything else. Ephemeral annuals can be used in pockets to prolong the season. Bulbs come and go, showing themselves at opportune moments before melting underground. Climbers can scramble over neighbors covering up dull characteristics and can also clamber up supports, taking up very little lateral space while providing columns of color.

Plantings can have movement or be stiff and architectural. They can be tropical, colorful, harmonious, or seminaturalist. Their flexible nature makes it possible to achieve schemes that are relatively low-maintenance. These types would lean heavily on more static elements like trees and shrubs, whereas high input–high output versions will favor ephemerals like annuals and half-hardy plants and will also rely on bedding out within a permanent framework. The ratio of one to the other depends entirely on your requirements.

In this book, Scarfone analyzes the mixed bed and its evolution, role, and function in the garden and landscape. He looks into maintenance factors, the role of succession, and the elements of composition. Practical matters, such as calculating the bed depth, infilling, and identifying positions for structural plants, are all covered. *Professional Planting Design* is analytical and inspiring, tackling the subject matter in a unique fashion by examining aspects through the eyes of a designer. The principles of design and design theory are linked with the world of the plantsmen. Complex but fascinating, the subject is pertinent for people who wish to train the eye to perceive line, form, color, rhythm, and balance, as well as recognize aesthetic qualities in a landscape and in turn, weave personal ideas and sentiments into a design of their own.

Fergus Garrett
Head Gardener, Great Dixter Gardens
Northiam, Rye
East Sussex
England
October 2006

Introduction

IMAGINE A PLANTING WHERE PERENNIALS are permitted to lean on shrubs, bulbs are planted to punch through annuals, vines are encouraged to climb small trees, tenders are placed in voids, tropicals are interspersed throughout, and self-seeders are allowed to remain where they sprout. In this same landscape, envision seasonal plants supported by a cast of more permanent plants—perhaps large deciduous shrubs or small trees. These serve as the backbone, or structure, for the composition which, in turn, "carry" the space during down seasons. Plants that have long off-seasons are strategically positioned so as not to disrupt the overall balance when they are underperforming.

This is the high art of mixed planting. When done successfully, it represents the pinnacle of planting design—it becomes a living work of art.

For centuries, humans captivated by the allure of plants have attempted to capture their beauty in words or pictures, doing their best to portray the subtleties of combinations of colors and textures in prose or paint. The French realist painter Gustave Courbet said, "The beautiful is in nature, and it is encountered in the most diverse forms of reality. Once it is found, it belongs to art, or, rather, to the artist who discovers it." No matter how eloquent the words or adept the artwork, however, nothing can compare with the *feeling* of place created by plantings and nature by actually participating in the scene. Sensory pleasures derived from beautiful plantings, especially mixed compositions, produce immediate reactions and require little of the participant because the human connection is instinctive. Experiencing the many moods of a garden and nature can have a profound, positive effect on the human mind and body.

This pleasure is also perceptual. Depending on the state of mind of the participant, these perceptual sensations may be emotional or intellectual, deriving from the composition the physical components of the scenery—line, form, texture, color, rhythm, and balance. All humans perceive these naturally, but without formal training in design, few have a conceptual awareness of these elements or the role that they play in eliciting such responses. Fortunately, the untrained eye and mind can be taught and conditioned to recognize the aesthetic qualities in the landscape that trigger such responses from humans. This awareness makes it possible for professionals, those trained in planting design, to re-create those conditions that elicit such responses from humans in a plant composition.

For a designer to develop mixed plantings that form artistic compositions, he or she must have the skills necessary to effectively select, modify, and arrange plants and plant compositions in the landscape, either to re-create a mood inspired by nature or to create a desired mood. In this way, the practice of planting design becomes the practice of a visual art.

Therein lies the focus of this book: the *artful design* of mixed plantings that create an ever-changing succession of interest in a landscape. Whether you are a serious gardener, an aspiring designer, a horticulturist, or a landscape architect, these pages will show you, first, how to *think* about the planting design process; then you'll learn practical techniques for developing mixed planting compositions in the landscape and selecting plants that evolve and succeed one another over time.

The design process described in *Professional Planting Design: An Architectural and Horticultural Approach for Creating Mixed Plantings* is simple and forthright—it clearly and concisely uncovers the principles of design theory and design linking them to solid horticulture. You'll see these concepts come to life through photographs, process diagrams, elevation drawings, and perspective sketches, all designed to illustrate the process for developing mixed plantings.

A primary concept described in this book, which is based on a pragmatic process for analyzing horticultural, functional, and aesthetic objectives, is the importance of specifying *plant characteristics*—as opposed to choosing individual plants—that meet both the physical aesthetic and horticultural requirements (soil types, exposure, spatial, and size limitations, etc.) for the planting composition. *Professional Planting Design* will give the necessary background in planting design principles to help you develop the ability to visualize and diagram abstract planting compositions, to specify plant characteristics and horticultural requirements. This knowledge will enable you to successfully choose and combine small trees, shrubs, perennials, grasses, climbers, bulbs, annuals, tropicals, and ground covers to create harmonious mixed plantings in the landscape that provide a succession of interest throughout the seasons.

Planting Design: A Unique Design Profession

Throughout my career I have had the good fortune to work with a variety of professionals—contractors, nursery staff, horticulturists, gardeners, designers, and landscape architects. Too often, however, I've found that individual professionals generally will focus on one particular aspect of plant design—either the plants or the design. This is understandable because it is difficult to become fully adept in both, and lines drawn between professions are often rigid, hence difficult to cross—it takes a conscious effort and ongoing study and observation. Thus, an individual who has developed the skills, knowledge, and expertise in both plants and design is special.

It is ironic that this line between expertise in plants and design is drawn because you can't possibly begin planting design without knowing and understanding the requirements of your medium—in this case, the plants—and without thoroughly understanding design principles. Gertrude Jekyll (1843-1932), the influential British garden designer, wrote in her book *Colour in the Flower Garden* (first published in 1908), "I am strongly of the opinion that the possession of a quantity of plants, however good the plants may be themselves and however ample the number, does not make a garden; it only makes a collection. Having got the plants, the great thing is to use them with careful selection and definite intention."

Planting design is different from other design professions in that we are designing, using living entities that respond to their environment and which change over time. They are growing, changing, environmentally interactive organisms. Plants, plant communities, and planting compositions are in constant states of flux, responding to their surroundings and influenced by their physical environment. The weather affects their growth rate, form, foliage density, and flower and fruit production. Sun exposure, quality of the soil, relationship to neighboring plants—which may introduce shade or competition for soil nutrients and water—also affects a plant's performance. These factors, which are external to plants, are beyond our control, yet we must learn how to work with them.

Environmental stimuli influence the genetic program of a plant, and each one will respond differently. Growth cycles vary widely among plant types, from the natural rhythms, such as the opening and closing of flowers, to the emergence of new foliage and the changing of color in the fall as plants prepare themselves for winter dormancy. Plant designers must be able to fully understand and take advantage of the changing nature of their medium, and that requires a carefully trained eye capable of noticing the myriad factors that influence a landscape or a garden and the plants that fill it. Designers need to understand the distinctive characteristics of each stage in the life cycle of the plants they are using and how environmental factors will influence and affect those living entities.

Equally important in the approach to planting design is the need to understand the architectural and design component of the planting design "equation." Principles of design are not new and are the result of centuries of conscious study and application to a variety of man-made elements from architecture to interior design to flower arranging. Regardless of the medium, harmonious compositions are achieved through the use of the principles of, among others, repetition, variety, balance, emphasis, sequence, and scale. Planting design particularly underlies the processes of combining planting elements, developing color schemes, and, ultimately, forming planting compositions.

All visual art forms, including planting design, can be analyzed using these principles. In practice, they become the physical manifestation of a common universal language and, as such, help us to understand the ordering of the visual elements inherent in any design. The resultant visual effects can be perceived by anyone, regardless of training, culture, or personal experience. But it takes training and an understanding of these principles to be able to analyze the visual "grammar" underlying a planting composition and to identify what exactly creates the perceived beauty. A good general place to start to gain this training is an art appreciation class, where a designer can begin to really "see" and to understand the significance of what he or she is looking at. More specifically, a student about to enter the design field will learn the principles of design and elements of composition, to help him or her develop the critical skills necessary to understand what makes a landscape beautiful, and how they can then use those skills to create their own works of art.

Practicing the Art of Mixed Planting Design

As described, planting design is a visual experience, both in how we apply the plants to the landscape and how we interpret it. It is the physical representation of the principles of design and elements of composition as expressed through the use of plants. Planting design as a visual art can be described as a three-part practice: *ability*, *process,* and *product*. According to Lois Fichner-Rathus in her book, *Understanding Art* (1986), as *ability,* it is our capacity as humans to create beautiful environments; as *process*, it is the act of creating; and as a *product*, art is the completed design.

ABILITY

To create an artistic composition in the landscape, planting designers must be able to both understand the complexities of a particular site and its context to the surrounding landscape and utilize plants to reinforce the spatial and structural aspects of the design in a beautiful and harmonious manner. Designers must also be able to project their own experiences and feelings into the designs they create, through the medium of plants as applied to the landscape. To achieve this, designers need the ability to first perceive and then respond to a number of visual elements—line, shape, form, texture, and color. They must have a firm understanding of the materials being used so that they can systematically apply those materials to a landscape to create the desired visual effect.

At the same time, designers are required to address the needs or program of their clients and functionally solve the problems of the site. Planting design, then, is much more than artistic expression; it is also a problem-solving undertaking, one in which the designer applies artistic principles to a set of given criteria to create the artistic composition.

PROCESS

As noted, art techniques can be taught and learned. Whether carving a piece of sculpture from a block of marble or painting a picture on a blank canvas, there are steps and techniques (the process) specific to the medium being used that aid the designer or artist in producing a finished work of art. Planting designers follow a systematic process that leads them to transform a barren or overgrown site into a richly planted landscape or garden.

This process must always begin with assembling the facts—that is, conducting a "survey" of the site whose results will affect how the designer will proceed. These results are related to the existing conditions of the site, as well as to the client's design program (the desired elements to be included or objectives of the design). The second step requires that the designer begin to make value judgments about the effects of various site components against the client's program. This is the "analysis" phase of the process. The third step, or "synthesis" phase, requires that the results of the previous two steps be evaluated in order to formulate a comprehensive solution (Rutledge 1985). It is this third step, which actually comprises a series of sub-steps, that is the primary topic of this book, for it is during this part of the process that the principles of the art of planting design will be applied.

It is important to point out that the process must always remain flexible, so that the designer has the freedom to apply his or her skill and knowledge to the best effects possible. A designer's natural artistic inclination, knowledge of the medium, and experience in the profession will all be significant variables in the developing and refining that process. Every designer will develop a particular method of structuring the process. Some prefer to make decisions before they begin actual implementation, while others are more comfortable moving from one step to another in what would appear to be a random process. Regardless of the individual process, fundamentally it will be based on envisioning, then weighing, possibilities. As renowned landscape architect and environmental planner John Ormsbee Simonds said in *Landscape Architecture—A Manual of Site Planning and Design* (1983), it is "an empathetic process—a creative act of the intellect."

PRODUCT

The final stage of the process is, of course, the resultant composition of plants in the landscape. In that composition every object is viewed in relation to every other object, because unlike other forms of art, planting design is *participatory*. The design comprises a series of spaces choreographed to elicit sensual and emotional responses from the participants. The plants used to construct these spaces should have texture, fragrance, and color, emanating from a variety of individual plant attributes. The composition, like a gallery in a museum, is to be walked through and seen from many different angles. No object in the composition will be viewed in isolation from one another. Moreover, this is a composition that will constantly evolve—daily, seasonally, annually. But though its appearance will never look the same, it will always be a place designed for work, play, rest, or pleasure.

Throughout the pages of this book, you will be led through a process that builds a planting composition from the ground up. Through detailed discussion of the principles of design, you will gain an understanding of not only how to look at a planting composition and "see" how it is working, but you will be able to create one on your own. Once you have mastered these basic principles, your craft will become a life-long process of observation and creation in the quest to create planting compositions that make a sensual and emotional impact on the viewer 365 days a year.

1 | Mixed Planting Basics

THE STRENGTH OF A MIXED PLANTING is its ability to extend the beauty of the composition from one season to the next, so that winter and spring can be as beautiful as high summer. By layering plants it is possible for one plant to, essentially, take over for another, creating varying interest in the same spot throughout the year to reflect the uniqueness of each season. The objective is to create a *succession* of *interest* from *foliage, form,* or *flowers*—the three F's—whose characteristics will change with the seasons.

Mixed plantings never use plants in isolation. Rather, plants are always chosen for their ability to be "good neighbors"—how well they coordinate with the color, texture, and form of others. Each plant does, however, maintain its own individual character. In successful mixed plantings there is always a balance between the plants as a grouping and each plant as a specific point of interest.

Mixing and Matching

In designing mixed plantings, the goal is to interweave a variety of plant types to get the best value and visual impact out of the available planting area over the longest period of time. We are striving to create plantings that display a wide range of textural, color, and seasonal effects that continually evolve in appearance throughout the year (see color plates, Figure 1.1). Thus, a mixed planting generally will contain an eclectic mix of vegetative and floral types assembled in varying degrees and percentages. A mixed planting might combine, for example, small trees, shrubs, evergreens, grasses, perennials, bulbs, climbers, annuals, and tropicals to maximize and extend the visual impact throughout the seasons. Clearly, no single plant type can achieve this.

But it is not just the variety of plant types that make mixed plantings so visually interesting—it is the evolution of the characteristics of the individual plants throughout their seasons of growth. So, seasonal layering of these various characteristics also can serve to extend interest throughout the season. It is the progression of time, coupled with an emphasis on the seasonality of the plantings, that provides the magic. As one plant characteristic fades, another blossoms; one plant dominates in one season, then fades into the background in the next. The challenge of creating successful mixed plantings is to first capture, then maximize, the power of that phenomenon. This challenge is what separates planting design from all other design media.

SUCCESSIONAL GROWTH

As noted above, a primary objective of mixed planting design is to ensure ongoing interest in the planting area. *Successional growth* refers to the pairing of plants in a sequence so that as one plant fades a neighbor is just entering into its prime. Timing is of the essence here: The growth sequence must be carefully programmed. And this applies not only to flowering plants but to any principle aesthetic function that is expected of a plant. Needless to say, accomplishing this would be easy if we focused on a single time of year, in particular late spring and mid- to late-summer, when most of the commonly known plants are in high bloom and everything is contributing to peak performance. But remember, the point of a successful mixed planting is to reach peak performance levels of various plants 365 days a year. To ensure the aesthetic objectives of the mixed-bed planting style are met requires a designer to have:

▷ Knowledge of plants and their characteristics

▷ An understanding of climatic conditions

▷ Being informed on the capabilities of the stewards of the landscape

▷ Grasp of the clients' objectives or goals of the project

▷ Horticultural awareness of existing cultural conditions

▷ Keen understanding of the basic principles of design and composition

Understanding the context and objective for the mixed planting in the landscape will better enable the designer to create mixed plantings that meet the requirements of all involved—least to say the plants.

Evolution of a Planting Style

EARLY MIXED-BED PRINCIPLES: WILLIAM ROBINSON

The concept of mixed plantings is not new. Some of the earliest principles on mixed-bed plantings were espoused by gardener and journalist William Robinson (1838–1935) in his book *The English Flower Garden*, first published in 1883. In it, he specified a variety of methods to combine shrubbery with perennial and ground-cover plants. Robinson suggested that mixed plantings are best created "in naturally disposed groups, never repeating the same plant along the border at intervals." He further recommended, "Do not graduate the plants in height from front to back . . . but sometimes let a bold plant come to the edge; and, on the other hand, let a little carpet of a dwarf plant pass in here and there to the back, as to give a varied instead of a monotonous surface." His philosophies were considered revolutionary at the time, when formal interpretations of Italian and Dutch gardens were in vogue and the bedding-out of annuals was the dominant form of planting with flowers.

GERTRUDE JEKYLL AT MUNSTEAD WOOD

Similarly, Gertude Jekyll (1843-1932), who experimented at her home at Munstead Wood in England in the late 1890s, employed mixed planting techniques " . . . where the copse and garden meet." There, natural stands of birch were thinned and supported with carefully placed groups of rhododendrons, to form the backdrop for drifts of ferns, hosta, and dicentra. It was here that she began to lay the foundation for her now-famous design principles. Thin strips, irregular patches, and drifts (massings) of individual plant types characterized her plantings (see Figure 1.2). Massings were interwoven so that their "tail" disappeared as it moved into the neighboring drift. Specimen plants were located at strategic points to add an element of excitement and to serve as points of emphasis. The concept of the repetitive flow of these drifts revolutionized the philosophy of planting design. But Jekyll's predominant focus was on greater percentages of perennials—mainly to achieve desired color effects.

CHRISTOPHER LLOYD AND GREAT DIXTER

More recently, Christopher Lloyd (1921–2006) evolved a modern interpretation of mixed plantings at his home and garden, Great Dixter, in south England (see Figure 1.3). More than six decades of experimenting led to his philosophy of succession, with mixed plantings at the core. Christo, as he was affectionately called by friends, together with his head gardener, Fergus Garrett, took the high art of the mixed planting to an extreme. They believed that the secret to creating captivating and ever-changing displays is in the extensive use of hardy and tender perennials, as well as bulbs, annuals, and biennials to supplement seasonal color displays. These plants are all added to beds where more permanent anchor plants have been carefully located. As such: perennials are permitted to lean on shrubs; bulbs are planted to punch through annuals; vines are encouraged to climb small trees; tenders are placed in voids;

Figure 1.2.
A border plan developed by Gertrude Jekyll, showing the irregular drifting of plant masses.

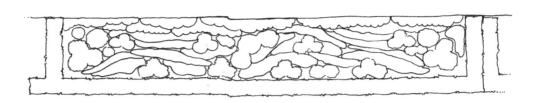

Figure 1.3
The sunken
garden at Great
Dixter in England
illustrates the
extreme in mixed-
bed compositions.

tropicals are interspersed throughout; and self-seeders, selectively edited, are permitted to remain where they sprout. This is mixed planting design and gardening at its pinnacle.

At Great Dixter, mixed planting is an adjunct to good gardening. It requires careful observation over time, to meticulously scrutinize individual plants as well as collective performance. Every plant type imaginable to the modern gardener has been used liberally. The result: a revolving display of a variety of plant characteristics all year long. Christo said the objective "is to keep the show going for as long as possible, with one highlight immediately succeeded by another." The garden never looks the same. This style, of course, requires a very intensive gardening regime, backed by deep horticultural knowledge and a very high level of maintenance, which most landscape managers and gardeners do not have the time or expertise to sustain over time.

CHANTICLEER AND THE NATIONAL SCULPTURE GARDEN

Other interpretations of mixed plantings can be seen in varying degrees of complexity and with alternating percentages of plant types at Chanticleer, a public garden outside Philadelphia, Pennsylvania. Gardener and horticulturist Dan Benarcik relies heavily on the use of tropicals and annuals in one area of the temperate climate garden (see color plates, Figures 1.4 a and b). Seasonal plantings garner support from permanent Zone 6 plantings, which include flowering trees, small and cut-back shrubs, and perennials. The garden's framework is founded on regionally hardy plantings, but the overall composition is enhanced with tropicals, annuals, cacti, and succulents. This, too, is an intensive way of gardening.

In contrast, the plantings at the National Sculpture Garden in Washington, D.C., designed by the landscape architectural office of the Olin Partnership in Philadelphia, Pennsylvania, use more permanent plantings that consist of massings of perennials, shrubs, and ground covers. To add focal points of interest, specimen flowering and evergreen trees are interspersed throughout. The trees, aside from the bed edges, give structure and help to form spaces. The infill mix of hardy perennials, shrubs, and ground covers represent planting types better suited for larger, more public landscapes. These generally require less maintenance than the previous garden examples illustrate. The plantings at the National Sculpture Garden illustrate that mixed plantings can be successful when only a few plant types are used in large masses. It also demonstrates that the selection of plant species, cultivars, and varieties are paramount to success, for the plants here are all superior cultivars of hardy species that have exceptional ornamental characteristics. Many have extended or longer-than-average flower periods; bold foliage, texture, or foliage color; and a variety of characteristics that change the appearance of the plant as the growing season progresses (see Figure 1.5).

Figure 1.5
A mixed composition at the National Sculpture Garden planted with large blocks of hardy species of perennials, shrubs, and trees.

Mixed-bed plantings can thus vary in their degree of complexity, from a few plant types interwoven with bold massings to a menagerie of choreographed plants. The more types of plants that compose the mix, the greater the design and horticultural skill will be required to achieve the desired successional effect. Additionally, an appropriate level of maintenance will be necessary to ensure that the design intent will be sustained over time. A mixed planting that is overly designed for the level of maintenance it will receive can rapidly deteriorate into a jumbled mess. In summary, the mix and number of plant types used must be appropriate to both the planting area and maintenance available.

The Theory Behind Mixed Plantings: The Role of Dynamism and Diversity

Too often, mass expanses of monotonous ground covers or evergreens are used unimaginatively in the landscape; when sheared by untrained gardeners they become nothing more than dreary colonies of junipers, forsythia, or azaleas. In such compositions, typically "fallback" plants have been selected—those most durable and most commonly known to the less experienced or knowledgeable designer—generally due to the misconception that plants with special or unique seasonal characteristics are difficult to grow or maintain.

Though it is true that many plants fit into the category of high-maintenance—requiring deadheading, cutting back, pruning, dividing, etc.—there are just as many plants whose unique attributes need minimal horticultural attention. Certainly, the level of maintenance that will be available for a particular landscape must be a consideration when choosing which plant types to use and the extent of planting for each type. This should not be an excuse, however, to limit the use of a *diverse* range of available plants. It is possible, even when using masses of evergreen and deciduous plants, to vary the aesthetic by adding herbaceous plants and providing accent with ornamental grasses and spring and summer-flowering bulbs. These plants will add a softer, more colorful, and seasonal dimension to an otherwise uninteresting composition.

The ephemeral qualities of plants should serve as the philosophical pretext behind the mixed plantings we design. Designers should cultivate and capitalize on an appreciation for each plant as it progresses through its life stages during the seasons. In short, we must strive to capture and present the best in each plant. Understanding how a plant evolves over time, both as an individual and in relation to other plants, is critical component to succeeding at succession. This can only be accomplished by the judicious selection of superior plants to support, complement, and emphasize one another as they progress from one season to the next. Trees, shrubs, climbers, ground covers, perennials, grasses, bulbs, tropicals, and annuals all can be combined at different levels to create rich and interesting mixed plantings. It is plant diversity working in a cohesive manner that contributes to a beautiful and memorable experience in the mixed planting composition.

It is also essential to take advantage of the *dynamism* of plants. They change color, texture, opaqueness, and overall character, often within one season's growth. The crux of good planting design lies in the ability to work with this aspect and exploit it to the fullest. It is these dynamic qualities that enable us to create the aesthetic we are looking for. But we must pay particular attention to the growth of plants—specifically, how they develop, change, and evolve over time.

Of course, the dynamism of plants also makes them more challenging to use effectively, whether because of the brevity of the blossom on one, for example, or the dramatic alteration in appearance of another over the course of the season. As designers, we must be concerned not only with how plants will appear and function at their peak, but also the role they will play throughout the remainder of the year; we must learn how to choose, place, and overlap plants based on seasonal attributes. These are some of the issues we will explore throughout the course of the book.

Our goal is to properly design a mixed planting so that it provides a strikingly different appearance as plants emerge, leaf out, bloom, transition into fall, and lie dormant in winter. We must choose and place each plant to have a particular effect—whether en masse or as individual specimens—based on their ability to play an appropriate role in a particular season or series of seasons. It may be a plant's shape or the berries it produces, or its seed heads, bark, flowers, leaf color or texture, or fall color or winter interest that dictates how we place each plant within the overall composition to function as part of a collective scene or to provide accent as an individual or group of individuals. In summary, proper mixed plantings should provide:

Visual interest The planting composition should be engaging and hold the attention of the observer. The variation of the plants' height, depth, texture, and color are combined to stimulate the senses. Care must be taken not overwhelm, to create a menagerie of individuals. Rather, a core framework must be established to "hold plantings," such as theme plants or massings of evergreens. These massings should then be intertwined with a variety of plant types to become a living tapestry of textures and colors.

Seasonal variety Plantings should vary in appearance over time and change with the seasons. Continually evolving sequences of floral and foliar events should take place one after the other. This need not require vast numbers of individual changes, but rather a continual evolution of change through the year.

Support to neighboring plants All plants have a "downtime," so it is essential to have a basic framework to serve as a backdrop or setting against which adjacent plantings can "rise and fall," to display their best seasonal attributes throughout the growing season. Careful placement of "friendly neighbors" will either complement other plants during their bloom time or will take over for them as they fade.

Throughout the course of this book we will examine how a variety of plants can be combined to create interesting effects throughout the seasons, and how levels of different plant types and varieties can be accommodated without sacrificing durability.

Making the Most of the Mix

Creating mixed plantings is a sophisticated form of planting design that, as stated previously, requires both a comprehensive understanding of design and thorough knowledge of plants. To be successful at this form of design, we must keep in mind that, with few exceptions, plants have a number of seasonal attributes, not just one brief period of "show," and that the exceptions should be reserved to function as structural plants for the composition.

Using plants with multiple seasons of interest also enables us to maximize the square footage of bed space we have to work with, which is very important to creating a successful mixed planting. When we select plants with multiple attributes, we can extend the period of visual excitement. The plants we choose must have a sustained length of performance, so we must leave behind plants that normally bloom for a seven- to ten-day period in favor of new and improved cultivars that bloom for fourteen- to twenty-day periods. We must also be sure to include in the composition plants that have beautiful flowers, bold and colorful foliage, strong form, and attractive seed heads or berries.

But choosing plants that look good is only the beginning. Behind any good design is solid horticulture, meaning that the plants look and are as healthy. That requires meeting the plants' cultural requirement for soil composition, moisture, and nutrient content. While it is not uncommon to modify some of these conditions, over the long term the plants will be better served if the existing conditions form the basis for the selection of plants.

Although we have been talking a lot about choosing the right plants in a mixed planting design, it is in fact the last step in the design process and will be detailed in later chapters. In preparation, we first need to delve into the other functions of plants, beyond creating beauty for ornamental value or art's sake.

The Role of Plant Functionality in Design

Many, perhaps most, of the functions that plants serve have a practical purpose as well as an aesthetic one. For example, some serve as physical barriers to control pedestrian traffic, or to minimize glare and screen objectionable views; others help to prevent soil erosion. In short, plants play a functional role in the landscape to improve our environment and to protect and support the functions of nature.

When designed well, a planting composition is an expression of the function and the needs of both the site and the users. Depending on whether the site is in a natural setting, on private property, in an intensively used landscape, or in an urban center, the uses will vary from site to site and client to client, and may include domestic activities, play, work, study or contemplation, and active or passive recreation. One thing they have in common: All require a functional and aesthetic environment that responds to the individual site and accommodates the purpose. It must provide, among other elements, the right amount of open space for the intended use, the right microclimate (e.g., shade or sun), and the right aesthetic character.

As designers, we must train our eyes and minds to view all landscapes pragmatically; from this vantage point, we will see that most landscapes are poorly designed and even more poorly maintained. Too often, planting design is done by nonprofessionals, whose love for plants may be genuine but whose understanding of design and knowledge of horticulture are sorely lacking. That is why we see plants located where they will grow too large for the space they occupy and crowd sidewalks or hide buildings, or plants that block or interfere with attractive views, block critical sight lines, or break up areas of usable space. Ultimately the plants in these instances become disfigured, unattractive, and a nuisance—and lead to increased maintenance costs or are a safety hazard.

Mixed Planting Bed Functions

The most successful use of plants comes when we, as designers, fully understand both the artistic and the functional value that plants can add to the project. This comes from asking questions such as:

▷ Do we fully understand the habitat where the plants will be placed?

▷ How will people use and participate in the landscape?

▷ What will be the planting and construction process?

  ▷   What level of maintenance can and will be provided? Are the assigned stewards capable of effectively maintaining the plantings?

These questions should make clear that mixed planting beds are part of a comprehensively planned landscape; they are not, generally, stand-alone features. Typically, this principle is not emphasized strongly enough, frequently designers and gardeners think that design is only about plant combinations. The form that a mixed planting bed can take will be as variable as the plants available to fill it. Likewise, the function will vary, depending on the role it plays in the overall landscape.

The intensity of the plantings within the particular mixed bed will depend on the purpose of the bed and the level of maintenance available to maintain it. For example, a mixed planting designed as a focal point in an overall garden composition will have significantly more varieties of plant types, texture, and color than would, say, a mixed planting intended as a backdrop for a sculpture. A rule of thumb is that the more impact a bed will need to make in the garden or landscape, the more diverse the plantings within the bed should be.

By understanding the possible roles mixed planting compositions can serve in the overall landscape, we will learn to use plants to their fullest potential. The purpose of plants, whether used individually or in groups, falls into three categories: *architectural, aesthetic*, or *functional*.

Here are some of the ways mixed plantings can be used to carry out those purposes:

As an artistic composition Here the designer or gardener can express his or her creativity through the use of plants. Beds created as an artistic composition are usually located in high-visibility zones or impact areas within an overall landscape or specific garden setting set aside for this purpose (see color plates, Figure 1.6). Located in a garden compartment or room these intensively gardened areas are created for the sole purpose of artistic expression; they are meant to be visual showpieces. Generally, they are labors of love and are intended to be intensively gardened—modified and refined over time.

As focal points These are small areas or zones located in the larger landscape at special points of interest. They are specifically designed to be an attraction as a point in space or to highlight an element or object—a piece of sculpture, an entrance to a building or special garden area—or to be an element itself. Focal points tend to be highlights of a garden or landscape and are generally more intensively planted with a greater variety of plant types than surrounding areas (see color plates, Figures 1.7 a and b).

For spatial organization This is a fundamental principle used to create enclosure in the landscape. Mixed plantings can be used as a form of garden "architecture" to create outdoor "rooms." Walls, ceilings, and floors can all be created by the judicious use of plant material.

The creation of space in this way is dependent on the actual or implied enclosure, and can be accomplished by modifying the vertical, overhead, or ground planes. Plants can be used to imply spatial definition through variations in height and material types (e.g., tree canopies, low vs. high shrubs, etc.). Plus, bed edges can suggest limits of space that can be further reinforced by the plantings contained within them (see color plates, Figure 1.8).

As buffer plantings Buffer plantings create, define, and screen edges. Visual barriers or buffer plantings can be created to screen objectionable views or direct the viewer toward a more desirable "framed" view. As such, buffer plantings are designed to accomplish functional objectives in an overall planting scheme. But a buffer's functional use can also become an aesthetic amenity by using a variety of plant materials with various colors, textures, and shapes (see color plates, Figure 1.9).

As backdrop plantings Used as a backdrop, plantings provide a visual foil between two areas to create a setting for an object or to stage a space for a foreground use of special interest. For this purpose, plants should be selected to minimize the potential visual competition between the foreground, the point of emphasis, and the background. Thus, the background mixed planting should have a relatively even color and texture and a minimal variety of plant types (see Figure 1.10).

Mixed Planting Bed Types

The size, shape, location, and purpose of a mixed planting bed is one of the first things you must consider when you are planning a garden or landscape. It is here where all of the plantings will be located. In most instances, however, the beds are not just places to put plants; they also perform a variety of functions that give shape and character to an overall landscape. We will discuss bed layout principles more in Chapter 6, page 125.

In addition to understanding the artistic and functional value of plants in a mixed-bed setting, we, as designers, need to familiarize ourselves with the roles of various mixed planting bed types, so that we may put them to their best use. These types include: borders, landscape beds, feature beds, islands, and edge or screen beds, which are discussed in turn.

BORDERS

Traditionally one of the most common types of mixed bed, borders were first popularized in England in the late twentieth century and they continue to be a favorite form today. Border beds tend to be rectangular and usually follow the lines of a hedge or a wall. The depth of the

Figure 1.10
This low mixed planting provides a backdrop for the sculpture at the National Sculpture Garden.

bed is consistent along the entire length and can range from between three to twelve feet, though the exact measure will be based on the space available and the intent of the overall design.

Narrower borders limit the amount of planting types due to the restriction of allowable planting depth. Therefore, predominantly small shrubs, smaller perennials, small grasses, ground covers, bulbs, and small annual plants are appropriate for narrow borders. As the depth of the border increases so, too, does the possibility for greater variety in the plantings and, consequently, a more diverse effect. Additional types of plant materials can be added. The greater the depth of the border, the greater height can be achieved, as the two are generally related to one another.

Border plantings are linear elements, and as such will generally lead the eye to a terminal point, even when the plantings within the overall composition are highly varied. By their very nature, linear plantings have a somewhat specialized and narrow purpose within a design. A border, as the name implies, is best suited for edges or long narrow planting areas, such as space perimeters, foundation bases, walls, fences, or hedges. In these areas, a border provides a transition between the horizontal and vertical planes and functions best when the movement desired is from one end of the garden to the other. The pace at which the observer traverses the space will depend on the intensity of the border plantings; for example, a very intense array will slow the pace by providing an array of colors, textures, and visual depth and height, to maintain interest (see color plates, Figure 1.11).

LANDSCAPE BEDS

Landscape beds, considered the general "workhorse" planting element, are the most commonly found in our landscapes and gardens. They are used to create spaces, soften architecture, direct movement either visually or physically, emphasize, or contain. Their design objectives are both functional and aesthetic. Landscape beds also can provide links to various site elements, effectively tying the garden or landscape together. They are planted to provide general enhancement of routes of passage through space. Sequential opening or closing, and increasing or decreasing the height, density, and width of the planting, can add richness to a landscape. Very flexible design elements, landscape beds can be effective as foundation plantings or as part of a larger garden plan; they can provide edge definition or buffering, or simply provide spaces for ornamental plantings (see color plates, Figure 1.12).

FEATURE BEDS

Historically, feature beds were component parts of larger specialized gardens, usually located within a framework of architecture (e.g., walls, courtyards, building massings), or central to spaces or "rooms" created by other landscape beds. These beds are generally focal points in a particular type of garden and so are often themed with a certain color or planting style. Feature beds can be both island plantings or linked to backdrop planting beds, which usually form the structure or framework of a particular garden. Feature bed plantings are usually dominant to the surrounding plantings (see color plates, Figure 1.13).

ISLANDS

Islands are freestanding beds that are either surrounded by lawn or hard-paved surfaces. There are no backdrops to island plantings, making them visible from all sides. Islands are often used to break up larger expanses of lawn, creating smaller areas of interest. Island plantings can link disparate elements of a landscape, such as irregularly located groupings of existing trees, or associate architectural elements such as outbuildings or structures together.

Island beds should be developed with consideration to the scale of the larger landscape. The size of the island should be in proportion to its surroundings. Care must be also given to the size and type of the plants chosen for use inside the island. The overall size of the island bed itself will dictate the criteria for the selection of the plants. The shape of islands can vary, but should follow the style or theme of the surrounding bed types (see color plates, Figure

1.14). Organic shapes tend to work best in larger gardens or open spaces, while formal geometric shapes function best in smaller spaces or those contained by a larger formal shape (see color plates, Figure 1.15).

EDGE OR SCREEN BEDS

Edge or screen beds are those that buffer landscape and garden areas from adjacent properties or garden areas that are considered unattractive in a viewshed, or are otherwise undesirable. Created for utilitarian purposes, screen beds provide a welcome opportunity to create visual excitement in what are normally rows of dreary evergreen plantings. Edge plantings can also create architectural spaces within a garden.

The extent to which these beds are developed into mixed plantings depends on the intended use of and objective for the space where they will be planted. Care should be exercised not to create a too-highly ornamented planting at the edges and distract from the main focal point of the garden. Thus, the level or amount of planting types will need to be minimized so that the purpose of the space is not overridden by the edge. That said, there are situations where the edge of a property will need definition. Screen beds in such cases offer an opportunity to incorporate mixed plantings as a method of presenting variety and generating excitement. This makes for a much more interesting planting than one comprising only evergreens, trees, and shrubs (see color plates, Figure 1.9).

Cultural and Maintenance Considerations as Part of the Design Process

Before we can begin to design a mixed planting, it is critical to understand the level of horticultural care that the composition will require as a whole, as well as from an individual species and plant variety viewpoint. Simply put, the success or failure of the entire composition depends on it. Proper plant selection and plant maintenance begin with in-depth knowledge of a site's cultural conditions.

Soil types and mechanical composition (sand, silt, clay percentage), mineral and nutrient content, soil moisture, and exposure to sun and wind are all horticultural factors that will affect plant performance. Deep and fertile soils afford endless design opportunities for a wide range of plants, whereas infertile soils (usually light and thin) lose moisture and nutrients quickly, making for a very challenging growing environment. Sandy soils lose water quickly, while clayey soils hold on to water for long periods. Exposure to sun and shade will further narrow the selection of plants. Fortunately for designers, the types of plants that can be used in each of these distinct conditions have been well documented.

Once we understand the cultural aspect of planting design, we can then turn our attention to the composition of planting types. The composition will, in part, determine the level of maintenance required. Generally speaking, the more plant types we include the greater the maintenance level and skill required. As stated previously, evergreens, shrubs, and ground covers are the most common planting types used for simple mixed-bed plantings because they typically require little maintenance. By selecting such durable plant types our designs will need the least amount of upkeep and have the best chance of success. Add more plant types to the mix (perennials, grasses, annuals, etc.) and the equation becomes more complex, thus increasing the effort and skill required to maintain such plantings. Another complicating factor is that within any one set of plant types are select groups of species and cultivars that are more durable than others. For example, the iris, daylily, and peony are all perennials that have proven to be quite durable. These plants return year after year with little care. Among durable shrubs that require little attention once they have established are, for example, the juniper, fothergilla, and clethera.

Clearly, the composition of our plantings—the amount of plant types (shrubs, perennials, grasses, etc.) as well as specific species and cultivars within each plant type—is strongly correlated to the level of attention and care the mixed planting will receive. For inexperienced gardeners or for those unable to ensure a high level of care, the general guideline is to minimize the diversity of the planting types and to choose durable and relatively carefree plants. Conversely, when the desire, knowledge, and resources all are available to provide the care required to maintain a mixed planting, the design possibilities are limited only by our imaginations.

The point here is, being aware of the species of plants within each category that require low, moderate, and high levels of maintenance will aid in your ability to properly select the plants that match the level of skill and attention required to sustain your mixed planting design over time. We will discuss the various types of maintenance that may be necessary in Chapter 9, page 237.

Moving on with the Planting Design Process

William R. Nelson, Professor Emeritus of Horticulture and Landscape Architecture, University of Illinois, Urbana-Champaign, said of the planting design process in his book *Planting Design: A Manual of Theory and Practice* (1985), "Planting design is a sequence of steps a designer must fully understand and be able to apply in any landscape setting. The process involves a purposeful integration of specific principles with orderly procedures to assure satisfying results. The successful integration of principles with procedures distinguishes one planting design as an art form from another that is haphazard, disorganized, and confused."

Planting design is fundamentally an analytical process, one that requires us to be both objective (when we will use our training and knowledge) and subjective (when we will be informed by our life experiences, natural artistic inclinations, and skills of observation). Making decisions during the planting design process is as much about feeling as it is about knowing; we will need to learn to switch between the right side of the brain and the left side.

Every process, especially those that rely heavily on the interpretation of design principles and application of creative thought, is open to modification. The design process described in this book for developing mixed planting designs is very linear and organized, but once mastered it can be altered and adjusted to suit the individual designer and project. This is normal for most creative processes. The key words here are "once mastered." Initially, it is best to follow the design process as described, as closely as possible. Only after you gain experience should you begin to deviate from it. In most cases, as you gain confidence in your abilities, the process will evolve naturally to serve as a general guide or direction for you to follow. In the next chapter, we begin the process by learning more about the concept of succession.

The Power of Succession

AS DEFINED IN THE PREVIOUS CHAPTER, in the context of mixed planting design, the term *succession* refers to the physical manifestation of the passing of time by plants, so any mixed-bed composition should include a variety of plants whose main show periods occur at different times of the year. Time is our canvas; plants are the artistic medium.

Planning for Succession

Planning for succession calls for sensitive choreographing of form, texture, color, and bloom sequence over time. It is, therefore, important that designers become familiar with the temporal aesthetic characteristics of plants at various stages of their life cycle, as their appearance may vary dramatically as they evolve through the seasons—from the opening and closing of flowers to the annual rhythm of the seasons. Aggressive new growth, reproductive maturity, and senescence are generally distinguished by different size, habit (pattern of growth), and form of the plant. Consequently, the role that each plant will play in the overall composition changes markedly throughout the season.

Preferably, each plant in the composition will exhibit multiple characteristics that provide extended moments of glory. Designers have to plan for the overlapping of these characteristics through time in order to create planting compositions that remain attractive throughout the seasons. We must plan for specific periods of impact for each plant to achieve striking combinations of plants, as well as successions of display. One of the most reliable methods for implementing this concept is to develop a table (see Figure 2.1), which details the various types of seasonal interest offered by the various plant attributes over time. Broken down by season, it becomes easy to visualize when a particular seasonal characteristic will come into play. Include the specific plants intended for use in the composition in such a customized chart. This will clearly illustrate the respective periods of flowering, fruiting, autumn leaf color, and winter stem color. This also helps to assess the overall composition and to determine where succession periods may be weak. We will discuss this process more in Chapter 8, page 218.

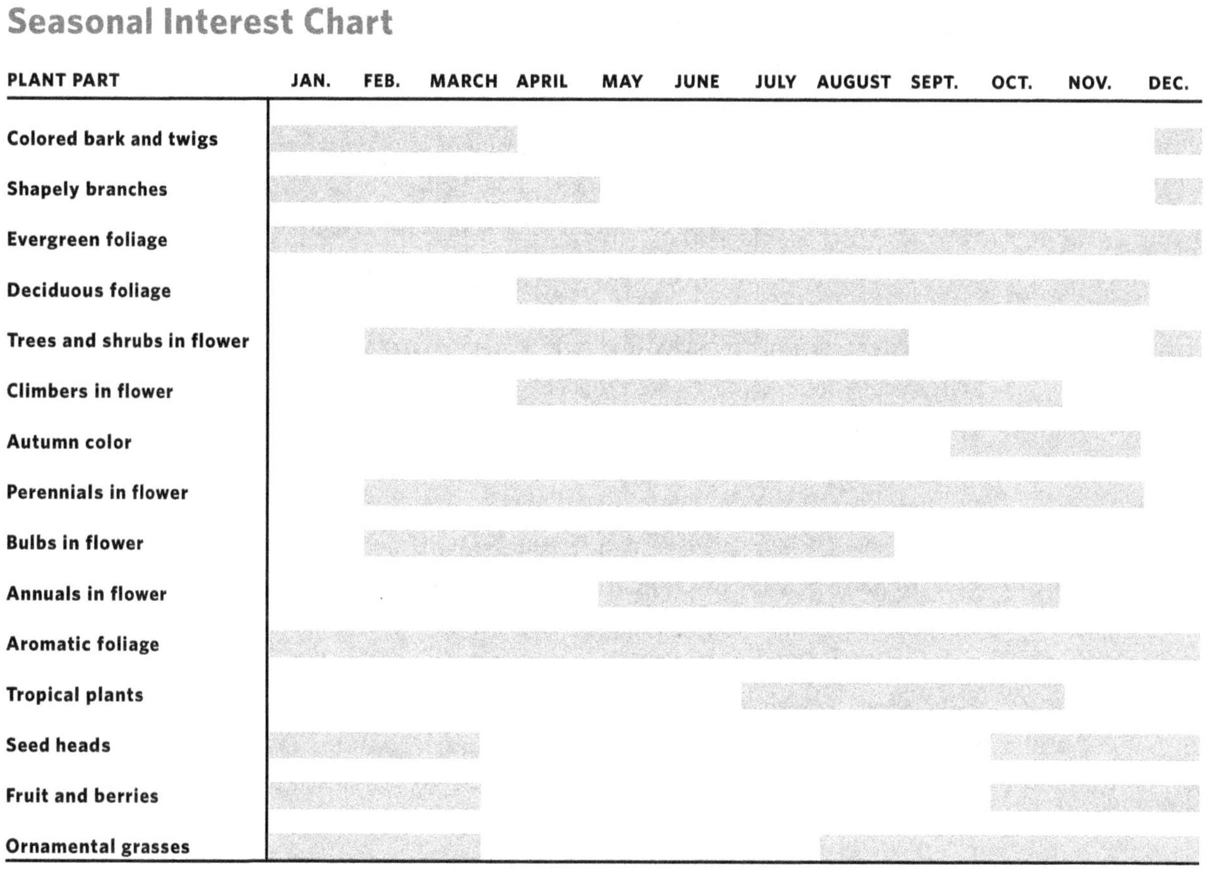

Seasonal Interest Chart

PLANT PART	JAN.	FEB.	MARCH	APRIL	MAY	JUNE	JULY	AUGUST	SEPT.	OCT.	NOV.	DEC.
Colored bark and twigs	�	▪	▪									▪
Shapely branches	▪	▪	▪	▪								▪
Evergreen foliage	▪	▪	▪	▪	▪	▪	▪	▪	▪	▪	▪	▪
Deciduous foliage				▪	▪	▪	▪	▪	▪			
Trees and shrubs in flower		▪	▪	▪	▪	▪	▪	▪				▪
Climbers in flower				▪	▪	▪	▪	▪	▪	▪		
Autumn color									▪	▪	▪	
Perennials in flower		▪	▪	▪	▪	▪	▪	▪	▪	▪	▪	
Bulbs in flower		▪	▪	▪	▪	▪	▪	▪				
Annuals in flower					▪	▪	▪	▪	▪	▪		
Aromatic foliage	▪	▪	▪	▪	▪	▪	▪	▪	▪	▪	▪	▪
Tropical plants						▪	▪	▪	▪	▪		
Seed heads	▪	▪	▪							▪	▪	▪
Fruit and berries	▪	▪	▪							▪	▪	▪
Ornamental grasses	▪	▪	▪			▪	▪	▪	▪	▪	▪	▪

Figure 2.1
The chart graphically depicts the times of the year that the various plant characteristics are on display. A similar customized chart can be developed for a specific planting composition.

Components of the Mixed Planting

The advantage of designing a mixed planting is that there are so many plant types from which to choose. In fact, there are generally no restrictions: A mixed planting can include small trees, shrubs, evergreens, grasses, perennials, bulbs, climbers, annuals, tropicals, and even cacti and succulents. Each plant type chosen should have a number of visual attributes—perhaps wonderful flowers, foliage, and possibly berries or attractive seed heads that prolong seasonal interest. On plant selection, William Robinson, the famous nineteenth-century garden writer, had this to say in his book, *The English Flower Garden* (1933): "Select only good plants; throw away weedy kinds, there is no scarcity of the best."

While it is highly unlikely that you will be able to fill the entire planting bed with highly ornamental plants, you should start out thinking of plants that possess some or all of these traits as a point of departure. For example, rather than choose a daylily that has a bloom duration of five to seven days, opt for the cultivar that blooms for fourteen to twenty-one days and occasionally repeats itself all season such as *Hemerocallis* 'Stella d'oro' or 'Happy Returns'. Any plants that don't have many advantageous characteristics should have at least one feature of extended seasonal performance. Aiding in this effort is recent scientific work in plant genetics and selective breeding, which has produced some remarkable plants with an amazing array of decorative attributes. The challenge is to find those plants that can be incorporated effectively into the overall composition of your mixed planting. As noted in the previous chapter, in addition to providing multiple seasons of interest, other selection criteria include choosing plants that can tolerate abuse or neglect and require minimal amounts of attention or maintenance.

It should go without saying that it is an unreasonable demand to have a planting that looks like something straight out of a flower show or one that is "on" every day of the year. But using our knowledge of horticulture and design skills, we can create a mixed planting that looks vibrant year-round. The key to accomplishing this is to develop a palette of plants that are representative of as many different plant types as possible given the restrictions of the site and to interweave seasonal interest so that as one plant begins to fade, another is taking over.

It is important to recognize that, at this point in the discussion, the individual plant species and cultivars are not yet relevant. Rather, we need to focus on the *types* of plants and how they must function in the overall planting composition. To do that, let us consider some of the plant types and the role they may fill in a mixed planting composition.

SMALL TREES

Small trees can add scale to a mixed planting and can link it to the surrounding landscape. Many small trees have attractive shapes or branching pattern. Others exhibit attractive bark or flowers during nonpeak times of the year. The particular type of small tree you choose for your mixed design should be in scale with the overall planting—specifically, it is the mature size of the tree that will determine its appropriateness. Small trees also can function in the mixed planting to create, define, or divide large spaces into smaller planting zones. Small trees add much-needed vertical elements to a composition. In larger planting schemes, they can help to create interest and "break up" plantings to avoid monotonous runs of similar planting heights.

For all their potential uses, however, small trees should be incorporated judiciously into

ABOVE: **Figure 1.1**
An example of a mixed planting
with varying degrees of plant types.

BELOW: **Figures 1.4a and 1.4b**
The Tea Cup courtyard at Chanticleer
planted in mixed fashion with greater
percentages of tropicals and annuals.

ABOVE: **Figure 1.6**
This border of mixed planting
at New York Botanical Garden
is positioned in the garden and
planted to be an artistic showpiece.

BELOW: **Figures 1.7a and 1.7b**
An entrance garden into the author's
house is planted in mixed fashion as
a focal point.

RIGHT: **Figure 1.8**
A mixed planting provides a buffer from the author's front yard on the left and the street on the right.

BELOW: **Figure 1.9**
A mixed planting provides a buffer from a neighbor's yard just beyond.

ABOVE: **Figure 1.11**
At Great Dixter the long border is planted in mixed fashion.

RIGHT: **Figure 1.12**
A landscape bed planted in mixed fashion at the author's garden.

Figure 1.13
The tennis court garden at Chanticleer contains five island feature beds.

ABOVE LEFT: **Figure 1.14**
Island beds developed with organic shapes tend to function better in larger-scale landscapes.

ABOVE RIGHT: **Figure 1.15**
A mixed planting developed in a formal island bed.

BELOW: **Figure 2.3**
Masses of shrubs used in proportion with massings of other plant types can create a bold composition.

LEFT: **Figure 2.4**
Planting bulbs at the base of deciduous shrubs and trees can make effective use of what is otherwise a dead space in the early spring.

BELOW: **Figure 2.6**
Evergreens of various sizes and shapes set in mixed beds, especially those with larger amounts of perennials, add stability and form to a composition.

ABOVE: **Figure 2.7**
Grasses can soften a
composition and occupy, if
necessary, large areas in the
foreground, mid-ground, and
background.

RIGHT: **Figure 2.8**
Large numbers of perennials
can be massed for impact.

LEFT: **Figure 2.9**
A succession planting of bulbs beneath a flowering shrub can add another dimension to the planting composition.

BELOW: **Figure 3.23**
Emphasis can be achieved by strategically locating plants with dramatic or differing forms.

ABOVE: **Figure 3.25**
The line of the bridge leads the eye to the weeping willow, which becomes the focal point of the composition.

OPPOSITE TOP: **Figure 3.26**
The masses of ornamental grasses drifting in front of other plant type masses provide a unifying element.

OPPOSITE BOTTOM: **Figure 3.30**
Variety in a composition creates interest; however, it must be tempered by a unifying element such as the foliage of the *Musa* (banana) in this example.

OPPOSITE TOP LEFT: **Figure 4.1**
Small trees positioned in a line can imply garden edges or walls.

OPPOSITE TOP RIGHT: **Figure 4.2**
A small tree "punching" through lower-level plantings can act like a pillar to define a boundary or mark a point in the composition.

OPPOSITE BOTTOM: **Figure 4.4**
One small tree used in a composition is balanced by greater numbers of other plant types that cumulatively have equal weight.

ABOVE: **Figure 4.6**
Structural shrubs are planted among herbaceous plants, establishing a structural framework.

RIGHT: **Figure 4.7**
The vertical evergreen provides a striking accent to the composition by its dramatic change in line.

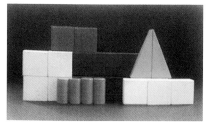

TOP: **Figure 4.9**
Contrasts in foliage texture can make dramatic statements.

LEFT: **Figure 5.2**
Evergreens most dramatically illustrate the limited number of plant forms.

ABOVE: **Figure 5.7**
Children's blocks can be used to experiment with creating compositions with various shapes, massings, and layering.

ABOVE: **Figure 7.8**
Accents or focal points, such as this geometrically sheared juniper, provide a striking contrast to the adjacent billowing grasses.

RIGHT: **Figure 7.11**
Contrasting surrounding plants with dramatic forms or foliage-shaped plants, such as the *Colocasia* 'Black Magic' and *Musa* pictured here, provide a setting for them to stand out as feature plants.

ABOVE: **Figure 7.14**
Locating several plants
together in a group
attracts attention, but
it is the space between
that provides a setting
for a plant's unique
form or characteristic
to read.

LEFT: **Figure 7.16**
Perennials are used as
filler material between
the evergreen planting
in the foreground and
the deciduous shrub
planting in the
background.

the mixed planting design. They should be located at strategic points in the composition to serve as punctuation points or to demarcate points of interest. Having too many small trees may cause the general picture to become spotty. Additionally, the type of trees used is a critical factor, for as they mature small trees will begin to compete for available sunlight and root space. They will then either shade out neighboring plants or take precious water away from other plants' root zones. After a time, plantings in these areas will need to be reevaluated and often replaced with more shade-tolerant plants and those that require less soil moisture.

A more recent horticultural trend is to "create" small trees by *coppicing*, or cutting back, larger trees to the ground each spring. This rather severe practice distorts the plant's normal growth patterns, concentrating the plant's energy into producing foliage growth with larger-than-normal leaf structures and additional stems. Often, these plants become thick adjuncts in the planting composition, whose powerfully bold foliage contrasts beautifully with its neighbors.

SHRUBS

As a medium-sized plant material, shrubs provide structure and stability to a mixed planting. Alone, they lack excitement; but by selecting certain species for use in combination with other support plantings, shrubs become the backbone of a mixed-bed planting. According to Robinson, again from *The English Flower Garden* (1933), "The shrubs should not form a hard line, but here and there they should come full to the edge and finish it." He goes on to say, "One can have the finest things among them if the bushes [shrubs] are not jammed together. The ordinary way of planting shrubs is such that they grow together, and then it is not possible to have flowers between them, nor to see the true form of the bushes, which are lost in one solid leafy mass."

Shrubs are often multistemmed and may have few or many branches. They can be deciduous, semi-evergreen, or evergreen. Seasonal effects from shrubs may result from foliage, stems, flowers, or fruits. Though diverse, there are fundamentally four types of shrubs that can be used to build a mixed planting: *structural, foliage, flowering*, and *dwarf*.

Structural Shrubs

Structural shrubs may be either deciduous or evergreen; both have their place in the mixed planting as a foundation plant. As medium-sized plants they can be used to provide backdrops, create planting compartments or bays, separate planting types or zones, and highlight points of interest. Generally, shrubs used for structural purposes are better massed in groupings, where they provide the necessary "filler" in large square footages of bed space. They can be massed to any scale, but the number of plants within any one group should be in proportion with the overall square footage of the bed space. Grouping plants in this fashion can result in a greater impact than when a single plant is used. In larger mixed planting beds, structural shrub massings are best planted in large overlapping drifts, much like massings espoused by Gertrude Jekyll. This massing technique can help to lead and transition the eye from one group to the other. It also creates pockets for other plantings.

Shrubs must be positioned carefully so as not to appear too spotty (see Figure 2.2). Only a few shrubs planted as individuals, generally separated by ground covers, can be used in any one scene for emphasis or accent. Structural shrubs planted as a loose grouping of individual specimens will function as a mass when viewed from a distance. They provide the visual weight needed to let other plant types—such as perennials, bulbs, grasses, and tropicals—project forward into space while still allowing the individuality of each plant to resonate (see color plates, Figure 2.3).

Planted at the edges of beds, structural shrubs can define as well as buffer the bed from other areas. Smaller than evergreen trees they are better suited for this purpose in smaller spaces or garden. As Robinson advocated, "In such plantations one might have in the back parts 'secret' colonies of lovely things which might not be well to show in the front

Figure 2.2
Shrubs planted too far apart to ever mass together create a "spotty" appearance.

of the border, or which required shade and shelter that the front did not afford." Here he makes reference to the use of evergreens as structural elements in the planting that create pockets or areas behind, allowing them to rise above and over the shrubs at select times of the season.

Foliage Shrubs

Foliage shrubs offer a great deal of shape, texture, and color variety. This is evident in the leaves of tiny rosette clusters of alpines, the bold fans of palms, the fleshy leaves of succulents, the narrow needles of evergreens, the variegated colors of deciduous plants, and the striking colors of purple, gold, or glaucous foliage plants. The diversity of foliar forms also offers interest and has great ornamental value to the designer, as their effect is long-lasting and they can be exploited in ways that have many practical advantages. They provide interest as a stand-alone, often serving as focal points. Foliage shrubs can also serve as a foil or background against which flowers and other features can be displayed, offering the durability that seasonal or temperamental flowers cannot, and having textural and visual value that can affect the mixed planting.

Flowering Shrubs

The use of flowering shrubs in the mixed bed provides an added characteristic to the structural shrub that makes it multidimensional and, thus, valuable as a sub-plant type. Whether used en masse or as an individual specimen, the flowering shrub can present a bold display during its season of bloom. In the mixed planting it is imperative that the seasonal bloom times of the shrubs be staggered so that no two shrub types are flowering concurrently. A designer can use early-spring flowering shrubs such as *Hammalis* or *Corylopsis*, late-spring flowering shrubs such as the *Viburnums*, summer-flowering shrubs such as shrub roses or *Hydrangea*, and late-summer to early-fall bloomers such as *Rhus*. Many of these shrubs also have a variety of forms that enable the designer to create additional interest, rather than relying on the flowers alone.

Individual specimens can be displayed in two methods. First, as part of a smaller mixed planting, they can be used cumulatively with other plant types. Used in this capacity the flowering shrub should be coordinated with adjacent plantings that support it during nonflowering periods. This might include, for example, underplanting with bulbs that will bloom before the shrub leafs out (see color plates, Figure 2.4). The second technique is to treat the shrub as an individual piece of sculpture, placing it within a sea of ground-cover plantings. This allows the unique ornamental characteristic of the flowering shrub to be prominently displayed, as shown in Figures 2.5 a and b. If used en masse, flowering shrubs should be incorporated in generous bold sweeps. This planting style, however, is usually best reserved for larger landscapes.

Figures 2.5 a and b Individual plants positioned in relative isolation in a sea of ground cover can create an interesting sculptural effect.

Dwarf Shrubs

Dwarf, or compact, shrubs can contribute long-lasting color, shape, and texture to the mixed planting without dominating companion plantings. They serve prominent roles while they are in their peak season, then retreat to a supportive role once their showiest stage has passed. Dwarf shrubs are generally maintenance-free, and their various qualities and characteristics will be emphasized according to their treatment. Many qualify as both foliage and flowering shrubs, and some are noteworthy for blooming early and taking on fall color late, thereby extending their characteristics into multiple seasons. Still others are used for their foliage effects, among these *Berberis* 'Crimson Pigmy' or *Spirea* 'Gold Flame'.

By nature of their size, dwarf shrubs, especially those smaller in scale, are best used as edge plants along the front of the mixed planting. In this setting, they stand out crisply in the composition, without the danger of being smothered by surrounding plant types. But dwarf shrubs also often take on the role of a structural shrub when situated among low perennials and ground covers. Many types can be displayed in both formal and informal settings. In smaller plantings or intensive mixed plantings, they can be used to break up a long string of one plant type such as a perennial or ground-cover massing. Dwarf shrubs can also be used as individual specimens in a repetitive fashion to bring attention to a particular characteristic such as color or texture. Used en masse as an interesting ground cover, dwarf shrubs will give a bit more height and textural interest to the composition vs. a traditional ground cover.

EVERGREENS

Evergreens are the quintessential workhorses of the mixed planting. They are the threads that tie a composition together. They bridge the seasons by providing consistent structure and interest. Robinson said, "Charming gardens might be made up of such shrubs, not lumped together, but in open groups, with the more beautiful American hardy flowers between them . . . and bulbous flowers of all seasons. The light and shade and variety in such beds of choice evergreens and flowers mingled are charming . . ." (see color plates, Figure 2.6).

In the spring, the new growth stands out because many other surrounding plant types have yet to begin their show. In the summer, evergreens assume a backdrop position, allowing more dominant and splashy plants to take center stage. Fall is when their true strength is revealed—their dark greens, blues, and yellows contrast with the deciduous foliaged autumn reds, oranges, and yellows. And in the winter, their forms dominate, maintaining the composition until the blooms of spring start the cycle all over again.

Frequently, evergreens have often been relegated to screen or backdrop positions due to their neutral and, at times, rather dull appearance. They traditionally are used as anchor or filler plantings, wherein they assume a subordinate but no less important role in the larger composition, setting the stage for other plant types to display flowers, seed heads, colorful bright foliage, or berries. Neutral evergreens are often used as fillers in larger mixed plantings where they are relatively maintenance-free and lend structure to the composition. In this capacity, they should be placed somewhat evenly and in massed drifts throughout so that they help create balance and repetition, as well as provide planting bays for other planting types or vignettes.

As intimated above, evergreens can contribute reliable color throughout the year. There are many color variations available for use in mixed plantings, in addition to the customary dark green fine texture of plants such as *Buxus* or *Taxus*. Greater effects are possible when conifer color variations—ranging from the golden yellow of a *Chamaecyparis obtusa* 'Aurea' to that of the silvery blue of *Juniperus scopulorum* 'Moonglow'—are incorporated in a planting. When viewed from a distance, however, the forms are what dominate, not these bold colors and textures.

Evergreens come in many different forms and shapes: rounded or mounded, flat, prostrate, conical, or cylindrical. The height and corresponding shape provide important visual elements in the overall composition, although their relative importance or prominence will vary depending on the season and the status of the surrounding plantings. Designers must be cautious: Too many differing forms generate unrest, confusion, and competition among each other. A general guideline is that evergreens with strong forms should be used sparingly as focal elements within the overall mixed planting. A single evergreen with a unique form such as a pyramidal or columnar, can be repeated at equally spaced intervals throughout the composition to provide a sense of formality.

GRASSES

Grasses look good nearly all year long and embody many of the qualities that meet the requirements for mixed plantings. They lend beauty to the garden when most other plant types have begun to fade. For nine months of the year they evolve in appearance, subtly changing only as they age. Some continue to look good into late January, depending on the snow load in colder climates. Grasses add a softer, more natural feel to the composition and often contrast with surrounding foliage types. The late summer and early fall are when grasses are most effective. As grasses mature and move into this period, the flower heads mature, turning into long-lasting seed heads for an exciting change.

Most grasses are grown for their form and texture of foliage. Some have good-quality evergreen foliage, while others are variegated. Others have fine, narrow leaves, while others are straplike. All offer flower heads that vary in weight of appearance such as the light and airy seed heads of *Stipa* or *Molina*, contrasted with the bold, fluffy appearance of pampas grass, *Cortaderia selloana*. Their wide-ranging height variability makes them appropriate for either the front or back of the planting composition (see color plates, Figure 2.7).

Grasses not only add aesthetic value to the garden; they have practical advantages as well. Because many grasses available for use are warm-season varieties, they often do not show significant growth until the weather begins to heat up—usually in mid-June. This makes grasses an excellent companion plant for spring bulbs and early-flowering perennials that go dormant in early- to midsummer. As the foliage of those plants begins to die off, the foliage of grasses begins to billow and take over the vacant space. Lower grasses make great foreground foil plantings for larger-growing shrubs or perennials that have "leggy" or bare bases.

Grasses have several uses in the mixed planting: as specimens; en masse, as ground covers; and as accent plantings. Some of the bolder grasses, including *Miscanthus floridus* or *Erianthus ravennae*, can be used effectively as a single focal element among smaller and gently contrasting plants. Grasses also can be used en masse in larger landscapes to create a sea-like effect. And as a green foil contrasted against brightly colored early-flowering shrubs or perennials, ornamental grasses recede and allow other plant types to shine. Later in the season the very same foil turns into a sea of plumes, which appear to float above fiery autumn foliage and colorful berries of other plant types.

As ground-cover plantings, grasses break up larger masses of mixed plantings, lending stability and establishing a place for the eye to rest. Against structural evergreen plantings, they provide a stark contrast in texture and a dependable and reliable combination of plant types that provide multiseasonal beauty. Teamed with taller perennials, sturdier grasses can act as a support, providing natural staking for weaker-stemmed plants.

PERENNIALS

Perennial plants are those that are nonwoody and die down in the winter, only to reappear the following spring. Perennials display a wide range of colors, forms, and textures. The range of size, flower type, and bloom time is practically limitless. Their season can stretch from early summer to late fall. The rise and fall of the life of perennials is quick, which is both their strength and weakness. Designers must account for this quick life cycle by taking care to layer plantings so that as they fade, early-blooming species are masked with later-blooming species. In doing so, perennials must be strategically interwoven and interplanted with other plant types.

Robinson had this to say about perennials: "A scattered, dotty mixed border along the face of a shrubbery gives a poor effect, but a good one may be secured by grouping the plants in open spaces between the shrubs, making careful selection of plants, each occupying a bold space." Large numbers of one plant type should be used to create plant massings in this type of space, though the actual number of perennial plants within each massing will vary and be dependent on the garden's size and the power of the desired effect (see color plates, Figure 2.8). The size of the space allocated for each species within the composition will be, in part, determined by the overall size of the bed. Larger landscapes often call for large massings of plants in one group that can number from the tens to the hundreds. In contrast, small gardens may warrant that a single specimen be used, or a small grouping of three to five. The scale of the overall design will determine the appropriate proportion for each plant species.

Functioning with structural plants such as shrubs, evergreens, and small trees, perennials provide seasonal variation, size range, and habits necessary to generate a variety of occurrences throughout the year. Their variations of color, size, and flower type are virtually limitless. Perennials are also design-flexible: They can be situated in the front, middle, and rear of the composition and can range in height from eight inches to eight feet. Their form can range from low-spreading to shrubby-mounded to tall and leggy, making them perfect candidates for layering in the mixed planting. Their wide adaptability makes them perfect companion plantings for other plant types.

BULBS

The exuberance of spring is often associated with flowering bulbs. Most of the commonly known bulbs bloom in the spring or early summer, revealing a succession of color before the summer when flowering shrubs and perennials reach their peak. Additonally, there are many summer- and fall-blooming bulbs such as *Allium, Lycoris, or Lilium*, which offer the potential for additional bright highlights or subtle contrasts of color and form. Autumn- and winter-flowering bulbs such as *Galanthus* or *Crocus* add color and variety to the planting during a time when most plantings are fading or already dormant. Bulbs have the unique ability to start the early season and finish the late season, thereby effectively lengthening or enhancing the traditional flowering period.

Bulbs are the most reliable source of color in the garden. They can be treated as annual plantings, to be swapped out later and replaced by the traditional early and late summer annual rotations or with tropicals. For the less intensively maintained mixed plantings, bulbs can be just as effectively used as perennial plantings, located throughout the bed as accents. Many late-flowering bulbs are taller and more dramatic than their spring cousins. These bulbs, often thought of as perennials such as *Crocosima* or *Liatrus*, hold their own among small shrubs, perennials, grasses, and tropicals in the mixed bed, making bold statements of color.

The use of bulbs to extend short-lived flowering seasons of perennials or shrubby plants is a valuable design technique. Bulbs can be incorporated into the mixed planting in a number of ways:

▷ They can be designed to create an overall scheme, repeating a pattern where they become the focal point for a specific period. In the early spring when beds are open, bulbs play a dominant role when used in this manner.

▷ They can be underplanted beneath plants that are slow to leaf out in the spring.

▷ They can be "tactful infillers," as Christopher Lloyd refers to them (see color plates, Figure 2.9), in which case small quantities of bulbs are used in between two plants to bridge the gap between leafing out, flowering, or reblooming periods.

▷ They can be used in mass drifts to create bold swaths of color. These masses can be combined with other plantings or with other bulbs to create a more saturated presence of color.

Perennial bulbs should be located in a planting bed where they are least likely to be disturbed such as among late-awakening sturdy perennials, with low ground covers that are late to emerge, or under deciduous shrubs. Species such as *Eranthis*, *Galanthus*, *Scillia*, *Crocus*, and *Muscari* all bloom early and poke their heads above the soil and flower before other plants begin to sprout foliage. Summer-flowering bulbs including *Lilium*, *Dahlia*, *Agapanthus*, *Lycoris*, and *Alliums* can be planted to pop through lower varieties of perennials, as well as in groupings for a bolder effect in a mixed planting.

CLIMBERS

Climbers have an ability to occupy narrow spaces that often occur above the overall planting, providing an additional layer of planting and excitement. They can be used to sprawl over vast horizontal surfaces, cover up low points, or take over the show when a host plant has completed its display. Both annual and perennial climbers can be trained over other plant types or up a variety of supports. By carefully selecting a companion host plant, usually a small tree or shrub, designers can plan for vines to trail up, through, and over their hosts—assuming their hosts are strong enough to support the weight and shading created by the climbers. Of course, not all climbers are suited for this use. Climbers come in a multitude of sizes, shapes, and colors, and their growth rates vary from several feet a day in high season to a few feet a year. Their use in a mixed planting composition will vary accordingly and is dependent on their hosts or supporting mechanisms.

In nature, climbers work their way up and drape themselves over trees and shrubs. This behavior can be mimicked in the mixed planting bed. In the garden, the most common supporting mechanism for climbers is a pole or tripod, whose height must be matched with the climbing capability of the plant. Used in this way climbers can be treated as vertical elements in the garden, taking up a minimum amount of horizontal space. The climbing structure becomes a focal point in the composition and so must be placed in relation to other vertical elements in the composition.

In the loose mixed planting, climbers can be encouraged to trail up hedges, through and over trees, through perennials or roses, or over ground covers or low-spreading shrubs. It is important to remember that climbers are often like blankets over a fire: They can easily smother what is beneath them. The type of climber must be matched to its support. Perennial climbers must have a host that is well established and possesses a solid framework that will support such a neophyte. This requirement is often met by mature trees or large shrubs that have open canopies.

Many perennial vines vigorous in their growth can be treated as cutback plants, to be trimmed back to the ground each year. Only certain vines will tolerate this type of treatment, however. Annual vines such as *Ipomoea* or *Tropaeolum* grow fast enough to do their magic but stop just short of jeopardizing their host plant before the season is over.

As with tropicals and annuals, climbers add an extra dimension to a mixed planting that is simply not possible with trees or shrubs. Their ability to create interest to the vertical is unmatched, except by small trees, and their remarkable ability to weave through plants can make for striking visual drama. But before working with climbers, gardeners must take into consideration the labor and time required for training, pruning, and general oversight.

ANNUALS

Annual plantings contribute dependable splashes of color in spring and summer and into autumn. Annuals have the flexibility to be quickly changed from season to season. The key to using annuals in the mixed planting is to have them support, not dominate, the landscape. By relying on other planting types to provide structure, shape, and texture in the mixed planting, annual plantings can be counted on as a consistent reliable color accent to the composition. They often fill temporary gaps and voids as other permanent plants transition from season to season or flowering period to flowering period.

During the Victorian era, annual combinations of garish colors were often used with tropical foliage plants. Low-growing, often tight-formed varieties of annuals were used to "bed out" planting beds for the season. Plant beds of all shapes and sizes were often placed in open lawns. Many of the more architecturally designed formal gardens used annuals to create or enhance geometric patterns located within the confines of highly formalized garden rooms. The weakness of this type of use is that annuals are slow to take, often requiring three to four weeks of precious early summertime before they begin to put on any substantial display. The result was a tendency toward monotony.

Although a designer today has a more extensive selection, more options, and better opportunities to be creative, annuals are still often presented in rather boring and unimaginative displays. Most are simply blobs of color placed in areas of high visibility such as building or doorway entrances, in front of signs, or near high-traffic areas. With such a concentrated display of color to enliven a space, their predominant role is to draw the eye to a specific point in the landscape. Coincidentally, the dramatic color attraction is made possible by the surrounding plantings, which are quite often bland and lack interest. The lack of interest is generally precipitated by the stagnant use of groupings of shrubs with similar leaf texture and color. These examples only exaggerate the untapped potential that more creative plantings and the interweaving of annuals could make.

Designing annuals into today's mixed plantings can be informal and loose, or formal. The key to successful annual plantings will depend on the type of mixed planting you are creating. This will, in the main, relate to the scale at which you are designing (small or large) and the type of landscape (public or private).

In a small mixed-bed planting, annuals are best planted in small pockets and let to intermingle, grow through, and spill into the surrounding plantings. For the more intensive gardening regimes, annuals can be planted to alternate and correspond with neighboring flowering periods. This requires that annuals be located and sequentially added to the garden throughout the course of the year. While some annuals are developing, others may require replacement; while some neighbor plants are in full swing, others may be ramping up. Again, the key is to locate annual plantings in voids where they will accent a neighbor or pick up its slack. The "threading" should be so seamless that the casual observer should not be able to distinguish the annuals from other plantings.

Designing with annuals in larger landscape plantings could not be more different. Often it is best to minimize locations of annual plantings due to the associated costs. This requires that larger massings of one type of annual be used, so that less intermingling occurs. Annuals should be integrated into the overall planting composition as elongated amebic shapes that blend or mimic the size and shape of the massings of surrounding, more permanent plant types. If the planting style has regular or geometric plant massings, then it follows that annual massings should match that style. When the annuals are required to be more localized such as in areas of high impact, interweave them with permanent plants as tightly as possible in order to avoid the color blob syndrome.

While the advantages of incorporating annual plantings in the mixed planting are great, they come at a cost. Intensive amounts of time and labor are needed to install and maintain them. Forethought is needed to select the correct varieties, procure them, and sequence the timing of the rotation of the next planting. Often, multiple rotations are needed each year to achieve the desired color splash, and require time to fully develop—leaving down periods in the mix. And because annuals require rich soils high in nutrients, extensive soil preparation and ongoing fertilizer regimes are needed prior to each planting rotation to maintain peak performance. Plus, watering is necessary—often several times a week.

TROPICALS

When we think about the garden, flowers are what mostly come to mind. However, the boldest of all displays in the garden seem to be those plants that are grown purely for their dramatic foliage. Tender tropicals with their exotic and unusual beauty make a powerful presence and can prolong the period of interest. There is the wonderment, a connection to the tropics, to which most of us are mysteriously drawn. Come late summer, when the traditional bedding plants begin to look tired, tropicals are entering the peak of their performance, still developing fresh new growth, which in northern climates will continue until frost. The wide range of species and availability of tropical plants, along with their relative cost-effectiveness, have made them increasingly popular. Many of these tropical plants grow so fast that they can make a feature plant after a few months of germination; and if started during the winter months in a greenhouse, they can have an almost immediate impact.

The use of tropical plants as annual bedding plants is not new. The Victorians were fond of adding bold foliaged tropical plants to summer bedding schemes (see Figure 2.10). The practice started when many of the palms that were grown in the conservatories of the time were moved into the garden for the summer. Their popularity grew and spread into the garden as more mobile bulbous and rhizomous tropical plants became available. They were often used as focal points within other annual plantings or as centerpieces within more permanent and formal parterres. The creativity of using these often-grotesque looking plants with other plant types was limited, however, as strict adherence to fashion was often practiced.

With today's ever-shrinking distance between climate zones, some of the world's boldest foliage plants have emerged as preeminent contenders in temperate climates. They are often associated as seasonal bedding plants or placed in containers that are moved indoors during the cooler months. Some palms such as *Trachycarpus fortunei* tolerate moderate levels of frost. Other plants, including the bulbous *Canna* and *Colocasia*, can be lifted and stored in a dormant state until the next season when they can be replanted. Even some of the more typical exotic bedding plants, including the caster oil plant (*Ricinus communis*) or the fig (*Ficus carica*), may be shrubs or perennials, depending on which climate zone they are grown in.

Cannas, with their bright colors and bold foliage, complement annuals. Their upright form contrasts particularly well with low-spreading or shrubby-formed plants. Other plants such as cordylines, agaves, and bananas add foliage shapes and sometimes colors to the mix that are difficult to find with hardy plants. They provide striking alterations in texture, which help to take the pressure off the designer, who may feel compelled to focus on flowers as the

Figure 2.10
Tropical foliage plants used en masse or individually for their form or color add an interesting dimension to a composition.

dominant design element. The tropicals' power to create drama is unrivaled so they are often most useful as statement-making focal points within an overall planting. Their downfall is that they must be treated as an annual and either be discarded after the season or be moved indoors, an expense of both labor and time.

Permanent vs. Temporary Plantings

Temporary plantings, regardless of the plant types chosen, are used to mitigate the lows associated with other plants that may not perform all season or have significant down periods. Temporary plantings fill gaps or voids between other plantings, give a solid base or accent of color, and constantly change the appearance of the plantings through the ease in which we can swap out one planting for another. Temporary plantings offer great flexibility and variety and enable the bridging of gaps from spring to fall. A variety of different plant types can be utilized for temporary plantings.

In newer plantings, there will initially be significant gaps between these plants as we wait for them to mature. These gaps provide welcome opportunities for temporary plantings to fill the void until the more permanent plantings mature and begin to fill that space. Any plant can be used in this circumstance as temporary fillers. Temporary "infill" compositions are created with the knowledge that in future years these plants will be either transplanted to other sections of the landscape or simply removed. This practice typifies the essence of gardening.

By virtue of the level of maintenance, permanent vs. temporary plantings will differentiate those landscapes requiring active gardening from those requiring less attention. The design approach and the attention given to maintain the plantings for each could not be more different. Actively rotating annuals, tropicals, and—in more intensively gardened areas—even perennials, define those compositions made up of temporary plantings. In this type of mixed planting, the planting bed is literally a living canvas where the scene is constantly being edited with the addition and deletion of plants. It is an ongoing work of art, constantly being evaluated, tweaked, and improved upon by the designer or gardener.

Tropicals are often used in the temperate garden to create a seasonal impact. Best used as "solo incidents," as Christopher Lloyd refers to them, the stout and often bold foliage of tropicals provide a striking exotic contrast to the more restrained foliage and flowers of other plantings. Tropicals are often late to come on because they need the high heat of the summer before they begin to make their presence felt. Realizing this, it is best to plan for that impact for the late summer and early fall garden, utilizing other plantings both temporary and permanent to bridge the gap. This illustrates how one type of temporary planting can be used in the garden to offset another.

Converse to this practice is planning for permanent plantings in the mixed bed. This can be done both small- and large-scale. In the smaller landscape or garden, there will be plantings that we fully intend to be permanent and will probably comprise 80 to 90 percent of the composition, with the remaining areas set aside for active gardening or temporary seasonal or revolving plantings. In larger, more public gardens and landscapes, or for those where active gardening or high levels of maintenance will not be available, the majority—if not all—of the plantings will be treated as permanent. In landscapes that are planned to be permanent, the use of annuals and tropicals are often not considered in the mix, and the use of perennials and climbers is limited if not removed completely. The driving force behind this decision, again, is the level of maintenance activities a landscape or garden will be given over time. The less maintenance available, the greater the degree of permanent plantings that should comprise the composition.

3 | **Applying Design Fundamentals to Planting Design**

DESIGN IS THE ORGANIZATION OF VISUAL elements in space. The time-tested principles that guide design, which are based on natural phenomena, assist the designer in assembling the elements necessary to create an artistic composition. The fundamental principles are the same for all fields of art and design, including architecture, industrial design, interior design, painting, and sculpture. In these design fields, however, the finished product is static; it remains constant over time. This is not the case in planting design, where the artistic medium changes over time, reacts to the environment, and is participatory. It is, as mentioned previously, a dynamic form of artistic expression.

The medium of the planting designer grows and evolves over time, in size, color, texture, and form. The appearance of plants is modified on an ongoing basis by ever-changing patterns of light, shade, and shadow created by their environment. Furthermore, because landscapes are participatory, their appearance and impact change as well as observers move through, in, around, and under them. Not surprisingly, then, applying design principles to planting is a more complex undertaking. In fact, the factors just described combine to make plants one of the most complex media to work with. To do so effectively, it's important to first understand how the various elements of design and composition come together in a planting composition.

Elements of Composition

The elements of composition—line, form, texture, and color—are the basic visual attributes of an artistic composition, which individually and together exert visual forces to which the mind and eye react. As a designer it is critical to understand the human response to these forces. In this case, of course, we will be talking about the elements of composition as they relate to plant materials—the size and configuration of the vegetative parts of plants when viewed in composite. Once we understand how the human mind and eye responds to these elements, we can then begin to learn how to use them effectively in our designs.

Each of these elements is described in turn below, pointing out how each might carry greater or lesser prominence in a given composition—that is, how the relative visual weight of each will vary, based on the design.

LINE

The line is the element of art most familiar to us. We have been creating lines since we were children; it was probably the first thing most of us ever drew. In art, a line is defined as an infinite number of points; it is a moving dot. This would suggest that a line is dynamic; it connotes movement. And because our eye will follow a line through a landscape, the potential to express movement in our planting designs becomes obvious.

The line makes it possible to accomplish an infinite variety of design objectives. Lines can be used in the landscape to create or control patterns, direct a viewer to a focal point, or control movement. Lines can be real (actual) and perceived (implied). Perceived lines are created from a series of points or objects organized in such a fashion as to make it seem an actual line is present. This can be accomplished in the landscape by using the plant forms or masses to imply a line. A silhouette of a group of trees as seen against the evening sky, for example, will imply a line where the tops of the trees meet the horizon (see Figure 3.1). Real, or actual, lines are formed by clearly delineated edges of objects. These may also be expressed in the landscape by bed edge or a hedgerow.

Figure 3.1
The tops of a tree canopy follow the contours of the land establishing a line along the horizon.

One of the most important characteristics of lines is the implication of direction. A line will always carry the eye along its route, whether it be horizontal or vertical, upward or downward, straight or curving.

By recognizing the attributes of various types of lines (see Figure 3.2), a designer can control the visual movement of the observer, directing attention to whatever point in the landscape he or she so chooses. Consider:

Horizontal lines, representing the horizon, imply quiet and repose. Creating horizontal lines in a landscape elicits a general sense of ease or peace.

Vertical lines are seen as more severe, as having more activity and giving emphasis. Think of the exclamation point and its use in grammar.

Diagonal lines most strongly suggest motion. They are transitional, connecting one point in the landscape to another.

Curving lines encourage slower movement and are useful in informal designs. They are pleasing to the eye and connote relaxation.

Straight lines lack interest and are more "businesslike," compelling the eye to travel quickly from one point to another.

FORM

Form, the second compositional element, is established by a series of lines that create and enclose a shape. The result is the total mass that is created by the height, width, and depth of an object, giving it three-dimensional qualities. For a plant the enclosing outline of the trunk,

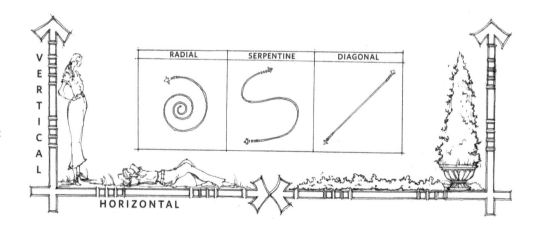

Figure 3.2
Each line type conveys a distinct feeling by leading or pulling the eye in various directions and design speeds.

branches, and leaves together create the total mass of its individual form. Form can be perceived through patches of color or texture juxtaposed against a background.

In a plant, form is the most enduring quality. Plants come in a variety of forms, including rounded, columnar, vase-shape, pyramidal, and a myriad of others. We will discuss these plant forms more in Chapter 4, page 75. In design, these basic forms are often repeated among the various plant types, mainly in shrubs, trees, and perennials, and come in varying degrees. The growth behavior of the plant will affect the personality and "trueness" of the form, meaning it may be more or less true to the form's basic description. Descriptors such as tight, loose, open, dense, and airy are often used to further define the character of a plant form.

Plants may also change form as they age or when they are grouped together in a mass. A zelkova tree on its own can be said to have a vase form; but when massed, this shape disappears and the form of the grouping takes on a more blocky character (see Figure 3.3). The same can be said of large planting compositions: When the composition is viewed as a whole, the individual combining forms become subordinate to the overall mass of the composition, thereby creating an implied form. In any one planting mass, care must be taken to ensure that the individual plant forms within the composition remain subordinate to the overall composition. They should not interfere with the perception generated by the overall composition or massing (see Figure 3.4). The sum should be greater than the parts.

As in the case of lines, certain forms have a more dominant presence in the landscape than others. Individual, clearly delineated upright or pyramidal forms carry greater visual weight, so they stand out more than other forms, as do vertical lines. However, if a row of upright forms were grouped together in sufficient quantity in linear fashion, the effective form would become horizontal (see Figures 3.5 a and b). The more striking the form in comparison to other forms, the greater its prominence in the overall composition. This will create interest in a composition. That said, too many striking forms within one composition will cause visual unrest and

Figure 3.3
The vase-shaped form of a zelkova tree as an individual becomes lost in the overall mass of a composition of multiple plants.

Figure 3.4
Individual plant forms can be perceived within, but it is the overall form of the composition that dominates.

create a disturbing scene. Thus, this design feature should be used judiciously and in full recognition of its impact on the surrounding composition. Neutral forms should be used to establish the bulk of the composition, reserving the more powerful forms for points of emphasis.

The importance of form in a design is dependent on the viewing perspective, which will vary depending the scale of the composition and the location of the observer. In a small-scale design, such as a backyard, the overall form of a large canopy tree becomes irrelevant when it is being used for shade and the total plant mass cannot be seen. But place that same tree in a park landscape where it can be viewed from a greater distance and the form of the tree will become a dominant element in the landscape.

VISUAL WEIGHT

Before designers can successfully combine and organize design qualities and their variations, they must fully understand how the eye perceives the relative importance of each element individually and as part of the whole. Line, form, texture, and color all have aesthetic characteristics, capable of producing certain effects. *Visual weight*, or *visual strength*, is the term used to describe the energy or force of expression of these various elements in relation to the other elements in the overall composition. The concept of visual weight helps to define how and why these attributes attract our attention, as well as which ones attract us more readily than others and hold our attention longer.

Figures 3.5 a and b
The direction of the line of force of a single upright plant will change when a grouping of them are massed together as illustrated by the photo taken at Ladew Topiary Gardens.

Each of the design elements will have varying degrees of visual weight (see Figure 3.6). Diagonal lines, upright forms, bold textures, and bright colors all are plant attributes associated with drama, dynamism, and a high degree of visual stimulation. These elements stand out, demanding attention, and thus are said to have a high degree of visual weight. Conversely, horizontal lines, prostrate forms, fine textures, and pale or dull colors are all considered restful,

Visual Weight Chart

DESIGN QUALITIES	LVW*	MVW**	HVW***
Line and Form			
Vertical			X
Columnar			X
Round		X	
Oval		X	
Horizontal	X	X	
Vase		X	
Weeping			X
Pendulous			X
Texture			
Fine	X		
Medium		X	
Coarse			X
Color			
HUES			
Warm colors			X
Cool colors	X		
FLOWER COLOR			
Red			X
Yellow			X
Blue	X		
Purple	X		
White			X
Orange		X	
FOLIAGE COLOR			
Variegated			X
Bronze-gold			X
Purple maroon	X		
Green		X	
Gray-Silver			X

LVW* = Low visual weight
MVW** = Medium visual weight
HVW*** = High visual weight

Figure 3.6
The chart illustrates the visual weight associated with various plant forms, colors, and textures.

therefore they play a more recessive role in composition. They are considered to have low visual weight and, logically, little visual impact on the composition.

The ability of the planting designer to successfully manipulate visual weight will be guided, in part, by the principles of design and composition. Each of a plant's attributes must be played against those of the others in the composition in order to achieve the full effect or impact of the individual characteristic to function within the design. Once you have begun to recognize—and learned to estimate—the visual weight of lines, forms, textures, and colors of the various planting elements in a composition, you can begin to use opposing and complementary qualities in plants to achieve balance, emphasis, and scale. Whether an overall planting composition will be designed to have high or low visual weight will be dependent on the purpose of the planting and its setting in the overall landscape. Areas of high visual weight will be the focal points of the design, generally created to emphasize a particular plant, attract the eye, or direct attention to a particular area. But the visual weight of a striking, bold-textured plant can only be fully appreciated if complemented by an area or other plants whose qualities are quieter, less showy.

TEXTURE

Texture refers to the surface quality of objects; it causes a tactile sensation often more perceptual than physical. Hence, the human reaction to texture can be both visceral and visual, and certain textures cause specific reactions. Designers can use the textural differences of plants as major components in planting design. For example, bold or rough-textured plants in a composition can impart visual strength and create textural accent effects, thus greatly reducing the need for flowers.

Plant material components possess a wide range of textural attributes, including leaf and flower shape and surface, bark, and twigs and stems. All of these can greatly enrich the visual quality of a landscape composition, thanks to the way that textural appearance is manipulated by various light and dark patterns and the way light is reflected from the plant's surfaces. This in effect will cause plant materials to appear coarse or fine, heavy or light, rough or smooth, opaque or transparent, rigid or fluid, thin or dense.

The visual distance of the observer to the plant also will be a factor in the perception of texture. At a greater distance, surfaces that appear to be relatively smooth. Upon closer inspection, however, they often will reveal themselves to be rougher and more varied and contain minute textural patterns. That said, the texture of a plant does not depend on the minute details but the overall textural quality or general appearance of the mass of the plant. Thus, objects that appear large in the near view become smaller as the distance increases, until they merge into one large mass or disappear entirely. The perceived texture, then, is the quality of light and resulting shadows on the mass.

Rough-Textured Plants

Rough-textured plants such as *Hydrangea quercifolia* or *Catalpa* will attract the eye and hold it for longer periods of time because the contrast between light and shadow is more striking. Such plants connote a sense of informality and are best used in loose drifts in informal plantings. Rough texture will "trump" color and form and is an important factor to consider in design. Rough-textured plants used in a small area will tend to make the space feel smaller, whereas in a larger area they might hardly be noticed. Rough-textured plants will also appear closer to the observer than fine-textured plants, which also serves to minimize distance.

Fine-Textured Plants

Fine-textured plants are generally dense and have little variation in their leaf shape. There are few or no shadows between the leaves, so that the overall appearance of the plants is consistent. Consequently, these plants tend to recede in landscapes. They are easy to look at and are often highly reflective. As a design element, fine textures can complement and reinforce color, form, and space, because their qualities are subordinate to the others. Fine-textured plants also can be used in design to provide a low-impact background planting for a distinctive feature and to emphasize depth in a landscape, according to Brian Hackett in *Planting Design* (1979). In this way, they let other more prominent plant attributes dominate.

COLOR

Color theory is extremely complex. The systematic study of modern color theory can be traced to 1810, with the publication of Johann Wolfgang von Goethe's book *Theory of Colours*. Since then, countless theories on color and color perception have been developed, almost as many as the number of color combinations possible from the color wheel itself (see Figure

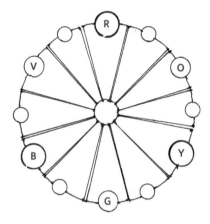

Figure 3.7
The color wheel diagrams the basic colors of the spectrum and their relationship to one another.

3.7). Most of that information is, however, beyond the scope of this discussion. We will address only those most applicable to planting design.

The first step is to understand basic color concepts—and develop a common language of color. Only then can we begin to recognize how colors react to and with other colors, how they appear in different light conditions, and how they affect people and can be used to create moods.

Color has a basic intrinsic appeal and the capability to provoke powerful emotional responses. Colors can impart a sense of peace and harmony or excitement and energy; colors can be used to convey warmth or coolness, light or darkness, happiness or sadness. In plantings, every color will appear different according to its surroundings, which are constantly being modified by changing atmospheric and environmental conditions. The relative quality of light on foliage, flowers, and branches and twigs will determine the quality and intensity of the colors. According to Penelope Hobhouse in *Color in Your Garden* (1991), designers can use their knowledge of color theory to blend and control the resultant effects in their mixed planting designs.

For all the theory and science of color, the appreciation of color is entirely subjective, and is heavily influenced by perception, personal taste, and experience. As H. Stuart Ortloff and Henry B. Raymore pointed out in their book *Color and Design for Every Garden* (1951), "Color is transient and capricious." And for designers, how well they understand the complex principles behind color theory will influence greatly their ability to evoke such perceptions by participants of the landscape or garden.

When it comes to design, too often color overrides other design considerations. It is not uncommon to see compositions that rely entirely on the use of color, to the exclusion of other elements of composition such as form and texture. But the brilliance of color is fleeting, so focusing a design strictly on color can very easily and quickly lead to failure. The true success of any garden or landscape lies in its basic structure and framework. Color and its impact should be used as seasonal highlights that support the more enduring elements of composition.

Fortunately, there are guidelines to follow for using color effectively, many of which were established for painting or graphic arts applications. In those instances, however, atmospheric conditions are more reliable. In the landscape, however, the changing conditions of light—for example, evening sun vs. morning sun, northern hemisphere light vs. southern hemisphere light, etc.—will change the appearance of the color, which is different from interior applications. Therefore, we need to take care not to turn the guidelines into "rules," which if followed to the letter can lead to boring and uninspiring compositions. Whereas in one garden we may have a subtle color scheme, such as using only greens to connote a relaxed atmosphere, in another we may design a color cacophony of loud and riotous colors, to impart a festive and joyful atmosphere. The choice will depend on the client, the location, and the purpose of the planting. Plant colors should be seen, as Hobhouse describes them, as tools "to extend and reduce dimensions, to give sensations of warmth or coolness, to provoke stimulation or induce moods of restfulness."

Notably, during the last decade, with the introduction of so many colored foliage plants and bold new floral types, a more informed use of color in the landscape has become increasingly important. The basic precepts of the use of color, the moods that it can create, and how it affects or is affected by neighboring plants are all factors that designers need to consider. In the mixed planting, specifically, color is used for interest, and so must be intricately weaved throughout the composition; and its presence must be extended across the seasons and at various levels.

Color is essentially the reflection, refraction, and absorption of various spectra of light, so the first precept to recognize is that color is perceived only when there is light. A color as seen by the human eye depends on the quality and brightness of the light that is reflected or absorbed by the surface of a given plant part. It is the wavelengths that are reflected from the plant part that determine the various colors or hues that we see. Objects essentially have no color of their own; rather, they reflect certain rays of white light, which contains all colors. Red objects, for example, absorb all rays *except* the red ones, so it is these are reflected to the eye. Black objects *absorb* all colors, while white objects *reflect* all colors. The significance of this to the designer is that the changing conditions of light as noted earlier—for example, evening vs. morning sun, northern vs. southern light—will change the appearance of the color.

Once we understand the relationship of light to color, we need to address what are considered the three fundamental qualities of color: hue, value, and intensity.

Hue

Hue is the attribute of colors that permits them to be classed as red, yellow, green, blue, or as an intermediate between any contiguous pair of these colors. The natural spectrum as represented on a color wheel is composed of six hues: red, orange, yellow, green, blue, and violet. Hue is a pure color—that is, it contains no white, black, or gray (shades or tints). The basic hues as represented on the color wheel are fundamentally pigmentation, not light. It is the application of light at various levels that causes differing hues. Pure hues in nature are rare, and to perceive a pure hue would require a flat, uniform surface, which in a landscape environment is equally rare. Most surfaces have a variety of textures and shapes that tend to reflect and absorb light in a way that makes the object's true color seem to change.

Hues are also affected by the size and shape of the area of color. According to Sandra Austin in her book, *Color in Garden Design* (1998), colors will often appear different when massed together in large groupings, vs. individually. In contrast, an individual flower color used singly, if its hue is intense enough, can carry as much visual weight as a larger massing of a weaker hue.

Rarely is a hue perceived alone; typically, it is seen in conjunction with other hues, so it is always affected by and will change according to surrounding colors. Even in the same light, a hue will appear different depending on the colors that are next to it. Similarly, lighting and the distance of the observer from the composition will influence the intensity of the perceived hue. Furthermore, some hues are more subject to change than others. David Lauer points out in *Design Basics* (1979) that hues such as yellow, orange, blue, and red will experience only slight changes in the perceived color, whereas grayed, neutral colors (called "broken colors") such as gray or green will change their appearance regularly depending on their context.

Designers also need to be aware that hues can convey an emotional value. Half of the color wheel is composed of what are known as the *warm hues* (red, orange, and yellow), the other half of *cool hues* (blue, violet, and green). Warm hues, which humans relate to fire, heat, and the sun, demand attention; in response, they generally provoke an exciting and stimulating effect. They also carry high visual weight because they can be perceived at great distances: The eye will tend to focus on the color, causing it to seem to advance toward the viewer (appear closer). When used as a background, warm hues will make all objects in front of them seem closer. For the designer, these are important attributes to keep in mind. Warm hues can be used to reduce the influence of large or distant spaces or, as just noted, to make objects appear closer.

In contrast, cool hues, typically associated with sky, water, and the forest, cause relaxing and calming sensations. They tend to recede in the landscape and promote the feeling of spaciousness. They have low visual weight and can be inconspicuous, in comparison to their warmer counterparts on the color wheel.

Value

Value, the second property of color, refers to the lightness or darkness of the hue. It is the result of the light reflected from or absorbed by the surface. Value is also known as brightness, lightness, or luminosity. Adding white or black to the base pigment (color) can alter the value of a hue (see Figure 3.8). According to Austin, white reflects most light, has the highest value, and is the lightest (known as a *tint*) whereas black reflects almost no light and so has the lowest value and is the darkest (known as a *shade*). The impacts of value can best be understood by studying black-and-white photographs, where values of black and white and the various shades of gray are used to create an image composed of the patterns and arrangement of light and dark.

Unlike painters, who can alter the color value of an object simply by adjusting the quantities of white and black in the mixture, adjusting color in the landscape is much more difficult.

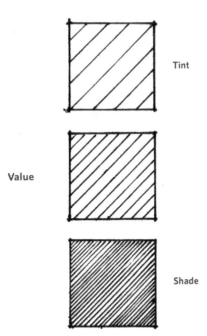

Tint

Value

Shade

Figure 3.8
The value of a hue is determined by
the levels of white or black present.

Rather than directly adjusting coloration, working with value in a landscape is more about being aware of the changes in perception than it is about directly adjusting coloration. As landscape designers, we have to account for environmental conditions that affect the appearance of value of color, which can appear lighter or darker based on their exposure the varying light conditions. A good way to illustrate this is to study the color of a plant that is partly in light and partly in shade: The part of the plant in the sun will appear to be lighter (have a higher value) in color than the part that is in shade, which will appear darker (have a lower value). The difference is in value, not color.

Value, like color, is variable and dependent on its surroundings for the visual sensation it generates. The contrast between color and value changes according to how the eye "reads" the various effects of light. Tints tend to be more prominent (have greater visual weight) when located close to the viewer, but have a low visual impact when viewed from a distance, when they tend to recede. By contrast, a shade of a hue has a higher visual weight and tends to advance, thereby reducing the apparent size of a space (Nelson 1985).

Intensity

The third property of color, intensity, refers to the brightness of a hue. Intensity is one of the most difficult aspects of color theory to understand because the definition changes with the medium. Also referred to as *saturation*, color intensity is the strength of a color and is determined by the quantity of the dominant hue.

As an example, a bright blue would be a strong intensity blue while a light blue would be a weak intensity. They both have the same value, but their intensity is different. Understandably, intensity affects the visual impact of a color. Weak intensity hues are visually undemanding and have low visual impact. The opposite is true for colors with strong intensities, those colors with a high visual impact, affecting distance, size, and force of attention (Nelson 1985).

The intensity of a hue, as with other qualities of color, can be influenced by other factors, including quality of light, surrounding hues, and the distance of the object to the viewer. Distance tends to gray colors. This can be witnessed by looking at mountain landscapes: As each range or peak recedes farther into the background its color progressively appears more gray or purple. This is due, in part, to the type and position of the light source on the object. When the light source is strong, the intensity of the color weakens, which is why landscape and garden photographers avoid photographing their creations during midday when all of the colors are washed out by the high sun. Instead, they take photographs during the early evening or morning hours, when the sun is low, so that colors appear rich and saturated.

Surrounding colors also have a strong influence on saturation and intensity. A very intense color may look bright and pure when placed against a dark green background, but that same color juxtaposed against other highly saturated colors will appear less intense because of the other, competing colors. To achieve a heightened degree of intensity, designers need to block out competing colors from the field of vision and juxtapose complementary colors.

Using Color in the Landscape

Sandra Austin, in *Color in Garden Design* (1998), identifies four phenomena that can be routinely anticipated when working with color in the landscape. These relate to how colors react to and with one another in different situations: simultaneous contrast, successive contrast, color assimilation, and color separation.

Simultaneous contrast When colors are adjacent to one another, their differences are emphasized, intensified, or otherwise tinged with the other colors. The contrast is appealing if the colors are complementary. For instance, when blue and orange appear side by side, both colors appear brighter because of the complementary nature of their relationship. This effect can happen between any colors, not just those that are complementary, but not all are attractive, especially when it occurs between analogous colors. Smaller patches of colors seem to be affected more by this simultaneous contrast than do larger massings of color.

Simultaneous contrast can be used to change the appearance of a hue by changing the darkness or lightness of the background. A hue will appear lighter when the background is dark, and darker when the background is light. An example of this would be to underplant red tulips with violet pansies, causing the violet in the pansies to seem more blue and the red of the tulips to move toward the orange range. If the pansies were yellow, then the red would move toward purple and the yellow toward green. In either instance, the colors would be intensified and their degree of contrast exaggerated.

Successive contrast This occurs when a color is influenced by a second color seen immediately beforehand, producing an effect known as an *afterimage*. To experience this, stare at an area of intense color for a brief period—say, a red circle. Then stare at a white wall. A complementary color, perhaps green, will seem to appear on the wall. The more intense the hue, the longer will be the effect of the afterimage. In a garden setting, areas with brighter hues and larger massings of colors will have a greater impact on the ability of the eye to perceive the "trueness" of adjacent colors. Thus, as Austin explains, if you were in a garden where green was the predominant color, and you then moved to an adjacent garden where the predominant color was red, the reds would look more intense and the green foliage adjacent to the reds more gray.

Color assimilation This phenomenon makes small areas of color that are not touching appear more alike. Due to their small size, the eye sees them in one overall field of vision. Hues in such spaces are read as an *average* of the hue, value, and intensity. The net result is a less vibrant and grayer composition. It was to avoid color assimilation that Gertrude Jekyll used large masses of colors in her color borders. Airy plants with fine texture and small delicate flowers that are spaced apart are more prone to color assimilation. Plants such as *Verbena bonariensis* with its lavender-purple flowers may make a composition appear darker from a distance while the light flowers of *Thalictrum* spp., for example, may make an overall composition appear lighter. From a distance, these plants tend to blend in with other colors, thus changing the overall color effect.

Color separation This occurs when colors that are separate but that appear within the same field of vision appear more alike. To counteract this effect in landscape design, "bridge" plants with neutral colors such as green or gray can be used to space out the colored plants. The result, especially when one general color scheme is used, is a greater degree of harmony in the composition.

COLOR SCHEMES

Familiarizing yourself with Austin's four concepts of how colors affect each other will be of inestimable value as you begin to design the color effects you want to achieve in your mixed planting compositions. But when it comes to truly understanding the complex relationships between colors and the outdoor environment, you will find experimentation—trial and error— to be necessary for determining the color schemes you will ultimately choose for your designs. Consider how Claude Monet, at his home in Giverny, west of Paris, produced scores of paintings of the same scene using different color schemes.

Color schemes, which relate to the position of the colors on the color wheel, can be divided into four categories: *monochromatic, analogous, complementary,* and *riotous.* They serve as the starting point for assembling plants with color.

Monochromatic Color Schemes

Monochromatic color schemes involve the use of only one hue of various values, for an overall visual effect that is harmonious and restful (see Figure 3.9). Creating monochromatic schemes is, without doubt, the easiest way to ensure a successful color scheme, but at the risk of being monotonous. Depending on the range of values used, the scheme typically transitions subtly from one value to another.

Monochromatic designs are simple and understated, yet require restraint by the designer to achieve the desired effect—typically an air of elegance. Because monochromatic schemes contain a single hue, shapes and textures become just as important as the color. When the eye of the observer does not have to change focus from color to color, other design features stand out more readily.

Analogous Color Schemes

Analogous color schemes combine several hues that are next to one another on the color wheel, as shown in Figure 3.10. To create an analogous color scheme, you simply choose any

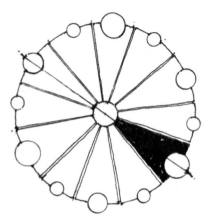

Figure 3.9
Monochromatic schemes are based on the use of one color at various intensities and values.

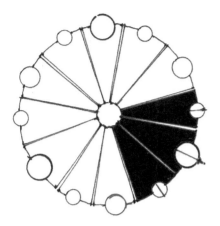 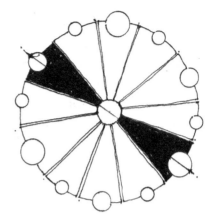

color and then use the color to the right and to the left of it. As in a monochromatic scheme, the values of the colors may vary in value. The colors may share a common hue, such as yellow, yellow-red, and red, or blue, blue-green, and green. Analogous schemes give the appearance of harmony and restfulness, as they usually are variations of warm or cool schemes. And because of the relative closeness of their hues, analogous schemes from a distance may appear to be a large-mass planting of one color. Therefore, if the intent is to create contrasting color combinations, the distance from which the composition is meant to be viewed must be given careful consideration.

Figure 3.10 (LEFT)
Analogous color schemes utilize any three adjacent primary, secondary, and tertiary colors.

Figure 3.11 (RIGHT)
Complementary schemes make use of any two colors aligned on opposite sides of the color wheel.

Complementary Color Schemes

In complementary color schemes, colors from opposite sides of the color wheel are combined (see Figure 3.11). Many people prefer vibrant color displays in which contrasting colors produce exciting patterns. As the term suggests, in these schemes, each color complements the others, making the saturation of the opposite hue more intense.

Complementary color displays are difficult to create, requiring the skill to transition effectively from adjacent colors. Too much contrast produces a jarring effect. The easiest approach is to choose a dominant color combination (say, yellow-blue, red-green, etc.) and repeat it throughout the composition, alternating other colors at appropriate intervals and using neutral-colored plants (white, silver, and green) as "bridgers." The value of the two dominant colors should be kept at an equal level.

Riotous Color Schemes

Riotous color schemes, as the term implies, follow no rules of theory or patterns established by the color wheel. Rather, they combine as many colors as desired to create a vibrant and bold composition. Producing a riotous scheme is the most difficult because it is all too easy to cause visual unrest—too many colors contradicting one another. Therefore, neutral colors and bold foliage plants are needed to create bridges between what would otherwise seem to be conflicting visuals. Repetition is also important in riotous color schemes, and is usually represented in the form of bold and neutral foliage plants located throughout the composition at regular intervals.

The Language of Design

A planting composition is not perceived as a set of distinct plants, but by virtue of the simultaneous interaction of all of the plants together it becomes a highly complex psychological and physical experience. Each element in the composition performs a function in the design and in turn exerts a visual force to which the mind and eye react. The purpose of this section is to show how and to what extent it is possible to analyze universal principles of design or what can be called the language of design. These distinguishing characteristics of design as applied to planting design include scale and proportion, balance, rhythm, emphasis, unity, and variety. We must understand this language if we are to successfully combine plants to create the particular feeling or mood appropriate for the landscape and the design intent.

SCALE AND PROPORTION

Scale essentially refers to the size of an object, whether large or small, based on a standardized unit of measure, such as 1 inch, 2 feet, and so on (see Figure 3.12). Proportion refers to the

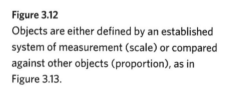

Figure 3.12
Objects are either defined by an established system of measurement (scale) or compared against other objects (proportion), as in Figure 3.13.

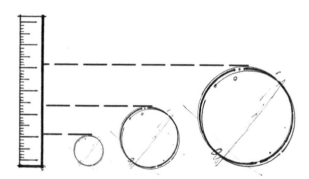

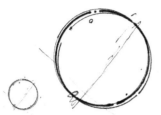

Figure 3.13
Proportionately, one circle
is larger than the other based
on their relative size.

relative size of an object as measured against another element or some accepted or relative standard (see Figure 3.13). Scale and proportion are similar concepts with slightly different emphasis, either absolute (scale) or relative (proportion). Scale and proportion can also be comparative values of line, form, texture, and color.

Proportion

Proportion can be comparative to separate objects or it can be the comparative relationship of the parts of the composition to each other and to the whole. It is the comparative relationship that is paramount in planting design.

Philosophers, artists, and architects have been defining and establishing mathematical rules for proportion since the time of the Greeks. The Parthenon was constructed according to the principles of the golden section, which states that the ratio of the whole to the larger part is the same as the ratio of the larger part to the smaller. The classical Greek artist Polykeitos sculpted athletic figures in which the height of the body was eight times the length of the head (Fichner-Rathus 1986). Leonardo da Vinci, too, studied relationships of proportion between parts of the human anatomy, then translated them to art, as shown Figure 3.14. Over time, using the human body as a means to establish pleasing proportions has become one of the leading frames of reference to aid designers in developing pleasing compositions. As Anne Bernat Sutter said in her book, *New Approach to Design Principles: A Comprehensive Analysis of Design Elements and Principles in Floral Design* (1967), "Good proportion is the pleasing variation of the dimension of one form or part thereof to the whole."

Proportion applies to space, color, and texture. As applied to planting design, it relates to the proper use of

Figure 3.14
Leonardo da Vinci used the human figure to establish a universal system of proportions, which were applied to paintings and works of sculpture.

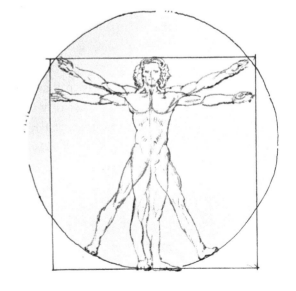

quantities or groups of plants in relation to others within an overall composition. According to Theodore Walker in *Planting Design* (1985), in comparing large-scale design (e.g., a park) to small-scale design (e.g., a private home), the plant massings in the design of a park would have greater quantities of plants in each grouping than in the home design. In the case of mass and void planting design compositions, proportion is the relationship of the open space compared to the planted areas.

Scale

Scale for a planting design can be determined before the components are placed in the landscape, based on a given reference. It can manifest in repetition, variation, or contrast of size (Sutter 1967):

▷ Repetition is achieved using like sizes.

▷ Variation is achieved using sizes that differ slightly.

▷ Contrast is achieved using sizes that differ sharply.

Scale is used in planting design to ensure that the size of the elements or parts within the design harmonize with each another and the overall composition. For example, in a small garden, the beds should be small, as should be the plants that fill them.

Scale is also used to compare the size and scale of the elements within the composition: It is relative to the overall area of the composition or elements within the composition. Thus, a large element in one landscape may be small in a larger one. An example would be to compare a *Cornus kousa* (Chinese dogwood) planted against a small cottage: the tree would appear large in scale relative to the structure. But that same tree, placed against a five-story building, would appear small in scale relative to the structure.

The three examples as shown in Figure 3.15 show how variations in scale can create a different impression of the composition. Having elements of differing sizes can create various effects, and thus can affect the result (Lauer 1979). In this way scale can be used to attract notice to the unexpected or exaggerated.

In Figure 3.16, the large circle would be called large-scale. This element occupies a proportionately greater amount of space given the overall dimension of the composition. It is, by comparison, *out of proportion* to the other elements. It is too large in relation to the other small elements and overwhelms the composition, demanding too much visual attention. It might or might not also be considered *out of scale*, depending on the intent of the designer. Such an element, when used to create emphasis in a composition, would serve as a focal point. An unusual proportion, generally large, in a design must, however, have a thematic or functional justification.

BALANCE

Learning to walk is our first real experience with balance. A sense of balance in humans is innate, and lack of balance tends to disturb us—hence the expression "throws us off balance." Whether we are aware of it or not, the mind naturally assumes a central axis, and we expect some kind of equal weighting, stability. The axis functions as a fulcrum, and balance is the equity expressed in the actual or visual weight about the central axis or point. It is the even distribution of weights, elements, or opposing forces that gives a sense of equilibrium.

Balance is generally categorized as symmetrical, asymmetrical, and perspective:

Symmetrical balance The most recognizable and simplest type of balance to create is symmetrical, where both sides of the axis or fulcrum are even or visually identical—a mirror image (see Figure 3.17), such as a row of street trees lining an avenue. In planting design, symmetrical balance connotes formality. Planting two trees, one on each side of an entrance drive for example, is an example of symmetrical balance. Studies have shown that children and

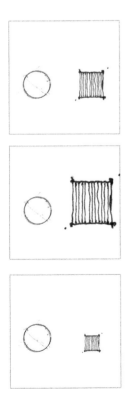

Figure 3.15 (LEFT) The circle in all three illustrations is the same size. Varying the size of adjacent elements affect the perception of its actual size, and will thus affect the relationships of the elements in the composition.

Figure 3.16 (RIGHT) The excessively large size of the circle is proportionately out of balance as compared to the other elements in the composition.

Figure 3.17
A mirror image of elements represents symmetrical balance.

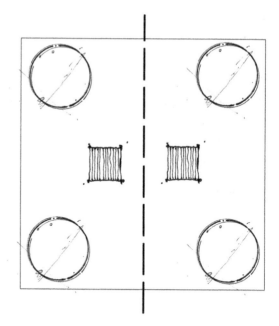

beginning art students will almost instinctively create patterns of symmetrical balance. This is attributed to the fact that our bodies are basically symmetrical and so we naturally apply this principle to everything we do (Lauer 1985).

Asymmetrical balance Asymmetrical balance renders a design that is visually balanced on both sides but using nonequivalent forms or masses, such as color, form, texture, or lines (see Figure 3.18). Asymmetrical balance is considered informal. A large shade tree on one side of a driveway might be balanced asymmetrically with three small flowering trees on the other.

Perspective balance Perspective balance relates to depth, and includes the foreground, midground, and background (see Figure 3.19). For example, if an element in the midground were designed to be of greater importance in the composition, the elements in the foreground and background would necessarily carry less visual weight. If any of the visual weighting were to change, the composition would lose its perspective balance.

Achieving balance is tricky, for the apparent weights of objects in space will vary. Our mind naturally comprehends this variation, though sometimes only on an unconscious level, and recognizing more subtle differences usually requires training. In planting design, denser and bolder forms—such as most evergreens—will appear heavier, as will brighter colors such as red and

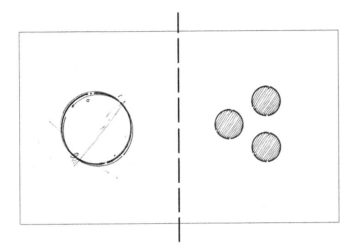

Figure 3.18
Different-sized elements
balance one another by
having equal visual
weight.

Figure 3.19
The large-leaved perennial in
the foreground, the deciduous
trees in the midground, and
the tall conifers in the
background all balance one
another (have equal visual
weight), creating perspective
balance.

orange. Larger-sized plants and coarser textures will also appear heavier. Smaller sizes and sparser forms appear lighter in weight, as do grayed colors and intermediate textures.

To achieve balance in a composition it's imperative that you appreciate the value and visual weight of the qualities of the various plant materials you will use. This will give you insight to both their inherent and opposing qualities. Position, shape, texture, value, and color are all critical factors to achieving balance. Some you will use exclusively, but more often than not you will implement more than one.

▷ *Balancing by position* refers to the apparent weight of an element, which will seem to increase the further it is from the axis. A smaller item placed toward the edge of the composition, for example, can balance a larger item placed closer to the center of the composition (see Figure 3.20). At first glance this may in fact seem to cause an imbalance, but it illustrates the well-known principle in physics that two items of unequal weight can be brought into balance by moving the heavier item toward the center of the axis or fulcrum.

▷ Color can be an effective tool to achieve balance. Studies have shown that our eyes are attracted to color and, given the choice, we will always gravitate to a colored object. Therefore, a small area of bright color, such as a grouping of flowers, can balance a larger area of neutral green foliage. The eye, drawn to the color, sees the bright spot as being visually heavier than the larger mass of green.

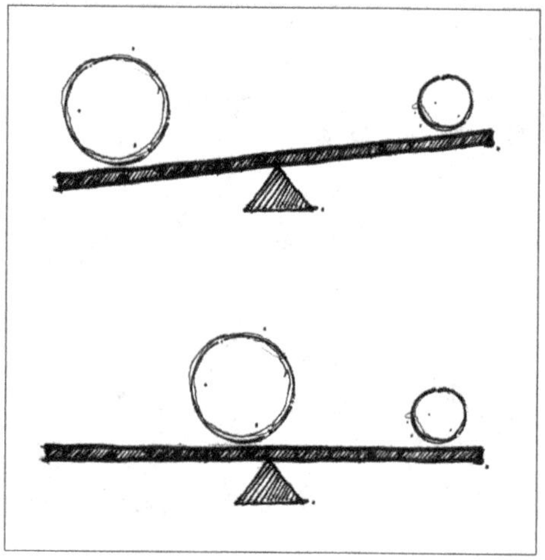

Figure 3.20
The relationship of an element to the central fulcrum point or axis line will impact its ability to balance another object on the opposite side.

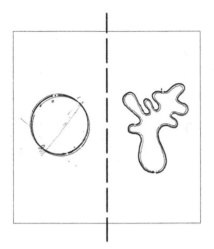 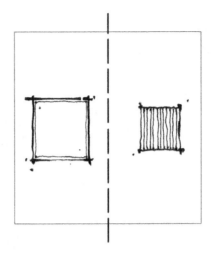

Figure 3.21
The intensity of the amebic-like shape or an element with a dark hue will have greater visual weight than simpler elements, making the picture appear out of balance.

▷ Using texture, shape, or value to help achieve balance is a more subtle technique for achieving balance in a composition, one based on objects being dissimilar. In practice, using these effects is much easier in painting, where the medium is more conducive to minute, controlled forms of manipulation. With plant materials as the medium, this is much more difficult, but nonetheless possible. A small, textured object might be used to balance a larger, untextured one; a small but complicated shape could serve to balance a larger, more uniform-shaped object; and a darker, smaller, element could appear visually equal to a lighter, larger one (Lauer 1985). These examples are illustrated in Figure 3.21.

RHYTHM

Rhythm is the organization of direction, which is movement in space. Nature is replete with rhythmic patterns, found in waves, sounds, the seasons, even the veins of leaves. Rhythm as applied to planting design refers to movement of the viewer's eye across recurrent aspects of the composition; it is the presence of a dominant, inferred direction. A design lacking rhythm is dull; a rhythmic design is dynamic. We can create rhythm in planting design in three ways: repetition, alternation, and gradation.

Repetition Rhythm can be established by repeating elements or groups of elements in order to create an obvious sequence (see Figures 3.22 a, b, and c). Repeating a vertical element such as a columnar juniper or a particular color along a border edge would illustrate this type of rhythm. The spacing, or cadence, between elements will establish the character of the composition.

Figures 3.22 a, b, and c
The three examples illustrate various types of rhythm.

Alternation Rhythm created in this way, as an alternating sequence of two or more motifs, produces a regular and anticipated sequence. This method of creating rhythm enables greater variation, hence typically generates more interest than a basic pattern of repetition. Consider, for example, a traditional architectural colonnade with its repeating pattern of light columns against the darker, negative spaces between.

Gradation Rhythm can also be achieved by gradual transitions, or gradations, from one quality to another. The change should occur slowly enough to create interest and never so quickly as to cause unrest. Gradation can be applied to color, texture, and form. Transitioning colors from hot to cool, or texture from coarse to fine would be examples of gradation rhythm.

Any rhythm prompted by planting design must be illusory, stimulated by design elements and the relationship between those elements.

EMPHASIS

Every composition must have a point of emphasis, a spot that stands out from the others. By making certain elements dominant, while subordinating others, an obvious focal point will become apparent to the observer. The objective of the focal point is to, first, attract attention and, second, encourage the viewer to look further. Thus, in using emphasis we must think in terms of dominance and subordination (Nelson 1985). No composition should be composed of parts whose visual weight is equal.

Emphasis can be achieved by:

Limiting the number of dominant points These points should have a higher degree of visual weight than others, and they should be few in number. This is what creates interest. Too many points of interest results in visual confusion.

Using accent planting This can be achieved by isolating individual plants serving as focal points, or by dramatically contrasting form, texture, or color. Accent plants are used to draw attention to elements such as entrances, steps, seating, statuary, or simply to create an interesting focus in the overall planting composition.

Introducing contrast Achieving emphasis by contrast is the most common method to achieve a focal point (see color plates, Figure 3.23). Using this method, one element in the composition differs notably or has greater visual weight than all the others. It "interrupts" the overall feeling or predominant patterns, thus it attracts the eye. There are many techniques for using contrast (Lauer 1979):

> A vertical form will break the pattern and become the focal point in a composition primarily composed of horizontal forms. The reverse is true as well.

> A grouping with a strong geometric pattern will break up, and become the focal point, in plant massing drifts of irregular forms.

> A grouping of plants with rough-textured foliage will serve as an effective contrast in a composition made up of predominantly fine-textured foliage.

> A plant that is significantly larger than the others will create a point of interest when added to a composition whose other plants are roughly the same size.

Isolating elements When one item is isolated or placed apart from others in the composition, it becomes the focal point. A small tree situated in a nearby lawn panel is an example of using isolation to create emphasis (see Figures 3.24 a and b).

Figures 3.24 a and b
Separating a plant or object from a grouping of similar elements can create a point of emphasis.

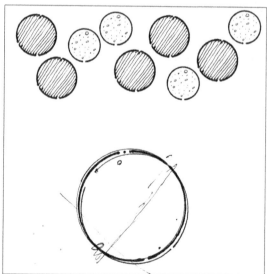

Placing plants purposefully If the general movement of a design points to one item, say through the direction of a line or by graduated sequence, the eye is directed there. By placing a special plant at that end point, it becomes the point of emphasis (see color plates, Figure 3.25). When using this technique, it is important first to identify where in the design you intend the point of emphasis to be. Once that point has been established, you can begin to build elements around it that will lead or draw the eye to it.

Clearly, there are many ways and opportunities to introduce points of emphasis in your planting designs—all the more reason to use restraint in this endeavor. Keep in mind that the point of emphasis must remain part of the design; it should not be so unusual that it seems out of place. Imagine a large ground-cover planting of *Liriopie* with an enormous *Miscanthus floridus* emerging from it: Here, the focal point would be too prominent and overwhelm the rest of the design. True, a specific theme may, at times, call for a very dominant point of emphasis. However, we must never lose sight of the general principle of unity to create a harmonious composition.

UNITY

As just stated, unity implies a harmonious pattern or order among the various elements of a planting composition. Within the composition each plant will play a specific role and have a meaning, but the viewer must first see the pattern of the whole, rather than a series of individual elements. A congruity must exist among the elements of the design. They should look as though they belong together having some visual connection or common thread.

Harmony can result from similar characteristics (of pattern, texture, form, etc.), an overall balance of the composition (no one part appears too visually heavy), or proper scale (the general size of the elements relates to the scale of the landscape setting) according to Nick Robinson in *The Planting Design Handbook* (1992). At the outset of the design process organizational themes must be identified to unify the different elements and to organize the elements of a composition to create a logical pattern.

Achieving unity in a planting design can be accomplished via several methods: creation of a theme, proximity, repetition (as with rhythm), and continuation (Lauer 1979).

Single theme When you invoke a single theme or idea in the design, the various elements used, despite their differences, will all have some basic linking characteristic that relates them. The theme may be color, such as the famous red border at Hidcote Manor, in Chipping Camden, England, or it may be expressed as in the planting designs of Oehme, van Sweden & Associates, where the predominant plant materials used are ornamental grasses (see color plates,

Figure 3.26). A historic theme is another possibility, such as creating an Italianate garden where the predominant style is one of geometric formality, with a heavy reliance on clipped evergreen hedges that form garden rooms and parterres. Other possible planting themes are seasonal, taxonomic, habitat, fragrance, annuals, and perennials.

Proximity Using this technique elements are located close together so that they appear as if they belong together, in spite of their individual characteristics, as shown in Figure 3.27. In planting design, proximity must, however, be used in conjunction with other unifying methods. For example, in a perennial border planting, where this method is often used, there would have to be some other complementary element, such as color, form, or texture, to support the proximity of the perennials.

Continuation Continuation is used to carry the viewer's eye smoothly from one element to another in the composition, such as a line, edge, or continuous surface treatment. Continuation is a standard method used in landscape design to connect one individual planting bed to another or to unify a group of disparate plants. Continuation can also be used to link or unify—proximate elements. In this way, a disparate group of trees or shrubs located in a panel of grass can be made to appear to float as separate elements or specimens, as shown in Figure 3.28.

A word of caution is in order here: Too much unity can result in a composition that is boring, as shown in Figure 3.29. To prevent this happening, unity must tie the composition together at the same time it incorporates variety. Translating this into design, repeating plants with similar shapes could be used to unify the composition, while shapes of different types or sizes could be used to add diversification. Or with color, in a predominantly blue garden, a range of blues from light to dark and all shades in between could provide the necessary variation.

Figure 3.27 a and b
The elements in Figure a (at left) are scattered and disparate, having no relationship to one another. Conversely, the elements in Figure b (at right) are in close proximity to one another and appear unified despite their differences.

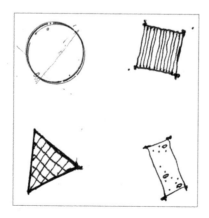
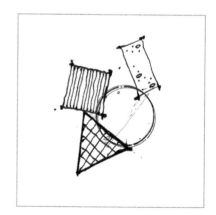

Figure 3.28
Unity can be achieved by using a single ground cover, in this case dwarf fountain grass, to link or tie together the separated shrub and evergreen plantings.

Figure 3.29
Too much unity as achieved by the repetition of a single element or plant, such as the ivy ground cover, can result in monotony.

VARIETY

As just explained in the context of unity, variety is the absence of uniformity. However, variety must be handled with care because too little leads to monotony and too much can cause unrest or confusion. Variety in design requires the use of a diversity of plant elements, characteristics, or types to result in change or contrast in the lines, forms, or colors of the composition (see color plates, Figure 3.30). It is variety that draws the attention and captures the interest of the viewer.

A mixed border that contains an assortment of plant types, or a perennial border that does not follow a particular color scheme but mixes a number of different colors, are examples of the effective use of variety in a planting composition. The degree to which you add variety to your designs will depend on the roles played by line and form, texture, and color in the composition. Sequentially graduating varietal changes will produce subtle designs that have a sophisticated calming effect. Dramatically altering the qualities will result in a design that is bold and dramatic. Ultimately, however, the effect of variety should never be so great that it disrupts the unity of the composition.

4 | **Structuring and Adorning the Mixed Planting Composition**

IMAGINE A PLANTING IN THE WINTER MONTHS, when there is no foliage or flowers on most plants. With the exception of some evergreens, the scene is drawn only by bare twigs, stems, and trunks. Though stark, these plant elements serve an important role: They reveal the "structure" or "form" of the composition, often also referred to as the "framework" or "skeleton" of a planting design. It is these structure plantings that create the "bulk mass" of a composition.

Imposing a Planting Structure

Structure plants establish a permanent framework for the garden or the landscape as a whole, as well as for the individual planting beds contained within it. When mature, it is the size, density, and shape of these plants that give the composition its overall form; and it is the mass and volume created by certain plant types that will determine the spatial quality of the beds and the overall landscape. Plants with good form, texture, and, in special instances, color all play important roles in achieving this objective. These plants must, of course, be placed strategically to create an effective, pleasing structure in the overall planting composition.

To begin to establish this vital structure, the first step is to "paint" the scene in broad brushstrokes, using a selection of structure plants—generally, small trees, shrubs, and evergreens, although in certain compositions large, sturdy perennials or ornamental grasses may fill this role. Essentially, structure plantings are the secondary background players in this scene, setting the stage for more flashy "star" performers. Let's examine each of these plant types in turn.

SMALL TREES

As structural elements, small trees help to create a vertical mass. The overall visual weight created by their height and generally upright form causes them to rise above other plantings and to create a point of interest and function as a defining element. Small trees generally comprise a small percentage of the overall composition, although this can vary depending on the objective of the design. Allocating between 10 to 15 percent of an overall planting composition for small tree plantings is a good general rule. In addition, an individual small tree or massing of trees in a mixed planting can be used to define an edge, enclose an area, set a point of visual interest, or create a visual ceiling.

As an edge plant in the mixed planting, a small tree can be used like a wall to reinforce or establish the symbolic edge of a space (see color plates, Figure 4.1). Collectively, they can be used as wall-like edges that define planting rooms; used singly, they can serve as plant pillars, acting like boundary markers denoting an edge (see color plates, Figure 4.2).

Small trees can also enclose an area, with their trunks and canopies forming semitransparent walls or ceilings that, in turn, create "compartments" (see Figure 4.3). To accomplish this design objective, however, fairly mature trees are needed. Within this framework other plantings become the dominant element in the landscape.

Small trees can become a point of visual interest, too. When a single small tree is located effectively in a small massing of shrubs or perennials, for example, it will stand out; or, in a larger massing of shrubs and perennials, serve to break it up (see color plates, Figure 4.4). When used in this way, careful thought should be given to the relative visual weight of the small tree, which should be balanced with some other element in the overall planting composition.

Another function of small trees in a planting composition is as neutral elements, in which case they allow other plantings to take center stage. They can set the vertical limit, the

Figure 4.3
In Central Park, small trees are used to enclose an outdoor "room."

"visual ceiling," in a planting composition, to channel the viewer's eye to the ground level to focus on lower-level plantings (see Figure 4.5). This is most effective when the design objective is to keep the eye at a certain level—for example, when the area behind the planting is distracting or unattractive.

SHRUBS

As structural elements shrub plantings provide the bulk of the mixed planting's compositional elements (see color plates, Figure 4.6). Typically, this means allocating between 20 to 50 percent of a composition to various types of structural shrubs. The percentage will, of course, fluctuate according to the use of other plant types such as perennials, grasses, and annuals; with the design intent; and with the level of maintenance necessary.

Structural shrubs have a number of possible functions in the mixed planting:

▷ They can serve as a visual platform, and other plantings can be displayed above, below, or behind or in front of this platform.

▷ Used en masse, they can become a unifying element, knitting other components of the composition together.

Figure 4.5
The canopy of large shade trees forms a ceiling over lower-level plantings.

▷ In larger beds, they are highly valued for their ability to occupy large amounts of space. In this capacity they serve as filler shrubs and establish the framework for additional support plantings.

▷ The number of species of structural shrubs, when minimized, will provide a neutral background and allow foreground and other plant types to stand out. In this fashion, structural shrubs can be arranged to define areas and create bays for other plantings.

▷ Structural shrubs with more ornamental qualities planted singularly or in small groups can function as specimens and provide a key feature or visual focal point in the composition.

EVERGREENS

Evergreens are the most effective and reliable structural plantings in a mixed composition, capable of maintaining the basic structural forms of the design. They provide an enduring framework throughout the seasons, even as neighboring plants types rise and fall. Most evergreens have dark neutral-green foliage, which provides a foil for foreground plants and never competes with that of others, as some deciduous shrubs do.

But there are some evergreen types that have colored foliage or unique shapes, characteristics that make them more appropriate as theme shrubs than as background plants. Incorporating these into the composition can dramatically influence the character of the design. Depending on their arrangement, for example, their shape can add an air of formality.

Geometric shapes or topiary can add either a formal or whimsical aspect to a composition. Their use in high-impact areas of the composition can make a dramatic statement. Understandably, however, these types of evergreens should be used judiciously, as they carry greater visual weight, and hence may compete with other areas of the plantings.

Punctuating with Decorative Plants

Decorative plants are important to a garden or landscape design because they act as "punctuation" in the composition. Though in essence a form of structure plantings, they have greater prominence. Decorative plants are those that have some distinctive quality that sets them apart from other plant types and forms, adding interest and variation to the overall composition. This quality will be some dominant characteristic that causes it to stand out as a focal feature in the overall composition, according to John Brookes in *The Book of Garden Design* (1991). Whether it is a distinct size, form, color, or texture that distinguishes it from its immediate surroundings, a decorative plant must also have sufficient "architectural presence" to serve its purpose year-round.

As elements that attract attention and carry heavy visual weight, decorative plant use should be restricted to those areas where a statement or change of rhythm in the surrounding plantings is desired. H. Stuart Ortloff and Henry B. Raymore in their book *Color and Design for Every Garden* (1951), suggest several techniques for incorporating decorative plants into a composition: accent by a change of line, emphasis by a change of position, accent by contrasting foliage textures, and accent by color.

Change of line A decorative plant located to effect a change of line may be a strong vertical form placed to rise above more rounded, lower shrub massings (see color plates, Figure 4.7). A form of this type, typically a columnar evergreen, will rise like a spire, drawing the eye and generating special interest. Spires may then be combined with other events in the composition to result in a unique combination of features at a particular point in the landscape.

Change of position This technique relies on breaking a particular rhythm established in the composition. For example, a particular plant placed in a grouping or massing may be moved forward and planted in isolation from, yet near to, the remainder of the adjacent group (see Figure 3.24, page 64). This emphasizes the plant's decorative features and distinguishes it from its massed counterparts. A decorative plant used in this way must have sufficient visual weight to justify its isolation, but also be similar enough to nearby plantings or massings to make the association obvious.

Contrast in foliage Decorative plants with contrasting foliage can be used as accent points in a composition—for example, locating a plant with coarse texture at a special spot among fine-leaved plants, or vice versa.

Accent by color Contrast by color is probably the most common method of providing accent. It is the most visually stunning and obvious. Color in a composition, especially one dominated by greens or with lesser vibrant colors than the accent color, creates areas of high visual energy in the composition, thus providing the accent. It is the most obvious technique but usually not permanent because is often accomplished with flowers. Using colorful foliage can minimize the temporality of flowers and create a more permanent impact.

By their nature as decorative elements, plants in this category can easily be misused or overused in a planting. Overused they can generate too much nervous energy by pulling and pushing the eye into many directions. Ironically, their overuse can also lead to monotony, as the decorative element itself begins to blend in with the remainder of the composition simply because there are so many of them. To avoid this, keep in mind that a decorative plant should never be used without a clear purpose.

Another important guideline is to distribute these plants evenly throughout the composition (for *compositional balance*) and, generally, locate them at punctuation, or emphasis, points. Effective places to incorporate decorative plants include: building corners, where a bed may change direction, bed bulb-outs (see Figure 6.50, page 173), ends of axis or view corridors, between plant massing types, or in contrast to hardscape elements. They can also be set to lead the eye through the garden.

We will discuss further in Chapter 7 how decorative plants, along with structural plants, will be among the first plant types to be located in a composition.

Working with Plant Forms

We discussed form extensively in Chapter 2 (page 20) in regard to successional growth. Here we will address how the form of plants affects the structural and decorative features in a mixed planting. When designing with plants, you must learn to look beyond the patterns, textures, and decorative elements that plants possess to determine their basic form. The form of a plant is important because all of design is fundamentally based on the arrangement of shapes or forms. The three-dimensional qualities of a plant's form provide you, the designer, with a myriad of opportunities. The participant will view the composition from a multitude of angles, therefore the designer must anticipate all the viewpoints from which the composition will be seen. Additionally, you must consider how other forms may affect the composition. In a flat, two-dimensional work of art, the number of angles from which the piece of art can be viewed will be limited, whereas the three-dimensional use of forms, as in sculpture, can be viewed from countless angles. With each passing step as the viewer moves through a landscape composition, forms are being seen in differing perspectives and relationships to one another. The visual experience is fluid.

Thus, to create a visual experience, you must master the materials of your art form: plants. Specifically, it is their visual appearance, individually and in combination with other plants, that you must understand. William R. Nelson in his book, *Planting Design: A Manual of Theory and Practice* (1985), said, "To achieve the goal of visual art, three factors are particularly important. They are the process of visual perception, an intimate knowledge of the materials to be used, and a systematic application of artistic principles and skills. Therefore, any design incorporating plants demands an understanding of the materials and sensitivity to the visual effects on the observer. This requires training your eye to critically observe plants and plant combinations."

Different plant forms will, logically, have different effects in a composition. Gaining an appreciation and understanding of how each form will create, influence, or define the scene will require you to apply your understanding of the principles of art to carry out the intent of the design. The key to successfully combining plant forms is the ability to design contrast and harmony simultaneously. A composition that is composed of only rounded forms will be monotonous and boring, whereas one that contains a variety of contrasting forms tied together by a unifying element or shape will be interesting yet harmonious.

The diversity of the form that a plant assumes is determined by plant forms is based on three primary factors:

Genetic makeup First, the genetic makeup of a plant predetermines its natural form and growth behavior or habit. This assumes, of course, that the plant has not been manipulated or changed by man, such as through pruning or shearing. It is always best to use a plant in its natural form unless a specific design objective is desired, such as to establish a hedge.

Environmental conditions Second, environmental conditions, especially light and wind exposure, can dramatically influence a plant's growth and its form. Planting a tree on a windswept mountain hillside will causes the branches to grow toward the leeward side of the trunk, for example. Or planting a tree or shrub in poor light conditions will force the plant to grow toward the strongest source of light, thereby distorting its natural growth behavior, or form.

Ability to change Third, a plant's form may change over time both through the seasons and as it matures over the years. A plant may start out with an upright form, and then grow to become a rounded form at maturity. Or a plant may seem to have a strong upright form when in full foliage, but in the winter, without its leaves, it may take on an oval shape.

Plant form is a key aspect of establishing the structure in a planting composition. Trees, shrubs, and grasses possess the strongest forms and should be used in the mixed planting to give shape to otherwise *amorphic*—shapeless—plants. From a distance, form will override all other design qualities (Nelson 1985). Therefore, the selection of a particular form must take into account the surrounding elements and plantings. All types of plant forms function best in a composition whose other plants complement or accentuate the dominant form of a particular plant; hence, this should be the first consideration in choosing a particular plant. For example, when massed together, larger deciduous and evergreen trees often lose their individual shape and form a collective mass.

A plant's form is determined by its silhouetted outline—the cumulative parts that result in mass and volume occupying three-dimensional space. Plant forms are generally grouped into nine categories, each of which has a distinct role in composition: rounded, spreading, columnar, upright, vase, pyramidal, oval, prostrate, and weeping, as shown graphically in Figure 4.8. That said, it's important to point out that not all plants fit neatly into a single category. Some, such as annuals and perennials, grow in rather amorphous ways and so resist assignment to a distinct form category. Moreover, within each classification there are variations in growth behavior.

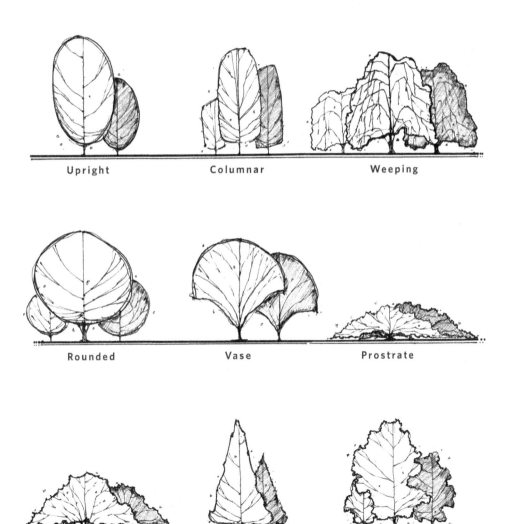

Upright   Columnar   Weeping

Rounded   Vase   Prostrate

Spreading   Pyramidal   Oval

Figure 4.8
Plants can be generally classified in one of nine basic categories of forms.

To refine the designation of a plant's form, descriptors such as loose, tight, open, dense, airy, solid, stiff, or leggy are applied. Similarly, the vegetative parts of the plant—twigs, bark, berries, flowers, fruit, and leaves—are used to establish the plant form's character.

Each of the nine forms has unique characteristics and applications in design, so they are described in turn in the following subsections.

ROUNDED

Rounded is the most common plant form and, generally, plants that fall into this category should constitute the majority of those used in a composition. Round-form plants are valuable for their stability. By virtue of their shape, they are nondirectional—they do not lead the eye. As such they can be used as anchors in a composition, acting as neutral backgrounds against which more powerful and dramatic forms can stand out.

Used en masse, rounded plants will grow together to form a solid block of vegetation and can instill unity through repetition in a composition. But they are flexible as well:

▷ They can be used as "bookends," to signify an opening or beginning and a closing or ending.

▷ Smaller forms of rounded plants can be placed individually as a specimen.

▷ When repeated along the edge of a border, rounded plants create repetition.

▷ When used in their natural form, they create unclipped deciduous screens.

SPREADING

Plants whose form is categorized as spreading are generally as broad as they are tall. This form is considered restful because it follows the horizon and often is in harmony with landforms. Unlike the rounded form, spreading plants direct the viewer's eye across the width of the planting. Therefore, designs can apply this effect across a horizontal plane to promote a feeling of spaciousness. Spreading plants are also used as "bridgers," to connect one massing of plant forms or plant type to another. Plants in this form category also make attractive companions to columnar or pyramidal forms through contrast. Much like rounded forms, spreading forms—specifically shrubs—function well as neutral plantings and so warrant consideration in a majority of compositions.

COLUMNAR

Columnar-form—or *fastigiated*—plants are narrow and taper to a point at the top. Understandably, they have a vertical emphasis, leading a viewer's eye upward toward the sky. When viewed from a distance, they appear even taller because of this powerful sense of verticality. Contrasted with lower rounded or spreading forms, columnar-form plants act like exclamation points, making a strong design statement. As focal points, they attract the eye to a point and hold it briefly before the eye moves on.

Their dramatic shape does, however, warrant a caution: Use them judiciously at selected areas intended as focal elements. Don't forget, too many individual points located through a design can cause visual unrest. However, the same quantity of plants used in a regularly spaced pattern or in logical intervals can impart a striking sense of rhythm.

UPRIGHT

Like columnar-shaped plants, plants that are upright also have a vertical emphasis, but their crowns spread slightly laterally and are rounded at the top. They are generally more contained and lack the pointed tips and narrow spires of the columnar form and are often quite bulky-looking in comparison to their columnar cousins.

In design, upright plants can be used to punctuate compositions made up of more regular forms, where their less severe form adds contrast to a composition but does not compete too dramatically for attention. Still, they need to be placed strategically, for optimum effect. They can also be used to demarcate entrances or exits or provide repetition along a border. Specialized plants of this form with unique foliage types or colors can be placed as focal points in a composition.

VASE

Vase-shaped plants are upright plants whose lateral stems arch from their own weight, forming a shape much like a V. These plants are often strong forms and so are frequently used singularly as focal points, though they typically have less of an impact than upright plants because of their looser growth pattern and rounded crown. And because their crowns spread, they need ample space to be fully appreciated.

For design purposes, it's important to note that vase-shaped plants are often described as "leggy," as their lower portions are usually devoid of foliage. Therefore, they need to be paired with lower plantings to hide their stems, or "legs." Another design issue with vase-shaped plants is that when are massed together, their individual form is lost, and the grouping assumes the form of a rounded or spreading mass.

PYRAMIDAL

Pyramidal plants have a vertical emphasis and are shaped much like an inverted cone, gradually tapering from the tip to the base. They usually possess a single straight trunk with a sharp and distinct outline, without any irregularities in the surface of the foliage. The branching behavior of pyramidal plants is usually regular, appearing dense or solid.

Pyramidal plants come in both evergreen and deciduous trees and shrubs types. Design-wise, the pyramidal plant form is best used for variety and contrast, as the conical shape offers a strong contrast between other rounded and horizontal forms. The foliage color variation in evergreens can offer additional contrast. However, because this is such a strong form, plants in this category should be used with caution—especially where this form does not exist naturally in the landscape. Pyramidal plants can, however, be used effectively in formal, architectural designs where stiff, geometric shapes are appropriate. In the mixed bed, they are effective as single specimens for contrast. Massed together, they often lose their prominent shape, except at the very top.

OVAL

The oval form plants, like the pyramidal and columnar, have a distinctively vertical emphasis because of their upright branching pattern and overall form. Typically, the width is narrower than the height and the overall appearance is somewhat egg-shaped. This form is most common in deciduous trees and is the result of selective breeding.

In design, the oval form—particularly the narrower plant varieties—provides a strong accent. And unlike the upright spires of columnar and pyramidal plant forms, oval-shaped plants blend more easily with rounded forms because the overall shape is contained within a soft outline. Their form also makes them popular for tight spaces or as street trees. In a mixed planting they should be placed sparingly, as punctuation marks for less regular forms. Oval plants are best anchored to the ground when surrounded with lower, rounded forms of shrubs.

PROSTRATE

Prostrate plants are low (under three feet), ground-hugging, creeping types that spread horizontally or at the ground level. They are generally fast-growing and follow closely the shape of the underlying surface, often forming neat, tightly massed foliage with consistent heights.

As design elements, their horizontal nature makes them an effective counterbalance to vertical and upright forms. They are also good filler plants for the front of the planting; and their often-neutral foliage texture and color make them beneficial as foils for more dynamic plant forms or types. They can serve as expansive neutral filler plantings between more intensive areas of the planting.

WEEPING

Weeping plants are generally rounded overall but have predominantly pendulous, or downward-drooping, branching patterning. This tendency leads the eye toward the ground, hence this category of plants is best utilized where the design intent is to direct the viewer to a specific downward location, such as a body of water. The weeping form is graceful and can add a picturesque quality to a composition, but it is also somewhat dramatic and so should be used only for accent, usually as a single specimen. Weeping plants function best along edges, where their pendulous foliage is encouraged to fall over the rim of an object.

Read more on the importance of form to design in Chapter 5, page 102.

Incorporating Leaf Characteristics

The importance of foliage to the mixed planting design cannot be overstated. As noted earlier, as a design element, foliage is more reliable and consistent than flowers yet offers just as much color and more variety in shape. Whereas the flower period of most plants is brief, foliage is present much longer and is, therefore, much more valuable as a decorative feature. In fact, if used properly, it is possible to construct a garden solely with foliage plants and still achieve interesting variety in color and texture. The diversity available to the designer from the vast array of leaf shapes, sizes, textures, and colors provide nearly limitless opportunities to combine, contrast, and develop complementary plant associations.

The more we, as designers, consider foliage with all of its various traits, the more important it will become in planning mixed compositions. Foliage can act as a neutral bridger between those plants displaying more dominant characteristics, provide interest in its own right, increase or decrease the apparent size of a space, or provide a background for which other plants or features can be displayed.

The overall appearance of any plant depends on the quality of its foliage, and each leaf has its own size, texture, and shape.

SIZE

Leaf size varies tremendously, from the tiny, smooth and lustrous leaves of *Buxus sempervirens* to the monstrously large, boldly palmate leaves of *Gunnera manicata*. The suitability of a specific type of leaf in a given mixed planting composition will depend on the design intent, whether it is, for example, to create a bold accent, to form a neutral bridge between two varying plant types, to establish a background, or to contrast with other leaf types. Leaf size also plays a role in establishing an atmosphere, to cast, say, an air of formality or conjure up an exotic feeling of the tropics. The largest leaves are most often found on perennials and tropical plants. Shrubs and trees with large leaves are less common.

Large-Leaved Plants

Generally, the warmer the climate the more leaf types that are available. Large-leaved plants are vulnerable to wind damage, so it is not surprising that large leaves, particularly on tropical plants, are found growing in moist, sheltered, and shady conditions.

Plants with large leaves can be used to dramatically contrast with smaller-leaved vegetation. Placing a single plant, or strategically spacing a number of plants, with large leaves in a mixed planting, can achieve a strong focal point. This is common practice for tropical plantings; however, as numerous types of exotic plants with large leaves have become more widely available, they are increasingly being used by gardeners and designers in other locations, as well.

Large leaves have the effect of foreshortening space, which can make long distances appear shorter. That said, large-leaf types should not be confined to big spaces, for when combined with other plants in a small garden, they provide not only contrast in size and foliar type but also give the illusion of space. In fact, large leaves are generally ineffective unless they are combined with smaller, more delicately leaved plants. But beware overuse: When too many large-leaved plants are incorporated in a design, the result can be confusion.

Small-Leaved Plants

Small-leaved plants are often well adapted for living in harsh growing conditions. Plants with a dense cover of small leaves make good foils or background growths for other plant types. They are generally visually undemanding (i.e., neutral) and dissolve into the background. Most small-leaved plants respond well to trimming or shearing and so make good hedging material. They also are excellent companions for plants with attractive flowers, as they do not compete for attention.

Small-leaved plants also have a tendency to recede from the viewer, giving a space the appearance of being larger than it is. This makes them particularly useful in small, confined spaces.

TEXTURE

Humans are, by nature, highly sensitive to texture, both visually and tactilely, so leaf texture in design can be a powerful element (see color plates, Figure 4.9). Texture in plants refers to the arrangement and character of its component parts—its size, shape, surface, etc. It may be the result of a pattern of lines or the scale of the leaf or twig patterns. On plants devoid of leaves, texture is determined by the twig size and the configuration and appearance of the bark. The arrangement of these plant components results in a texture generally classified as fine, medium, or course. But more specific descriptors are also applied to textural qualities, including heavy or light, rough or smooth, stiff or flexible, or thin or dense, according to Florence Bell Robinson in *Planting Design* (1940). It is predominantly the play of light and shade that highlights these details in the texture of leaves. The perception of leaf textures is detailed in Figure 4.10.

According to Norman Booth in his book, *Basic Elements of Landscape Architectural Design* (1983), texture plays a vital role in developing contrasting plant associations, and can affect planting compositions by its capability to affect unity and variety, foliage color tone, visual weight and interest, and overall mood. Texture in a composition must be given equal, if not more, weight than the use of color to initiate and maintain visual interest. As such, it is an important tool in developing planting compositions.

Texture in a composition can express a garden's personality, increase or decrease the apparent space, harmonize, and differentiate one plant mass from another. A mixture of textures adds a dramatic quality to a composition and provides a more stable, longer-lasting dimension to that of color. A composition of thoughtfully arranged and well-balanced textural patterns certainly is more intriguing than one composed of textures that are all the same.

Texture becomes more or less apparent depending on the distance of the viewer from the plant—logically, when closer in view, the details of the plant will be easier to perceive; when farther away, the texture will be seen more as the overall appearance of the plant mass. William R. Nelson described the effect of distance on texture this way in *Planting Design: A Manual of Theory and Practice* (1985): "The linear details of the branches begin to merge onto form; color details are lost except for the contrasts of the various hues of green; and texture becomes more of a general effect." From a greater distance, the details of the plant

Textural Perception Chart

PLANT COMPONENT	TEXTURE EFFECT*		
	F	M	C
Branching pattern			
Sparse			X
Dense	X		
Leaf type			
Short needle	X		
Long needle		X	X
Large leaf—general		X	
Large leaf—widely spaced or deeply sinused			X
Pinnate leaf			X
Cutleaf or deeply lobed	X		
Small leaf	X		
Fernlike	X		
Long petiole	X		
Grasslike—narrow blades	X		
Grasslike—wide blades		X	
Stiffly spikey or ribbonlike			X
Leaf surface			
Glossy	X		
Dull		X	X
Colored underside (white, silver, or light color)		X	X

*F = Fine texture
M = Medium texture
C = Coarse texture
X = Predominate perceptual texture

Figure 4.10
The chart illustrates the textural effects of various plant parts.

are lost and what is perceived are the reflections and shadows in, around, or reflected from the overall mass.

Coarse-Textured Plants

Coarse-textured plants attract the eye and engage the viewer for longer periods because of differences between light and shadow. Their value to design, then, is that they are highly visible, attract attraction, and provide rich contrast to other types of plant materials, and so are frequently used as focal points. Large leaves, thick, sparsely spaced branches, and open forms usually give the appearance of coarseness. Some examples of coarse-textured plants include oakleaf hydrangea (*Hydrangea quercifolia*), London plane tree (*Platanus occidentalis*), American agave (*Agave Americana*), and ornamental rhubarb (*Reum palmatum*).

Coarse-textured plants are especially effective when used with other, finer-textured plants that are to be seen from a distance, as the coarse-textured plant will make these more prominent—in essence, they provide visual relief as well as act as a counterpoint to fine-textured plants. Additionally, coarse-textured plants lend an air of informality and so are best reserved for informal massings in a naturalized setting, or singularly as a focal element. Their use in more formal settings should be limited to focal points.

Too many coarse-textured plants in a composition can quickly cause visual unrest. Therefore textural balance must be maintained throughout the entire composition—the visual textural weight must be evenly distributed. Additionally, the principle of sequence gradation must be introduced, to provide transition from coarse to fine texture—unless, of course, a dramatic contrast is desired for accent or drama (Nick Robinson 1992).

Coarse-textured plants tend to display colors better at great distances. The colors of these plants do not mix well with adjacent plants unless viewed from distances because of the variation in shade light, shade, and shadow reflected from the leaf and plant surfaces are so great, which affects the perceived spectrum of color. Moreover, coarse-textured plants with color have a disproportionately heavy visual weight, even though they may not be the largest group or occupy the greatest area. Consequently, they often appear to be the dominant color. Therefore, distance helps large-textured plants appear as larger blocks (Austin 1998).

Like large-leaved plants, coarse-textured plants give the feeling that space is compressed, thus making the apparent distance between the viewer and the plant seem shorter. As a design technique this effect may be helpful when the objective is to reduce the apparent size of an area to create a more intimate space. But caution must be exercised as well for too many coarse-textured pants in a small or confined space will cause a feeling of overcrowding or confinement.

Fine-Textured Plants

Fine-textured plants, those with small leaves or needles, are visually undemanding and have a soothing quality to them. Their soft and delicate appearance makes them less obvious in the landscape, especially from a distance. Few or no shadows are apparent between fine-textured plants, giving the effect of density and solidity. Examples of plants with fine texture include: horizontal rockspray (*Cotoneaster horizontalis*), honeylocust (*Gleditsia triacanthos*), shore juniper (*Juniperus conferta*), and painted fern (*Athyrium niponicum*). Deeply cut or divided leaves like those exhibited on Japanese maples will increase the appearance of the fineness. This quality provides fine-textured plants with the desirable design capability to act as a background foil or neutral bridge between more dominant plantings.

One important function of fine-textured plants is to make space seem to recede from the viewer. This makes fine-textured plants especially valuable in small spaces where the objective is to make the space appear larger. At greater distances they will blend with other fine- to medium-textured plants. Distance also affects the color perception of fine-textured plants: Their individual parts are easily seen up close or against a background of a different color; at further distances, colors of fine-textured plants are more difficult to distinguish tending to merge with adjacent colors.

Monotony is the primary caution against using too many fine-textured plants, especially in a composition generally viewed from a great distance. Fine-textured plants generally have a tight and controlled overall form, which dominates and overrides any other plant quality. It is this characteristic that makes them an appropriate form for more formal designs, where strict control of form and pattern are critical to the design intent. That is why they are so often used to create formal patterns as clipped hedges to contain more rambling types of plants, and to punctuate or designate a point such as an entrance.

SHAPE

Whether it is to introduce contrast, harmony, or direction, the importance of the shapes and patterns of leaves in a planting composition will become increasingly apparent as you learn to simplify your designs and reduce your reliance on color. You will find that leaf shapes and patterns can spark viewer interest and hold attention.

Leaves, of course, exist in a variety of shapes; but regardless of the shape, each leaf has a similar structure: It is made up of a broad, flat blade and a leafstalk attached to the twig or stem. Most leaves have one blade and are known as simple leaves. In compound leaves the blade is divided into three or more "leaflets." But whether simple or compound, leaves can be attached to the stem *alternately*, *oppositely*, or in *whirled* fashion. Alternately is generally the most common.

As many as nineteen different leaf types have been classified, but for the purposes of this discussion, we will focus on the seven largest general categories that affect design (see Figure 4.11). These include: palmate, pinnate, round, strap or ribbonlike, fernlike, grassy, and spiky.

Palmate leaves, as the name implies, are shaped like the palm of a human hand. All of the leaflets radiate from a central point at the tip of the stem. Palmate leaves are somewhat rare

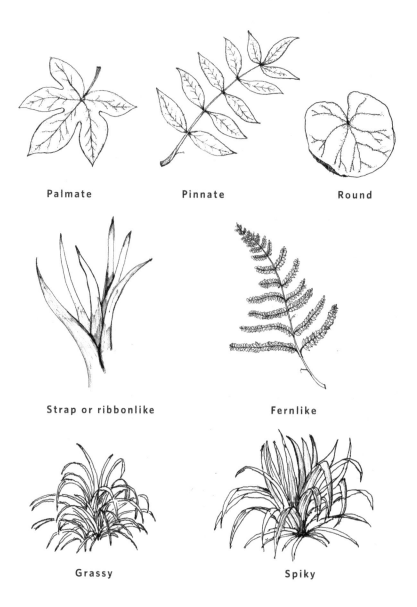

Palmate   Pinnate   Round

Strap or ribbonlike   Fernlike

Figure 4.11
Leaves are predominately classified into seven broad categories.

Grassy   Spiky

and are seen only on a limited number of perennials and shrubs. Consequently, most palmate foliage can be used to lend a dramatic contrast to other types of foliage. Smaller palmate leaves are dainty, with an elegant appearance, whereas large palmate leaves appear tropical. Because of their heavy visual weight, palmate leaves can add excitement to a composition. Not surprisingly, these plants tend to stand out in any composition, especially when paired with round or straplike foliage.

Pinnate leaves are unique because they have several leaflets along one central stem, giving the appearance of individual leaves. They can look rather tropical and are generally prevalent on trees and shrubs. Pinnate leaves provide a strong contrast to more simple leaf types such as round, strap, and oval types. Some larger-leafed species even have what can be described as a prehistoric appearance, giving them high visual weight. This is in contrast to many Asian plants that have very fine pinnate leaves with a delicate and ferny quality. The effect is further compounded with dramatic fall coloring.

Round leaves and their closely related leaf-shaped cousins, which include heart-shaped and broadly oval, comprise the largest category of leaf types. Round leaves mix well with other foliage shapes because of their neutral visual weight. Round leaves generally establish an area of calm, giving the eye a place to rest. Common on clump-forming, low-level perennials, and some shrubs, round leaves contrast well with spiky and straplike foliage. Too much round foliage, however, can result in a monotonous composition.

Strap or **ribbonlike leaves** are narrow and long, with a tendency to arch over and downward. They typically have parallel side leaves and end in a sharp point. Short and medium-sized strap or ribbonlike-leaved plants make for good contrast in a mixed composition, especially when surrounded by rounded or less articulated leaves. Most strap or ribbonlike plants do not mass particularly well and are best repeated through the mixed planting in small groupings at regularly spaced intervals. Many of these plants make favorable specimens for containers.

Fernlike leaves are deeply cut, which give them a very fine texture. They are, essentially, pinnate leaves but with much finer divisions. They produce a light, airy contrast to the more solid foliage types and to coarser-textured leaves. They can, in special circumstances, be used as focal points. Typically found on ferns and perennials, there are a few shrubs and trees with this type of foliage. They tend to be visually and literally lightweight, easily moved by a breeze. Fern-type leaves are best juxtaposed against bold, as well as round-shaped, foliage plants in a composition; overused, they can be monotonous.

Grassy leaves are similar to spiky and strap leaves but are much finer. They provide a soft, billowing type of texture and contrast nicely against bold foliage types of large-leaved and palmate forms. Grassy-type leaves are, logically, generally associated with grasses. They appear in several forms, which include tufted, mounded, and upright. Grassy leaves look good in a mixed planting either as a specimen or in large masses. Specimen plants are usually of a mounded or upright form, which can reach heights of four feet and greater.

Spiky leaves are much like straplike leaves with the difference being that they are stiffly upright, resembling swords or blades. These jagged accents contrast strongly with smaller-leaved plants and dissimilar forms. Typically, clumplike in form, spiky foliage plants make emphatic statements as single specimens. The leaves of these plants often occur on those from warm or dry climates and tend to have a tropical appearance.

Bold vs. Subtle

Although the wide variety of leaf shapes available to the designer today presents exciting opportunities, it also presents a sometimes daunting challenge. Therefore, it is helpful to think of foliage first in its broadest context, as to the ways it can be applied in the mixed planting for maximum effect. For this purpose, according to Noel Kingsbury in *Design and Plant a Mixed Border* (1997), it is a good idea to consider foliage as falling into in two broad categories: *bold* shapes and large leafs, and more *subtle* foliage usually composed of fine-textured plants.

Bold and dramatic shapes impart a lush atmosphere and add an air of exotic tropicalism to the composition. This category of plants includes perennials, tropicals, and grasses. Specific examples include: giant rhubarb (*Gunnera manicata*), elephant's ear (*Colocasia* spp.), indian shot (*Canna* spp.), and giant miscanthus (*Miscanthus floridus*). A few trees and shrubs can be added to this group, among them: oakleaf hydrangea (*Hydrangea quercifolia*), big leaf catalpa (*Catalpa bignonioides*), and horse chestnut (*Aesculus hippocastanum*).

Generally, these lush foliage plants are more prevalent in warmer, more tropical climates where a wider range and diversity of plants exist. However, today, many of these plants are available as tender perennials or annuals in more northern climates.

Large-leaved or bold foliage plants stand out in a composition, making dramatic visual statements either singularly or in combination with other plants of the same type. With that in mind, it is important to restrain the desire to design a composition entirely with these plants, as they will appear busy and so tire the eye quickly.

The more subtle foliage types play no less an important role than their bold and more dramatically shaped brethren, but for a distinctively different purpose. These foliage types are useful when you want to emphasize the characteristics of other surrounding features, such as a neighboring plant's form, flower, or colored foliage. Plants with subtle foliage generally minimize visual competition because their neutral, undemanding leaf shapes allow plants with more dominant characteristics to stand out.

Using Foliage Color

The color of a plant's foliage is one of its most notable characteristics—second only to a plant's form. When most people think of foliage, they "think green." But as designers we know there is an astounding array of foliage color, from variegated whites and yellows to reds, yellows, and glaucous blues and all colors in between. The color of some foliage changes with the seasons while others maintain one strong, dependable color throughout the year.

A plant's foliage color is the result of the pigment found naturally in a particular species or cultivar's leaves and of light being absorbed or reflected from the leaf surface. It is the latter that the designer has more opportunity to determine how foliage color will be perceived: By placing and exposing plants to either direct or indirect light, the intensity and effectiveness of the color will be determined. Additionally, because leaf surfaces are not flat, some portions of the leaf may be in direct light while others are in shadow. As described previously in the discussion on color, this play of light and shadow affects the human perception of leaf color. Those portions of the leaf in shadow have a darker color value and less intensity, while those in full sun are intensified or diminished, depending on the reflectivity of the surface (Nelson 1985).

A plant's foliage color can, of course, dramatically affect the mood of a composition. Plants with highly colored foliage stand out from their primarily green neighbors. As such, they present design opportunities to add contrast and excitement to a composition. Color variations, especially in the light ranges, are powerful and can often be seen from great distances, making for strong design elements that have the potential to be arresting visually (Booth 1983).

Colors like bronze, purple, chartreuse, glaucous blue, and variegated colors are quite noticeable because of their visual weightiness. A single, brightly colored plant placed carefully can add a dramatic touch to a composition. That same plant used en masse can create a bold, sweeping statement. Consider *Spirea bumalda*, 'Gold Flame', which is in prime in the late spring and early summer when the foliage is fresh and has not been scorched by the hot sun. Other foliage, such as that of *Cotinus coggygria*, 'Purpurea', stays deep burgundy all summer, only to morph into dappled shades of red, orange, and purples during the fall.

When it comes to design, however, green foliage and its numerous variations should always be the dominant color. Green unifies as well as sets off other colors. Variations in green hues are wide-ranging, and different shades can be used to accomplish a number of design objectives.

> ▷ Dark greens and other dark colors can impart a quiet, subdued feeling. They tend to move toward a viewer and shorten relative distances. Too many dark greens in a confined space will, however, give the impression that the space is smaller. It might also appear monotonous.

> ▷ Light greens and other lighter colors convey a light, airy, and uplifting mood. Bright colors will appear to recede from the viewer, making a space feel much larger. Adjacent, complementary colors, when viewed from a distance, will begin to gray, instead of appearing in vivid opposition when viewed at close quarters. Analogous colors used side by side and seen at a distance will begin to merge, and the average of the two will be perceived (Austin 1998).

An increasingly extensive selection of cultivated plants from around the world, in a wide range of colors, is now available to designers. So, when exploring the use of all the colored foliage that is now part of the designer's plant palette, the challenge will be to create bold statements with subtle effects, yet show restraint to ensure color variation without sacrificing unity. The following subsections present a number of design possibilities for colored foliage.

YELLOW, GOLD, AND BRONZE

Yellow, gold, and bronze foliage are always bright and uplifting and highly stimulating. In the early spring when the leaves are fresh, yellow-green foliage glows with an almost neon effect, whereas in the brilliance of the fall yellows are tinged with deeper tints of old gold and bronze. Plants that retain the best yellows are those grown in full sun. The downside, however, is that the leaves could scorch and, depending on the species, tend to lose their luminosity as the season progresses. Hard pruning of many of these plants in the winter may help to minimize this tendency.

A little touch of bright yellow may be all that is needed to intensify the overall planting. From a distance, yellow, gold, and bronze advance forward and dominate. Plants with these colors will appear larger than their actual size. Yellows and golds offer even greater relief when combined with colors on opposite sides of the color wheel, such as blues, purples, and even pinks. Blue always makes for a delightful contrast to yellow. Clear pink combined with yellows and golds can result in an unexpected and daring combination. Mauves and blues also make for soft, opposing combinations to yellows and golds. Pairing yellow or gold plants in a sea of dark green or maroon foliage companion plantings is the simplest method to allow this foliage color to "pop." A modest balance must be struck between these contrasting color combinations. This is usually accomplished when yellows and golds are used in modest quantities.

PURPLE, MAROON, AND BLACK

Purple, maroon, and black foliage used sparingly in contrast to other colors can make an emphatic color statement. Used en masse, they present a somber and dramatic scene. Purple and maroon foliage offer a tranquil backdrop that can intensify the contrast between other more colorful plants set in the foreground. But tread lightly when using single trees or large shrubs of maroon or purple foliage in a composition, as they can become a "dark hole." The foliage has a heavy visual weight and so needs to be counterbalanced with smaller, dark-foliage plants, typically perennials or grasses that are repeated in the foreground. Thus, they are best situated among light-colored foliage types so as not to get lost.

Dark-colored foliage generally works well against any other color. Companion color combinations include warm colors, which can intensify the color range and result in a themed color scheme. Used with silvers and grays, or peaches, corals, or rusts can make for pleasing and restful compositions. Used with chartreuse foliage they make a vibrant combination, but one that is severely contrasting, thereby creating high degrees of visual energy; so use these combinations sparingly.

SILVER, GRAY, AND GLAUCOUS

Silver, gray, and glaucous foliage colors are generally associated with plants that come from hot, dry climates. Gray foliage plants are often not true gray, but pale yellow-greens or pale greens and bluish greens. Plants with silver and gray foliage often have dramatically different textural surfacing, ranging from smooth and waxy to fuzzy and hairy. These surfaces tend to reflect the surface light differently and affect the coloration of the plant. The color is also affected by weather and temperature conditions—often appearing more green or blue in the winter, in shade, or when wet.

Silver and gray foliage plants are indispensable to the designer. Because of their neutral presence, they have the ability to calm riotous color combinations, creating peace in a busy composition. Used in contrast to dark colors, they lighten the grouping by their reflective and light-catching qualities. They can also function as garden bridgers, providing a neutral transitional color between more starkly contrasting colors or textures. Gray and silver plants "jump" forward and stand out in a composition. They also can do much to enhance flower colors. In short, silver and gray foliage plants are remarkably versatile and can be paired with pinks and mauves to create a pastel charm, or they can be combined with bright reds and oranges for a dynamic contrast in a composition.

VARIEGATED

Variegated foliage, which can be seen in color variations or in stripes, blotches, or patches, plays a dramatic role in a mixed planting. Most yellow-variegated plants hold their color until they drop their leaves, unlike their yellow- and gold-leafed cousins. Yellow- and white-variegated plants, which reflect light, illuminate shade and brighten up dark areas.

In terms of design, a number of guidelines apply:

▷ Set variegated foliage against a dark-colored background or in a less busy surrounding to make it an effective, eye-catching accent.

▷ Avoid planting more than one type of variegation color or pattern next to one another.

▷ Consider carefully before choosing a plant based solely on the type and pattern of variegation as a stand-alone feature, as it may be difficult to incorporate into the overall composition unless it is set in an area with a complementary color or green. Otherwise, the drama of the individual plant, which is generally the reason for its use, will be lost. The exception to this rule is if the variegation is distinctively different in color, texture, and form. Planting a tropicana canna (*Canna* 'Tropicana') next to a golden bamboo (*Pleioblastus viridistriatus*) is one such example.

▷ Use other colors to enhance or pick up the color of the variegation. Yellow and green variegated foliage, which impart a bright, sunny effect, are best combined with other warm colors or those that are opposite it on the color wheel. White and green variegated foliage tend to be more neutral and so work well with a greater number of colors and textures. The best of them can sharpen a garden and brighten a dark corner. The cool tones of white variegation go particularly well with flower colors in the blue, purple, pink, and magenta ranges.

EVERGREEN FOLIAGE

Evergreen foliage provides permanent structure in any planting composition. Evergreens are generally classified as either broad-leaved or coniferous. Broad-leaved evergreens have the appearance of deciduous leaves, but they remain on the plant year-round. Their leaf structure is generally much thicker than that of deciduous leaves and their surface is generally more lustrous, whereas coniferous foliage tends to look like needles and threads. Other evergreen foliage may have divided leaflike structures that have shorter needle lengths. Often described as having feathery leaf structures, these include plants in the *Arborvitae* and *Chamaecyparis* families.

Additional variations of evergreen foliage are seen in shape, texture, color, and reflectivity. The effect of light reflected from these surfaces depends on whether the plant's surface quality is matte, glaucous, or glossy. The thickness, shape, and color all affect the amount of light the foliage either reflects or absorbs.

Regardless of their foliage type or texture, however, evergreens are universally valuable for lending architectural solidity in a garden design. They are equally effective as backdrops for compositions of other planting types and as screens for privacy or view control. But unless evergreens serve a particular function, their placement in the mixed planting composition should be limited to a smaller percentage of the overall scheme—generally around 20 to 35 percent of the total plant mix. The maintenance necessary to maintain the design objective will dictate more specific percentages, but a rule of thumb is that those compositions that will receive less attention will benefit from a larger percentage of evergreens, because of their low maintenance requirements.

Evergreens should be distributed evenly throughout the composition, interspersed with other plant types. Otherwise, as with other heavily visually weighted plant types, evergreens can produce a spotty appearance. The following subsections detail more specific design criteria for each of the two evergreen types, broad-leaved and coniferous.

Broad-Leaved Evergreens

Broad-leaved evergreens generally possess the darkest foliage of the evergreen family. The surface of their leaves is usually glossy, which gives them a special reflective and glittery quality. Other, more traditionally green broad-leaved varieties of evergreens usually have enough reflectivity to brighten up a location. This characteristic can be used to good advantage in a planting composition. The surface glossiness adds a metallic sheen to those evergreens whose seasonal color may vary, such as those of Mahonia, Daphne, Pieris, or Rhododendron P.J.M.

Many of the broad-leaved evergreens produce brilliant spring flowers. And in combination with other types of plant surfaces, their shiny foliage becomes important highlights in the patchwork of the composition.

Coniferous Evergreens

Coniferous evergreens vary widely in their form, color, and texture, though overall they are generally dark and heavy in comparison to other foliage types. This gives them the appearance of being fairly massive and heavily weighted visually. Unlike broad-leaved evergreens, coniferous evergreen foliage is relatively nonchanging, remaining constant year-round. This quality makes them excellent counterparts to deciduous and perennial material, emphasizing the ephemeral qualities of those plant types.

Maintaining Seasonal Interest

The hallmark of any mixed planting is a composition that maximizes seasonal interest—which is to say, extends the period of interest beyond what is considered "peak." For designers, this can, at times, seem like a formidable task. One effective approach is to select plants that have a minimum of two periods of interest: This will maximize the value of each plant, ensuring that the composition will be "on display" beyond the so-called peak season. Another important guideline is to take advantage of the seasonal attributes of *all* the various vegetative parts of a plant.

It is the qualities of these vegetative parts that combine to define the character of the plant. The component parts are useful not only for identifying the unique characteristics of each species, cultivar, and variety but also for determining their use in planting design.

As designers we must consider how the ornamental qualities of plants, in conjunction with the other plant characteristics, can contribute to the tapestry of colors, textures, and forms that will make up the completed composition. We must ask what role each vegetative part will play throughout the year. And to answer that important question, we call on our knowledge of these seasonal attributes and vegetative characteristics, to organize and design plantings that take advantage of color, form, and texture; flowers, berries, and fruit; bark and stem texture and color; seed heads; fall color; and a plant's form.

But our knowledge must be informed by experience—years of careful observation, watching plants grow and transition between the seasons. Only then can we fully assess the contribution of each of the vegetative parts of every plant to determine which are best utilized to accomplish specific design objectives. In doing so, for any given planting composition:

▷ We must identify the dominant plant characteristics that attract attention and elicit an emotional response.

▷ We must take note of which plants have been used effectively in a setting, both in terms of their functionality and durability.

▷ We must pay particular attention to the plant's appearance as juxtaposed against other plant types as well as en masse. The character of a plant in isolation may change when surrounded by others or grouped.

In sum, to effectively assemble plants in a mixed planting, we, as designers, must be fully aware of each plant's characteristics: how it evolves, when it reaches peak performance, how long it remains at peak performance, what it looks like each season, what it looks like during down periods, and how it transitions between the periods.

To help with this important assessment, the following subsections describe the principle vegetative parts and their attributes.

BARK AND TWIGS

Bark

The bark of a plant serves a protective function, covering the trunks and branches of trees and shrubs. But to designers bark is also an ornamental characteristic—generally associated with trees, although some shrubs possess interesting bark and twigs.

Bark and stem color and texture can vary dramatically from species to species and even on the same plant. The distinctive textural and colorful appeal of tree bark and stem coloration is most interesting on deciduous trees and shrubs in the winter. As trees grow, they tend to shed their outer layers of bark. Certain species of plants may start out with smooth, nontextured bark, which begins to color, exfoliate, or deeply fissure as they mature. Many will peel away, for example, Paperbark maple (*Acer griseum*), Sycamore (*Platanus* spp.), Birch (*Betula* spp.), and *Eucalyptus* spp. On other trees, the bark will split or crack, producing what is known as fissures or furrows, as on Oak (*Quercus* spp.), Dogwood (*Cornus florida*), or Persimmon (*Diospyros virginiana*). These furrows assume various patterns that are distinctive to each species.

Many plant species are valuable to designers solely for the color and texture of their ornamental bark. Bark colors are typically earthy tones of browns and greens, but within that general categorization is a vast array of hues available to the designer. Gary L. Hightshoe in his book, *Native Trees and Vines for Urban and Rural America* (1988), classified eight basic bark colors: white, gray, yellow-orange, green, maroon-purple, red-brown, gray-tan, and brown-black.

Contrasted against an evergreen or light-colored background, bark color and texture combined can produce one of the most outstanding design elements in a winter landscape. Certain bark colors and textures are most effective when viewed from a distance, such as those of the birches. Others garner the most appreciation when viewed at close range, such as the shiny and pealing papery bark of *Prunus* or some of the *Acers*.

Twigs

Closely related to bark as an ornamental element are a plant's twigs. More typically prominent in shrubs, twigs, like bark, have a wide variety of textures: They can be thorny, velvety or hairy, smooth, or lustrous. But it is the color of twigs, rather than texture, that is of the greatest ornamental value to the designer.

Twig color is generally not as pronounced on older plants or on those that have been growing in poor soil. The most colorful stems or twigs are exhibited on young or new growth. That means plants will have to be pruned heavily in spring to promote the new, colorful, and vigorous growths desired. The most brilliant twig displays, of red, yellow-green, and yellow, are provided by the dogwood family.

FLOWERS

Flowers are the celebrities of the plant world. Humans are immediately and powerfully drawn to them, to their beauty and fragility and their many shapes, sizes, and colors. It is for this reason that flowers are the single most popular element of planting design. Their drawing power, coupled with the incredible diversity of shapes and colors available, offer unlimited design possibilities.

Flowers are borne on structures called *inflorescences*. Each inflorescence contains a number of smaller individual flowers arranged in some fashion, and it is the arrangement of these smaller flowers that create the visible display. There are a number of flower types, including spikes, racemes, corymbs, umbels, cymes, panicles, heads, spadixs, or solitary types. Each has its own unique design presence and, therefore, application.

The most common shrub and tree flowers display themselves during the spring, although a wide variety of perennials bloom throughout the summer. And a select few flowering plants from all categories of plant types have blooming periods that extend from late winter to early spring, even into late summer and early fall. By the careful selection of a variety of species, one or another type of flower can be on display virtually year-round. As a bonus, a select group of flowers produce fragrance. The spicy blossoms of fragrant viburnum (*Viburnum carlesii*), the sweet smell of butterfly bush (*Buddleia davidii*), or jasmine (*Jasminum* spp.), among others, can fill the air with wonderful scents, adding an extra dimension to the composition.

Establishing a bloom sequence is another important design criterion, but doing so effectively requires knowledge of bloom sequences and of length of flowering periods. For example, a witch hazel (*Hamamalis* spp.) will always bloom before an *azalea*, and an *azalea* will always bloom before a *viburnum* spp., regardless of where in the country they are located. The sequence of flowering will begin at an earlier date, however, in the South than in the North—both latitude and altitude affect bloom times. Unfortunately, according to Donald Wyman in *Shrubs and Vines for American Gardens* (1977), from a design standpoint flowering periods are unpredictable, depending on micro- and macroclimatic conditions for a particular location and season.

Complicating the design picture are the horticultural aspects of proper soil preparation and ongoing soil rejuvenation and fertilization to maintain peak performance, as well as proper maintenance (dividing, deadheading, pruning, etc.). In most situations, the number of flowers used in a composition should be directly proportional to the amount of maintenance that will be required to keep the plantings looking fresh and healthy. Poor maintenance is the downfall of many plantings that rely on flowers.

For these reasons, as discussed in previous chapters, designers are cautioned against relying on flowers to generate long-term interest in a mixed planting composition, and are instead directed to using other plant types and characteristics such as texture, foliage color, form, and all the other elements discussed so far to achieve success year-round.

SEED HEADS

With the first frost the colors and flowers of summer fade, to be replaced by other, equally attractive, points of interest: new earthy colors, seed heads, spent flowers, and foliage. Various plant parts are transformed into remarkable architectural shapes, some odd, others elegant. The landscape, too, changes color to assume the muted fall shades of browns, golds, rusts, and tans. In the absence of flowers, it is the structure of grasses and seed heads of various perennials, in combination with the winter form of plants, along with evergreens and berries, which keep the composition interesting until spring returns.

Nature's annual grand finale becomes the setting for these winter structures. In terms of purpose and durability, seed structures are more dependable, dramatic, and longer lasting than their colorful predecessors. They accomplish the final seasonal design objective in a mixed planting by extending beauty and excitement well into the winter months. There are predominantly two plant types that produce the majority of ornamental seedheads: ornamental grasses and perennials.

Ornamental Grasses

As fall arrives, ornamental grasses blanch into shades of brown, and their seeds become dramatic focal points, borne as they are on plumes that tower above the ground and move in concert with the wind. Used en masse or singularly as a specimen, these grasses create dramatic displays, especially when contrasted with evergreens. They accent other plants by their ability to capture light and display it through their finely textured seed heads. Grasses hold their form during and after frost and even through lighter snow events. Their vertical elements have soft, billowy crowns that soften the strong shapes and tones of evergreens. They also make excellent companions to lower perennials whose broad flat-topped seed heads are set on tall rigid stalks or stems.

Perennials

Perennials—with their brown, hard seed cases, domed seed heads, or bubble-shaped seedpods—are impressive dark accents against the lighter grasses and darker evergreens. Many perennials also possess stiff stalks that enable them to form a structured framework in the winter landscape; and it is this type, which can maintain a rigid structure or hold their foliage throughout the winter period, that makes the best design choice.

Like grasses, perennials are best used en masse, to magnify their visual impact. Massing plants can also serve as structural support as the winter winds and snow loads do their best to knock them flat.

FRUITS AND BERRIES

There seems no end to the ornamental fruits produced by a variety of plant types. Their size, colors, and shapes are as interesting and varied as flowers—many, in fact, surpass flowers in ornamental value. Species with brightly colored fruit or berries that are visible early in the season can add a welcome contrast to the early summer composition. Those that mature in fall and hold fruit until late into the year add bright spots to the winter landscape.

The appearance of fruit and berries is, of course, affected by geographic region: the length of the season, the amount of rainfall, and the type of soil. And just as there is a sequence of bloom periods for flowering plants, there is a sequence of fruiting periods, making it possible to provide a never-ending parade fruits and berries, from late spring throughout the summer and into the fall. It's important to point out, however, that not all fruits or berries have the same capability to make an aesthetic impact. Some plants, such as spireas and mock oranges, produce either inconspicuous fruits whose structure (size and color) blend into the background, or their foliage hides them. Nevertheless, a number of classifications and categories of fruit structures are worth consideration. The major ones are listed here.

DRY AND INDEHISCENT FRUITS (LEAST ORNAMENTAL VALUE)

Samara One-seeded fruits with a thin membranous wing or wings

Nut, acorn, nutlet Hard shell, partially or entirely surrounded by a husk or bur that may be papery, woody, leafy, or spiny in character

Strobile Slender pendant and erect catkinlike or conelike fruit with papery overlapping seeds

DRY AND DEHISCENT FRUITS (MODERATE ORNAMENTAL VALUE)

Legume Elongated pods that split open with maturity

Capsule Fruit with more than one chamber, usually splitting lengthwise along multiple seems from one end

Follicle Aggregate of small fleshy pods on stout, short, erect stems resembling a cucumber

FLESHY FRUITS (HIGH ORNAMENTAL VALUE)

Berry Fruits with soft fleshy covering over the seed

Pomes Fleshy fruits common to edible varieties

Drupes Known as the "stone fruits," with hard centers surrounded by soft fleshy often-edible outer covering

COMPOUND FRUITS

Cones Woody fruit borne primarily on coniferous plants that have stiff scales supporting naked seeds

Aggregate Similar to a cone, the result of multiple fruitlets massed on one receptacle

Multiple Small unwinged but sometime plumed one-seeded fruit compounded to form a ball-like head

The coloration of fruits and berries can affect a mixed planting composition as much as that of flowers, foliage, and bark. Coloration is considered for the period that the fruits and berries remain of ornamental value. Some may begin as one color and develop into another more ornamental one. Others fade as they age and so are of lesser value. Coloration is generally divided into ten color categories: green-yellow, yellow-orange, red, red-purple, purple-brown, tan-brown, blue, black, yellow, and white.

The most conspicuous fruit and berry colors are those producing red and yellow fruits. These can provide striking contrasts in the landscape, especially when set against dark green foliage. Some of the white-fruited plants also are effective if set against bright or dark green backgrounds. Yellow and white berries are less common but can, nonetheless, dramatic design features. Blue fruits are less noticeable, but can be amazingly beautiful when mature, especially if they have a highly reflective surface. Black fruits, generally thought to be the least effective and attractive, can be used to create an intriguing appearance (Hightshoe 1988).

FALL FOLIAGE

For sheer volume of color, fall foliage stands alone. The most brilliant displays occur where the first frost is crisp and the changes in length of daylight and daily temperatures are more dramatic. These light and temperature shifts trigger a plant's natural response to prepare itself for the onslaught of winter.

As anyone who has witnessed the glory of fall in the eastern United States knows, trees and shrubs can become as colorful as the most vibrant of flowers. But the quality of the color fluctuates. When rainfall has been plentiful throughout the year, coloration will be outstanding; in drier years, the color is notably less intense and long lasting. Availability of light, too, affects the intensity and extent of coloration, as it does flower production. Plants of the same species located in full sun will color much more richly than those of the same plant located in partial or full shade. Yellow coloration is typified in many of the ashes, maples, and hamamelis species. Brilliant reds and scarlets are typified by oaks, maples, and viburnums, and are intensified by just the right amounts of water, cold, and sunlight.

Through careful selection and arrangement, fall color can make for dramatic compositions of color contrast and accent. Fall color should be considered in terms of its color pattern along with the other seasonal attributes. The most striking combinations result when the brilliant reds and scarlets are contrasted against the golds and yellows. Designers need to be aware, however, that many of the yellow leaves appear first in the sequence of coloration and often will drop their leaves by the time the reds appear.

Careful observation of the sequencing of color and leaf drop is necessary to select the correct plants for the design intent. Another important guideline is to alternate as much as possible among the range of fall coloration of trees and shrubs, for too great an emphasis on fall foliage is risky, as the duration of color is brief—and some years more than others.

5 | Form-Based Approach to Mixed Planting Design

A SUCCESSFUL PLANTING COMPOSITION will be the result of the pleasing arrangement of forms—specifically, the individual and collective characteristics possessed by those forms (line, texture, color, and mass). In previous chapters we discussed at length the various types of forms and how they might be used in a mixed planting design. This chapter expands on that information to address in greater detail the importance of taking a form-based approach to composing a mixed planting design.

Understanding Form Relationships

The first step—and it's critical—in a form-based approach to mixed planting design is to understand the plant medium you are working with, from both a horticultural and architectural standpoint. That means focusing on how to perceive and assemble forms.

In her book *Planting Design* (1940), Florence Bell Robinson stated that line, color, and texture are essentially expressions of form, and that color and texture patterns are abstract and offer limitless arrangement possibilities. Form, however, is definite, hence it imposes limits. Geometry comes into play, and each object can be reduced to a simple shape. This is a commonly accepted principle in the art world and is the reason that form is stressed as the most important factor in composition. It is also the reason designers will almost always begin with some expression of form, usually represented by a line or series of lines that enclose a geometrical boundary. In the case of planting design, the plants within the composition are "drawn" with a series of geometric shapes, contained by an enclosing line or silhouette, that represent a plant's form, as shown in Figure 5.1.

Plant forms are the result of lines—straight, curved, or a combination of the two—and the textures of foliage, twigs, and branches; these determine the outline and main shadows, both internal and external, that give a plant its character. As designers we must train our eyes to perceive a plant's basic form as a simple geometric shape—a square, rectangle, triangle, column, circle, etc.—without the refinement of details such as texture or color (Robinson 1940). By doing so we eliminate distractions, enabling us to concentrate solely on the relationships of the various forms.

Basic relationships between forms can be found everywhere: in modern buildings, urban and rural landscapes, abstract paintings, and the graphic arts. These examples illustrate how

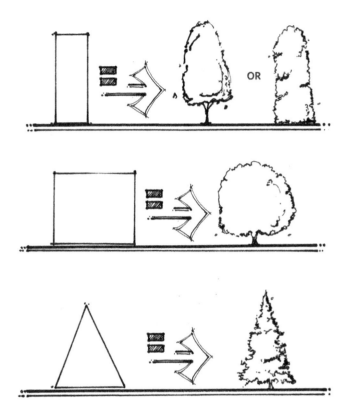

Figure 5.1
The various shapes of
different plant types can be
simplified into an abstract
massing block.

basic shapes can be used to create a composition, in any dimension, and to offer insight to the
important relationships that emerge between forms and lines and the effect they have on the
final "image."

PLANT GEOMETRY

As explained earlier, it is a plant's form, not color (as is commonly believed), that is its most
important feature. Plant forms, both distinctive and neutral, used wisely ensure that variety,
harmony, depth, and the illusion of scale are all achieved in a composition—fundamentals of
good planting design. A plant's outline, its silhouette, will determine its form; its overall mass
can be reduced to the most basic geometric shape that encloses it—the plant's form.

Recall the nine plant forms discussed in the previous chapter. Close inspection reveals
that a limited range of shapes are repeated in various heights in correspondence to the particular plant type, such as shrub, tree, evergreen, perennial, etc. (see color plates, Figure 5.2).

Defined in geometric terms, deciduous shrubs, for example, are generally classified as upright rectangular, square (for rounded, mounded, and vase-shaped forms), and triangular (for pyramidal-shaped forms), while evergreens are categorized as rectangular, square, upright rectangular, and triangular forms. At this point in the discussion, plant species, cultivars, and ornamental attributes are not factors in the design process. These characteristics will be considered at a later stage. We are concerned here only with a plant's form.

Recall also from the previous chapter the different effect various forms and shapes have on a composition or within a group of plants. To review, consider tall and narrow forms, especially in a grouping of herbaceous plants or among rounded forms. These will attract attention. When viewed from a distance they become "arresting perpendiculars" in the words of Jill Billington in *Planting Companions* (1997), leading the eye upward toward the sky. These forms will tend to stop the eye, causing it to pause for a moment the way a period ends a sentence. Horizontal forms, in contrast, take the eye across the width of the view—imagine the layered horizontal branches of a *Cornus controversa*. The same is true with long masses of rounded forms.

An important part of the process of understanding the plant medium you're working with is to study the masses and silhouettes of individual plants during all the seasons. Only then can you begin to hone the description of plant forms, to be able to see a simple geometric shape as representative of the overall plant. Needless to say, each plant will vary slightly, possessing subtle differences that make its shape unique. Some will be more open; others will be denser; still others will arch while others will be mounded.

In most cases you'll be able to identify a geometric shape contained in the plant form. That said, you will also begin to notice that many plants change form as they grow from youth to maturity. In the case of grasses and herbaceous materials, for instance, change occurs throughout the season, so assigning a form to these plant types will be a more abstract undertaking. For the most part, however, especially in the beginning, it is best to consider the form of the mature plant for design purposes. With experience, you'll be able to incorporate the evolution of a plant's form into your design process, which will increase your ability to successfully use plants in various capacities within your compositions.

PLANT BEHAVIOR

Studying plant forms will also enable you to become more aware of the *energized nature* of plants, referred to as a plant's visual or shape dynamic (see Figure 5.3). Each shape produces energy due to its imbalance in relation to the force of gravity. The form naturally thrusts outward while the ground naturally compresses. Edges, planes, or corners will appear to compress or expand outward, upward, or downward. This effect is the equivalent to the Chinese philosophy of yin and yang, where opposite sides, elements, or extremes are, essentially,

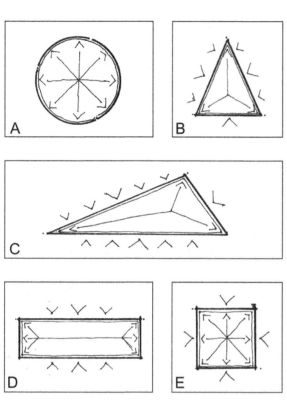

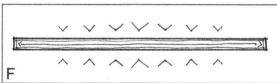

Figure 5.3
Inward and outward forces at play for
the various types of shapes.

involved in a balancing act. This interaction affects the human ability to perceive. The force
is fundamentally illusory but perceptually affects the way we see it. Thus, it has the power to
affect the movement of our eyes, both on the individual form and as part of the collective composition.

This is an important aspect to consider in your efforts to direct the viewer's eye through a
landscape composition in some fashion. Understanding the visual dynamics that various forms
and shapes play individually and collectively will increase your chance of success in creating a
desired effect.The behavior of forms, and the resultant forces generated—either individually or
collectively by the assemblage of these forms—conveys the appearance of movement. Note the
term "appearance of movement," for this is perceptual rather than actual. Nonetheless, it affects

Nature as Teacher

Historically, successful designers have developed their compositions by re-creating elements and phenomena they observed in nature. Many did not understand the complex mathematical measurements involved; rather, they used their acute powers to observe pattern and then to re-create what they saw.

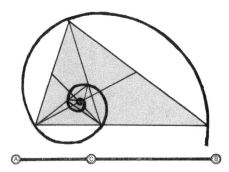

Figure 5.4
Good design is based on rules for divine proportions, which have been explained by mathematical relationships found in forms and shapes found in nature.

Proportion, for example, can be seen in the shell of a nautilus, in the branching of a tree, or the packing pattern of seed heads. Their pattern of organization is mathematically derived and based on a common set of proportions. It is these natural occurrences in all things that formed the basis for the *Golden Mean*, also called the Divine Proportion (see Figure 5.4). Theories on proportion, closely studied by the Greek sculptor Phidias, found a common relationship in all things as interpreted by the human psyche. It has been noted that these relationships have the power to affect emotional or aesthetic feelings within us. All forms of design have their underpinnings in these relationships and resultant phenomena.

Throughout the ages many artists, philosophers, mathematicians, and architects have developed various systems of organization to illustrate the principles of proportion. The Swiss architect Charles-Édouard Jeanneret, better known as Le Corbusier, devised a system of scale and proportion known as the Modular, which he described as a "range of harmonious measurements to suit the human scale, universally applicable to architecture and mechanical things." His interest was in finding proportional relationships in the basic forms and structures that naturally occur. His premise was illustrated by a human body and was based on a six-foot-tall man with his arm extended upright surrounded by a rectangle (see Figure 5.5)—similar to the method of enclosing plants. The system, in the tradition of Leonardo da Vinci's *Vitruvian Man*, and the work of the Italian mathematician Battista Alberti, is premised on the notion that there is a set of mathematical proportions based on the human body that can be used to improve the appearance and function of designed and organized elements.

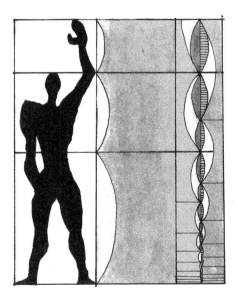

Figure 5.5
Le Corbusier's Modular illustrates the principles of harmonious proportions based on the human figure.

The purpose of proportion is to establish harmony among the particular elements of any composition in any medium. This is accomplished by the conspicuous use of line and form. Applying these theories to a planting composition would suggest that individual plant massings should have some proportional relationship to one another—both in the relationship of the size of the adjacent plants and in the number of planting types used in the overall composition. We will discuss this in greater detail in Chapter 7, page 197.

the way the viewer experiences a composition. This becomes clear by studying the dynamics of the forms, and by observing the tendency of the eye to follow and extend the edges of forms. According to David Piper in *The Illustrated Library of Art—History Appreciation and Tradition* (1986), this is referred to as *lines of force*.

Important as it is to understand and to be able to recognize individual plant forms and the forces they exert, we, as designers, must never lose sight of the fact that plants rarely grow in isolation and that we will rarely use them that way in our compositions. Native vegetation often grows in groupings or drifts; as environmental conditions change, the plant forms change, too, depending on the amount of light, soil, and moisture. These plants often overlap or interlock, growing adjacent to, behind, or in front of another. Designed by nature these plant massings are naturally pleasing and unified, and human designers would be well advised to learn the lessons taught by a master.

The point is, arranging plant shapes cannot be done in a vacuum—not if they are to be successful. You must draw inspiration from, then relate the massing and placement of individual forms to the surrounding landscape and architecture. Accent, highlight, or repeat the predominant forms you see in the environment where your composition will be seen to achieve greater success.

Blocking a Design Pattern

At the conceptual level of design, individual plants or masses of plants, treated as simple geometric shapes, can be blocked out as larger geometric units (see Figure 5.6). These units will, as with natural groupings or drifts, vary in size and overlap one another. Training your eye to see these massing blocks, first in natural landscapes and then in designed compositions, and

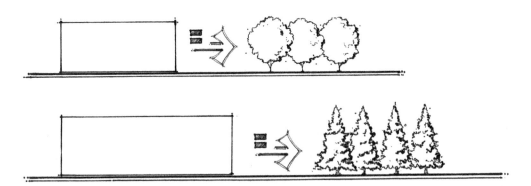

Figure 5.6
Individual plant forms when combined form large rectangular block masses.

studying the relationships and effects each has on others, will help you implement these concepts into your professional practice.

One effective way to begin to block a design pattern is to use children's building blocks. Experiment with a variety of shapes that resemble plant forms to see how each form in various combinations affects adjacent forms and the composition at large (see color plates, Figure 5.7). As you'll soon discover, each shape has a unique dynamic, and its visual weight and lines of force will affect the visual properties of adjacent shapes differently. By manipulating the arrangement of shapes you will quickly get a sense of how that impact might or might not affect a combination. You'll see elements of both harmony and discord displayed in planting massings (the aggregate of various combinations of individual forms and shapes) and learn how to achieve the former and to prevent the latter.

To attain harmony of form and mass, you'll have to create a similarity or a detectable sequence from one form to the other. To avoid a disruption to unity, you'll learn to make judicious use of sudden contrasts to serve as accents or focal points. A columnar evergreen placed in a sea of herbaceous plants, for example, certainly will attract attention, but often at the expense of the surrounding plants. Columnar spires among rounded forms or pyramidal forms among oval or flat-topped masses are other examples of how a unique form can provide contrast.

The work of architect Michael Graves illustrates the simplicity of form and purity of geometrical relationships. Strongly influenced by the essentials of Classicism and the grammar of antiquity, Graves has distilled the forms of and within his buildings into the purest of geometrical arrangements—triangles, rectangles, squares, and circles (see Figure 5.8). The intent is to break down larger building massings into smaller units, allowing for a more varied and interesting treatment. The contrast and play of light and shadow exaggerates the forms. Pure forms divide the building into vertical and horizontal planes, each of which is further subdivided. The repetition of windows and doors creates a rhythm throughout the massing. The relationships formed among geometric shapes, and the proportion and rhythm manifested in a particular building, represent the fundamental principles of composition—which can be translated into the design of planting compositions.

Creating Mass: Grouping and Arranging

As previously stated, plants in nature grow in groupings—groves, stands, clusters, and drifts. There is a sense of order and harmony about these massings in their natural settings. They seldom end in hard lines or have sharply defined edges; instead, they gradually fade or transition

Figure 5.8
Basic geometric shapes
(triangles, squares,
cylinders, rectangles)
have been combined to
create the Erickson
Alumni Center on the
campus of West Virginia
University.

from one grouping to another, with a variety of plant types morphing within from one to another. From examining such groupings, we can extract ideas about compositional arrangement for pictorial effect, manipulating mass and void, line and silhouette.

At the conceptual stage of design, we must conduct our studies in the abstract, that is, based solely on the groupings of plants en masse, not as individuals. That is the point of doing the exercise with blocks, as described above. Once we have set the massing patterns, we can begin to refine the composition to include texture and color. Only then can we begin to select plants that meet specific design requirements. We explain it in detail in Chapter 10, page 251.

As we begin to group plants together to form a mass, some guidelines are in order. First, base the height of the individual plant block on the mature height of the plant; then base the width of the block on the mature spread of the individual plant multiplied by the number of plants intended to be in that particular block. The resultant mass, in geometrical terms, will establish the dimensions or overall size of the block of plants.

Generally, the more plants we include in a massing block, the more blocky the massing will appear, as individual plant shapes tend to get lost when grouped together. For example, the vase-shaped forms of *Viburnum setigerum* or *Ilex verticillata*, when combined together en masse, get blurred, to become an overall rectangular block shape. The resultant lines created by the masses flow from one to another, carrying the eye from one part of the composition to the other (Robinson 1940). By working with blocks of massings in this way, it is much easier to develop a unified whole.

ACHIEVING BALANCE

Once we have combined individual plant forms to create a mass block, we must next consider the relationships that will be created by joining blocks comprised of various heights and lengths. It is highly advantageous to have plant materials interconnect and overlap, to create visual interest and harmony. In this regard, plant blocks should always touch or overlap in the horizontal, and progress upward or downward in the vertical, as shown in Figure 5.9. Think of a tapestry where all of the threads are woven together to form swaths of color.

The objective in the planting composition is to achieve a balance among all the components. Massing blocks should be balanced between open bays, light and shadow, and plant massings. Other elements of compositional balance to consider include connection of near

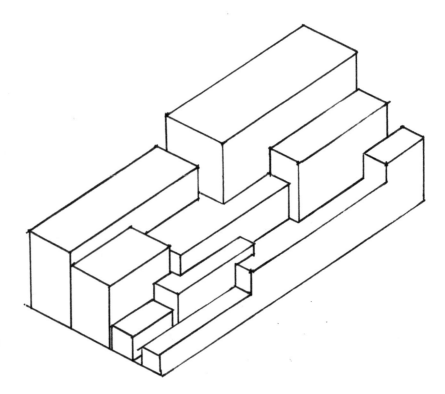

Figure 5.9
The abstract massing blocks represent plant masses and illustrate variation in height and depth in a planting composition.

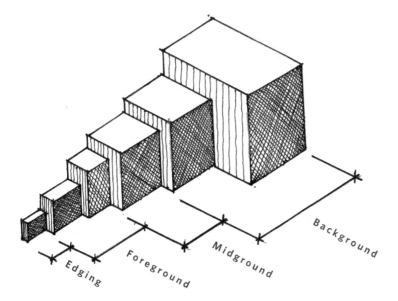

Figure 5.10
Plant masses (represented by geometric blocks) positioned in graduated sequence from the front to the back, illustrate the "traditional" method of layering plant masses.

with far, solid against the void, light against dark, rough texture against smooth, and bright against dull. In all cases, designers must balance divergent and contrasting elements within the composition, striving for a state of equilibrium (Simonds 1983).

From a design standpoint, in mixed planting compositions the relative size of the masses should always be developed in scale with the garden or landscape area in question. Smaller landscapes or gardens should have smaller massings of three to five plants; larger, more open landscapes can support larger, bolder sweeping masses.

From a maintenance standpoint, a large grouping of plant masses will be much more self-sufficient than singular plantings. By allowing larger masses to grow together we are not only growing larger plants, as determined by the overall size of the mass, but covering more bed space, as well, thus eliminating bare areas where weeds might otherwise cultivate. Additionally, shaded areas under the massings conserve water. It is important to resist the urge to shear, once the plantings have been installed—effective massing can only be achieved when the plant are permitted to grow together.

LAYERING

Guidelines for structuring layers of plant massings have their foundation in border planning. The traditional method was to design a progressive gradation in height from front of the border to the back, as shown in Figure 5.10. This type of arrangement was believed to be orderly, in that it allowed everything to be seen equally and so was the most effective way to display flowering plants. The fundamental flaw, of course, is that it relied solely on flowering plants, which as we've discussed throughout this book, have a limited range of bloom times, which consequently imposes limits for design purposes. It also resulted in a fairly regular and predictable composition, one lacking dimensional and multi-seasonal variation.

Today we recognize that in a mixed composition, flowers should be treated as "trimming," not the main theme. That means, in a mixed bed setting where interest is to be maintained year-round, it will be necessary to overlap, intermingle, blend, and overlap foreground, midground, and background plantings, for an overall mingling plant features. This not only softens the sharp definitions of the "layered look," but adds interest and intrigue, vertically and horizontally.

Three important factors come into play when layering the mixed planting: depth of space, time, and location. They are interconnected; each supports the others. Depth of space is created as various plant characteristics (flowers, foliage color, seed heads, etc.) rise and fall throughout the seasons—that is, through time. Consequently, the location of the various plants in relation to each other, based on when their design characteristics are in full display, is key as well. Therefore, a primary objective of layering in a mixed planting composition is to vary the vertical arrangement of plants in the horizontal plane, and vice versa. The elevations of the plant groupings in three-dimensional space and voids located throughout the composition will generate interest. For example, you might want some taller plants (mainly herbaceous, tropical, and grass types) near the front of the composition, to break things up and provide interest through contrast. Or, depending on the circumstance, you might want to place some smaller plant masses in front of larger plant masses. We talk more about composing the mix in Chapter 7, page 175.

LAYER STRUCTURING

Naturally occurring plant communities, especially fields in the midstages of succession, develop in layers of complex arrangements and associations. In these plant communities, a variety of permutations of plant types occur randomly at a number of levels. As designers, seeking inspiration from these plant communities, we must strive to develop ornamental plantings that re-create these variations but in a more controlled aesthetic. To achieve this, a variety of plant types must be used to develop the layers. Varying plant height will dramatically affect the scale, compositional interest, and overall framework of the design (Booth 1983).

The simplest way to begin assembling these layers is to consider planting in five ranges based on height and function: ground layer, foreground layer, midground layer, lower canopy, and background plantings. These are shown in Figure 5.11 and are described in turn in the following subsections.

Ground Layer

The ground layer is, as the name implies, the first layer of plants generally located in the front of the composition. It is used to develop a ground covering that links various bays or diverse ranges of plant types to produce a unified whole.

The ground layer contains low and compact plants, generally under 8 to 12 inches in height, which may consist of annuals, bulbs, low perennials, prostrate shrubs, ground covers, and some of the smaller grasses. These plant types should be selected specifically for their ability to maintain a compact growth habit. Many typically have early-spring blooms or late-summer displays. By repeating their form or color they act as a neutral foil, to visually link more complex planting patterns, textures, or colors. Additionally, they serve as a base, or platform, from which to display accent plantings. These plants can also hide the bases of leggier plants, or bridge two different plant types or colors. Or they can be used to develop low-level display layers that change with the season.

Filling this role are also seasonal plantings such as annuals, tropicals, and bulbs, which provide seasonal variation. Used in this way, the ground layer will take on greater importance, meaning that it will be necessary to balance the visual weight of the ground layer with the other layers in the planting composition.

Foreground Layer

Often positioned behind the ground layer, the foreground layer contains plants in the twelve- to twenty-four-inch height range. This layer marks the first change in level as part of the gradual

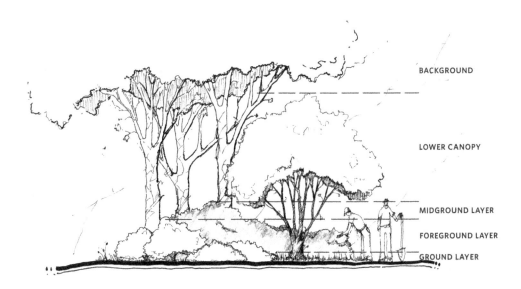

BACKGROUND

LOWER CANOPY

MIDGROUND LAYER

FOREGROUND LAYER

GROUND LAYER

Figure 5.11
An elevational drawing illustrates the relationships of the five basic layers of plantings.

buildup of the planting from lower to higher. Plants in the foreground layer may include small to medium perennials, small flowering shrubs, smaller grasses, larger annuals, taller bulb species, and smaller tropicals.

The foreground layer will often define smaller spaces in the front of the composition, creating "bays" for ground-layer plantings. Used in this fashion, they are valuable for establishing foreground and low-level interest without interfering with views to deeper portions of the composition. Like ground-layer plantings, foreground plantings can also act as unifiers. Planted in larger masses or drifts, the lines and masses formed by the drifts serve as links to other planting masses by their vertical connections—much like a wall.

Foreground-layer massings are also effective for reinforcing or infilling larger spaces created by the middle-ground layer immediately behind. And to create additional visual interest, some foreground plants should be encouraged to spill into the edge of the planting composition, weaving in and out of ground-layer plantings. This is the beginning of the planting tapestry.

Midground Layer

Plantings at the midground level establish the bulk of the planting composition and consist of plants that range in height from two to six feet. Depending on the plant type, massings at this layer serve three primary functions:

▷ Space definition or bay creation

▷ Infill

▷ Transitory linkage

The midground layer is generally established with medium shrubs (both evergreen and deciduous), medium perennials, large grasses, and some of the larger tropicals. And a significant proportion of its makeup (at a minimum, 50 percent) should contain structure plantings, generally evergreen shrubs or other shrubs with a marked woody structure and notable presence during the winter months. It will be important to evenly distribute various plant types throughout this level to achieve midlevel balance. Tropicals are generally considered accent plantings and are placed as highlights or focal points at this layer. A composition that has an even distribution of plant types tends to maintain interest better year-round.

Midground-layer plantings play a vital role in creating bays or planting compartments by forming midlevel "background" plantings. In essence, these plant masses encapsulate zones of ground-level and foreground-level plantings. This is an important concept because it subdivides larger planting compositions into smaller units, further creating interest. To unify the composition, two or three species should be repeated consistently throughout the composition. These plantings are predominantly neutral in character, such as evergreen shrubs like *Taxus* or *Ilex*. Often these plants, which knit the composition together, allow a more diverse range of plants to play out in foreground and background layers—they play a transitional role by connecting or bridging the various layers. Alternatively, they take on a secondary role as infiller, occupying neutral space between more interesting midground-layer plantings of perennials, tropicals, and grasses.

Lower Canopy

Lower-canopy plantings consist of large shrubs and small trees (over six feet) that are situated toward the rear of the composition. Two types of plantings comprise this layer: large shrubs, which have foliage mass that extends to, or almost to, the ground; and small trees, which have a canopy associated with them at some distance above the ground. This is an important distinction, as the latter will permit plantings underneath while the former will not.

Plantings in the lower canopy can play a number of roles depending on the scale of the composition. Predominantly, they occupy the rear layers or upper levels (hence, the term "canopy") of the composition. Occupying large amounts of space, they establish bulk mass. Depending on the height of the plant, they can imply edges or completely enclose space. They can, in certain instances, serve as background plantings or be located immediately in front of larger background plants.

Lower-canopy plantings also may define space in both the vertical and overhead planes. This is usually accomplished with small trees, which can be located at any position in the composition. In this role, they serve as visual and compositional accents, to provide contrast and make a vertical statement—usually as a focal point. In this regard, they should be considered in relationship to other plant massings in order to maintain visual balance.

Taller shrubs comprising the lower canopy layer can be used as landscape walls to establish larger landscape bays. As at the midground layer, tall shrubs in the canopy layer can accomplish the same objective of bay creation but on a larger scale. They can provide a neutral background for lower-layer plantings positioned in front of them. To be effective, the size of the massings and bays created should be in proportion to the scale of the overall composition.

As with small trees, large shrubs at this layer can be used as individual specimens set within lower planting types. It is sometimes effective to bring a canopy-level plant forward into a lower-level planting zone, as this will increase the visual interest by providing greater depth in the planting composition.

Background

The rearmost layer in the composition, the background, contains the tallest plants, usually ten feet or taller, typically large evergreens or shade trees. But this will depend on the overall size of the composition: In smaller-scale compositions, the background plantings should be in proportion to the available space. For example, plantings used for the background in the backyard of a townhome might be considered midground-layer plantings if used in a composition with a larger, more open landscape. The arrangement of the mix, evergreen vs. deciduous, will depend on the functional objective of the background planting, whether to screen objectionable views, frame distant views, or achieve some other desired design effect.

LAYERING SUMMARY

Layer structuring in elevational view is a teaching tool to help you reach the next level of understanding. As you fine-tune your visualization skills, using this technique to design a composition with plant masses will become second nature.

At this stage in the design process the depth and pattern of the planting bed is not important—of course, it will be later. Remember to draw the blocks to scale and to represent the mature height and spread of the plant type desired. This will enable you to visualize the heights and evaluate the various relationships more effectively than in plan view (Booth 1983). The actual horizontal bed dimension will be determined when the elevation is translated into plan view. We will discuss this further in Chapters 6 and 7, pages 125 and 175 respectively.

Assembling the Abstract Composition

When three or more plant massings are positioned together they become a composition. Such compilations of plants are *volumetric* expressions of a particular site situation in that they occupy a defined "volume" or area of space. In the third dimension this "volume" in turn defines and creates edges of space. It will be important to maintain this perspective as we work through the design process. As you know, all plants within a composition have a purpose to fill within the design; likewise, the composition has a purpose: to define and enclose spaces in the landscape. Such spaces must clearly relate to the character, mass, and purpose of the surrounding landscape and structures within it (Simonds 1983). That is, the composition must become a complete and balanced composition—not just an assemblage of plants for decoration.

At the beginning stages of creating a composition, it helps to think in abstract terms, to imagine the composition as a series of blocks, which represent the various types of plant massings. The next step, to effectively visualize and study the relationships between the abstract boxes (plant masses), is to prepare an elevational composition, to show the blocks in silhouette as viewed from the ground at eye level. Florence Bell Robinson first developed this method of study in *Planting Design* (1940). This technique enables us to study the compositional relationships among the height of abstract blocks, the proportional relationship between block masses, and layering relationships. This technique would later be refined by William R. Nelson, which he described in his book, *Planting Design: A Manual of Theory and Practice* (1985). Nelson coined the term "backward process," to define the stages of compositional planting design where essentially the last thing to be decided is which plants will be used. In summary the stages include:

1   The first step in the planting design process is to decide on the plant's size and form as it relates to the overall compositions.

2   Next to be specified are plant qualities such as texture, flower type, ornamental characteristics, etc.

3   Third, identify the existing cultural conditions of the soil such as soil type, exposure, moisture availability, etc.

4   The final step is to select those plants that are culturally suited for the particular location that fit the aesthetic criteria.

In a composition, the function of the individual block massing, aside from a plant's primary function as an individual, has many secondary functions that contribute to the overall composition. Compositional form, may establish bays or serve to bridge, emphasize, provide a neutral mass, or enframe. An analogy can be drawn from buildings to plants in a composition. Jose Luis Sert, author of *Can Our Cities Survive?* (1942), commented on the role of individual buildings within a cityscape: "City dwellings should always be considered as the component parts of groups of structures, or districts." Assembling the abstract blocks, as in developing a cityscape, should not be random; it must be planned, for the massing blocks will function differently according to their placement.

To create the most interesting effects, plant masses—at this stage abstract boxes—should establish depth and variety. The position of the blocks should be modeled, to produce a variety of silhouettes: to have openings and hollows, be irregular and varied, and create bays for decorative plantings (see Figure 5.12). The arrangement of the masses, their size, and spacing must alternate rhythmically, while never losing sight of the objective, which is to create a unified whole. While arranging individual plant masses, we need to think of them as either background or screens, of divisions for the establishment of areas or planting bays, fillers, or enframers or accents (see Figure 5.12).

At the same time, and regardless of their function within the composition, the masses must provide depth and vary in height. Large or dominant masses, small secondary groupings, and connective and filler groupings must collectively convene to comprise a series of patterns that make for a pleasing composition. By keeping these considerations in mind, we can begin to assemble various massing blocks to develop the abstract composition.

It is best to begin with a simple composition, then move on to more complex and layered ones, all the time considering depth and distance, opposition and balance, scale and proportion, and sequence and climax, if appropriate (Robinson 1940). The easiest place to begin is with the plant masses that will occupy the background, then build forward. At least in the

Figure 5.12
Layering of a variety plant types at various heights creates interest in the foreground, midground, and background as seen in both plan and elevation.

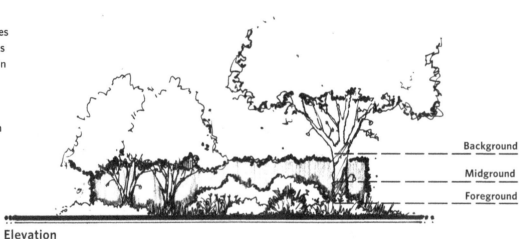

Background

Midground

Foreground

Elevation

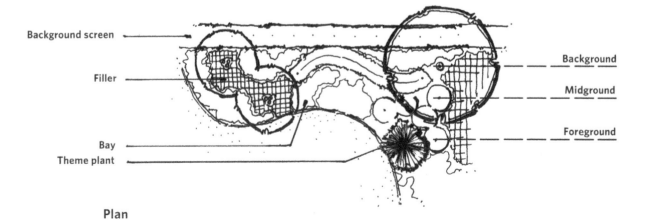

Background screen

Background

Filler

Midground

Foreground

Bay

Theme plant

Plan

beginning of the process, the blocks should generally be layered with the tallest in the background and the smallest in the foreground. The taller blocks will usually be representative of small trees or large shrubs. Once the taller blocks have been positioned in the background, we can proceed to add the intermediate blocks in the midground. These will represent medium-sized shrubs, large perennials, tropicals if used, and grasses. The last stage will be to add the foreground plantings representative of small shrubs, perennials, grasses, bulbs, and annuals.

Think of positioning the blocks in layers both vertically and horizontally—relating to the height and spread of the plant masses (see Figure 5.13). Masses should follow this rhythm generally, not strictly, to avoid monotony. As you become experienced with this process, and your comfort level with using more plant types rises, you can begin to experiment, even break the rules—for example, by inserting taller blocks in the foreground to add interest. But initially at least, it's a good idea to focus on a rhythmic progression from back to front.

Moving horizontally along the composition a much greater variation of rhythm should be established. Adding masses from left to right and right to left, locate blocks so that they vary in height from high to low to intermediate to high again, etc. This variation in rhythm creates a distinctive visual pattern and silhouette and is what Nelson termed "pleasing skyline" (see Figure 5.14).

As the designer, you must also consider the ability of the viewer to perceive any one length of the planting composition at one time. In larger compositions, those covering horizontal

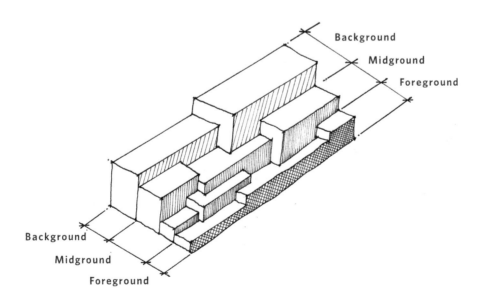

Figure 5.13
A layered planting composition illustrating variation in foreground, midground, and background layers.

distances of, usually, over twenty feet, it will be necessary to have smaller subgroups of plantings within the composition The distance of the viewer from the composition will have a direct relationship to how much of the composition is visible: The farther away, the more the viewer will be able to see, because the "cone of vision" becomes wider, as diagrammed in Figure 5.15 (Nelson 1985). This physiological fact warrants that larger compositions be broken down into smaller units to make them more easily perceivable. This requirement also helps to create interest in the composition and avoid monotony.

Distance from the observer to the composition also will be an important consideration for deciding how many layers are needed and how close the layer heights should be in relation to one another. Here, too, the farther away the viewer, the less evident the layers, because they merge into one another. Likewise, the greater the distance the viewer from the composition horizontally, the less apparent will be the difference vertically. Texture and color will, at this point, increase in importance, as these two characteristics aid in differentiating plant masses from one another. Therefore, the composition must be simplified so that it can be "read" effectively as a coherent scene. Height variations will need to be more defined stair-step with

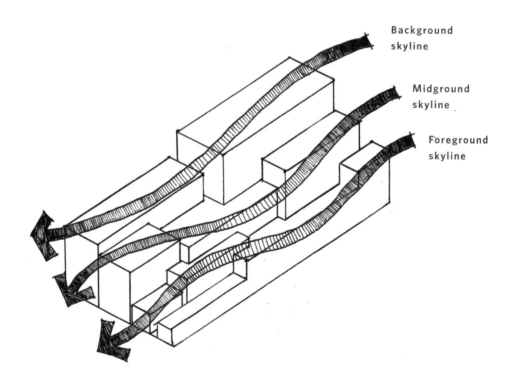

Background
skyline

Midground
skyline

Foreground
skyline

Figure 5.14
A smooth
transition made
between the
various plant
heights of each
level will create a
"pleasing skyline."

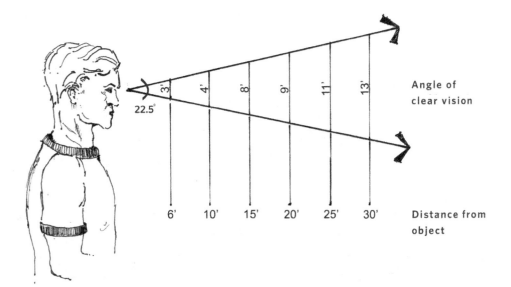

Angle of clear vision

Distance from object

Figure 5.15
The angle of clear vision is 22.5 degrees. As the distance from an object or composition increases, the span of vision will increase.
Source: William R. Nelson, *Planting Design: A Manual of Theory and Practice*

greater differences in height between each layer to counter the effect of distance. (This technique has ideal application for highway and buffer plantings where the composition is viewed not only from a distance but also traveling at high speeds.)

Returning to the cityscape analogy, think of your own experiences in viewing cities from a distance. What stands out first is the city skyline—the cumulative effect of the tops of the buildings creating a silhouette across the horizon. Many cities in the world—San Francisco, New York, Pittsburgh, and Sao Paolo, for example—are known for their distinctive skylines. Why? To answer that question we must study the forms of the buildings that contribute to the overall mass.

It is the relationships of the various heights and forms the buildings take that make the skyline so intriguing (see Figure 5.16). It is the juxtaposition of the various building shapes to one another, the contrast of one form against another, the rhythm created by the windows and other building elements that combine to make a memorable view. As the building massings become more complex and layered, each successive building massing in the foreground should have some relationship to, or complement, the one behind it.

Conceptually, as it relates to forms, the only difference between the appearance of a city silhouette and that of a planting composition silhouette in the abstract is the use of materials. In the cityscape both the lines and the forms comprise the composition. They vary in shape, direction, or both. This will be evident in a plant massing, as well. One plant massing may be flat-topped while another will be rounded; one will be upright, another low, etc. Variation from

Figure 5.16
The skyline of the City of Baltimore clearly illustrates how a variety of sizes and shapes of "building blocks" are combined to create a composition.

a dominant form or line, an accent, will prevent monotony. As such, accents should be used sparingly. As we've said so many times in this book, too many cause visual unrest; and poorly placed ones can destroy balance and pattern.

And always, always, remember to include one constant element to tie all the variations together—to make a unified whole. It may be form, direction of line, scale, rhythm, or color or texture. The ultimate goal of a composition is harmony. The methods used to achieve it will depend on the mood you, as the designer, are trying to establish with the composition. A composition that contains a large amount of bold foliaged plants will convey a tropical feeling; one that has numerous contrasting forms and shapes will convey excitement; still another with a predominance of cool colors will suggest repose and calm. All of these elements contribute to a dominant mood.

Harmony also can be achieved through the extension of lines—lines growing from lines. Changes of direction should be gradual (unless accent is desired) and rhythmic. In general, lines should relate to, not be in competition with, another. Or, if they are, they should relate through a transitional form. Keep in mind, it is the relationships among the lines and forms that will direct the observer to a place or a point of interest.

Evaluating the Composition

The basic principles of art are the foundation for the development of any composition. Those same principles will be used to evaluate it. Nelson, in his book *Planting Design: A Manual of Theory and Practice* (1985) offers a detailed checklist for evaluating an abstract planting composition:

Consider the relative number of blocks "staked" or "layered" in front of each other The greater the number of layers, the greater the bed depth will be. Smaller areas, where bed depth is not possible, should have fewer layers.

Evaluate the line implied by the tops of the planting masses This "skyline" should create a free-flowing smooth extension across the top of the overall composition and over each succeeding layer. Avoid ragged and stair-stepped lines.

Make sure to overlap blocks in planting masses Each succeeding layer should sufficiently overlap the preceding block so that no large gaps or open areas are created. Avoid openings or gaps between units, unless a specific effect is desired; otherwise, attention will be drawn to the "hole" in the composition.

Consider the distance the viewer will be from the composition The height of the massing blocks should have an obvious difference between those behind and those in front of it.

Avoid literal stair-stepping of blocks either vertically of horizontally There will be greater interest in varied heights and depths of the planting massing.

Consider the relationships between layers in the composition Specifically, be cognizant of the mature size of the plant and position it accordingly in the foreground, midground, or background layer. These various "grounds" should serve as a general guideline for the placement of various sized plants—for example, taller plants in the background, smaller plants in the foreground, etc. To increase the appearance of depth and create greater visual interest, however, you may want to allow some taller plants to "escape" into the foreground layers.

Simplicity, similarity of scale, balance, and sequence are essential components in developing compositions (Robinson 1940). The key to combining shapes to establish masses in a mixed planting is to provide contrast while creating harmony.

STARTING THE PLANTING DESIGN PROCESS in the abstract gives us a foundation from which we can begin to visualize the planting composition in three dimensions. In the previous chapter, the discussion on abstract compositions dealt primarily with the vertical arrangement (elevation) of plant massings and the juxtaposition of proportions in elevation. Working in elevation gives us a sense of how plants relate to one another, both in height and in proportion to their massing. The overall forms and outlines of the plant boxes, which we use to represent various species and plant massings, give us a three-dimensional view of volumetric relationships. According to William R. Nelson in *Planting Design: A Manual of Theory and Practice* (1985), using these "raw" forms helps us to, first, visualize and, subsequently, analyze a proposed composition based on the principles of design. Now it is time to consider the horizontal plane.

Going Horizontal

Most planting compositions are developed on the ground plan, or in *plan view*—looking straight down from overhead. Interestingly, plans developed in this manner are actually poor representations of the final composition, and will never be seen this way except at the planning stages. Nevertheless, working in plan view is important for designers, for two reasons: first, of course, because plants grow horizontally as well as vertically; second, because their position in the landscape is set against horizontal edges and boundaries (e.g., building lines, paving surfaces, property lines, etc.).

THE VIEW FROM ABOVE

Taking a bird's-eye view is the best way to describe the process of translating the abstract elevational study to plan view. So far we have focused on relationships in height and proportion of massings. Now we will begin to consider the third dimension, as established by the horizontal growth, or *spread*. This is what gives a plant its volume. The mature spread of a plant, which is represented by a circle in plan view, will become the prominent design symbol we will work with (see Figure 6.1). In this view:

▷ Plants such as perennials, ornamental grasses, annuals, or ground covers are represented as amorphous-shaped coverage zones.

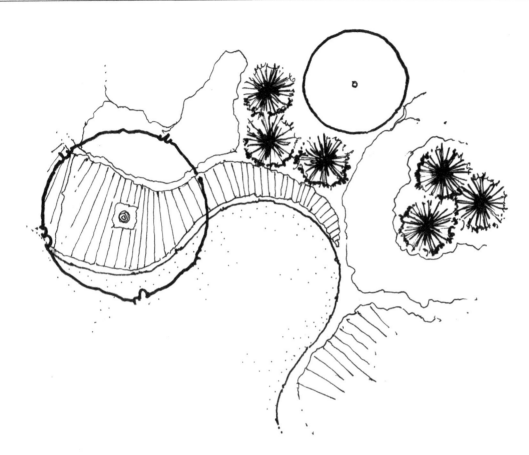

Figure 6.1
View of a planting plan that illustrates individual trees, shrubs, and herbaceous massings.

▷ The circle representing the plant (trees, shrubs, or individual specimens) should be drawn to scale at the size that represents the mature or desired maintained size of a plant.

▷ Coverage zones should be drawn to illustrate the full extent of the desired area of coverage.

Working in plan view enables us, as designers, to be much more effective in utilizing space to establish plant masses and create bays for accent plantings. At this conceptual level, we must envision massing forms within the planting composition. From there, we will position structural elements on the ground plane within the bed. We have the necessary perspective to ensure that spatial relationships between plant massings are fully considered. Ultimately, working in plan view also forces us to evaluate the relationship of the composition to the larger landscape—that is, how a particular bed under design will function, both individually and collectively, among other landscape beds and elements.

THE TRANSLATION PROCESS

Strictly working in elevation view will not give the complete picture of the composition. At this point designers must begin to understand the impacts that the abstract composition will have in plan view. Elements in elevational study, the abstract blocks which represent a single plant or a grouping of plants, must be transferred to the plan view (see Figure 6.2). The process will begin to allow us to visualize the relationship of the composition in the horizontal dimension ultimately leading to decisions regarding bed depth and layering of planting blocks. The primary objective is to establish plant masses and planting bays. We should be working only with desired sizes of the plant and plant types (e.g., evergreen or deciduous trees and shrubs, perennials, etc.). Focusing on these two characteristics first will help us to develop spatial relationships, proportion, and scale. To begin the process, follow these guidelines:

1   Beginning with the plants in the background, transfer the plant groups onto the plan view, adding each successive layer, culminating with the foreground plants (see Figure 6.3). Take care at this stage to ensure that each plant's position in the bed is accurately represented in plan view, as indicated in the abstract composition. That means, in most cases, the plants toward the rear of the composition will have the largest-diameter circles, as they represent the largest plant materials in the composition.

2   Pay special attention to transferring the boxes that overlap in elevation view. Place plant masses in plan view so that they touch, overlap, and blend into a cohesive composition. Note that not all plant masses represented in elevation will transfer neatly to plan view— at least not initially. The reason is that, in elevation view, the length of the boxes in the foreground may conceal the boxes that are overlapping in the background. You may see areas that are unresolved, have larger than appropriate gaps, or seem not to align as you envisioned them in elevation view. As the process evolves, you will need to resolve these voids or exposed areas, otherwise they will quickly become breeding grounds for weeds or other undesirable growth. To fill all of the voids, it may be necessary to adjust the number of plants you originally visualized in the abstract elevation study or enlarge or reduce the zone of coverage. Remember, the abstract study is a starting point; you can adjust each abstract plant box in plan view as appropriate. It is difficult to address these issues working in elevation, which is one reason we use both views. Further refinement will always be necessary during the transition from elevation to plan view.

3   As the translation continues, consider the placement of plants and the layering of plant massings in relation to the depth of the bed, which is determined by the mature size and spread of the plants, the numbers and types of plants, and the numbers of layers (see

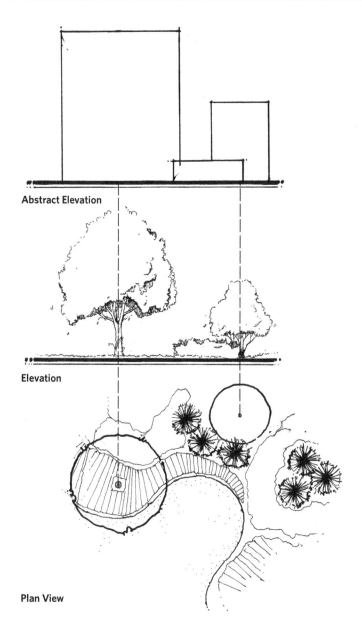

Abstract Elevation

Elevation

Plan View

Figure 6.2
The relationship between plan and elevation view can be seen when transferring plantings from the abstract composition to the elevation to the plan.

Figure 6.4, page 131). This factor is directly proportional to the number of layers in the abstract elevation. For example, an abstract composition that comprises predominantly grasses and perennials will require much less space than one using evergreens and shrubs.

Assume an abstract composition has these four layers: (1) a large deciduous shrub for the background, (2) a medium evergreen shrub, (3) a medium ornamental

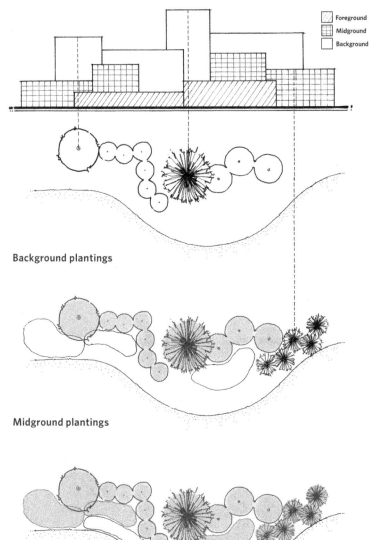

Background plantings

Midground plantings

Figure 6.3
"Layering" each
successive plant layer
builds on top of the
previous layer.

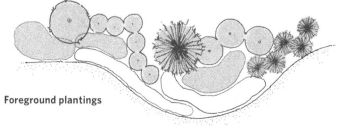

Foreground plantings

grass, (4) and a small perennial. In this case, the required bed depth to accommodate a mature planting would be approximately thirteen to seventeen feet, based on the Mature Plant Spread and Spacing chart. The greater the number of layers desired, the greater the bed depth needed to accommodate the plants. This is discussed in greater detail on page 138.

Mature Plant Spread and Spacing Chart

PLANT TYPE	MATURE HEIGHT*	MATURE SPREAD*	RECOMMENDED SPACING ON CENTER
Ground cover	1–4″	10–18″ +/–	6–12″
Annual	6–15″	10–20″	8–15″
Compact herbaceous plants	6–15″	15–24″	12–18″
Upright and vigorous herbaceous plants	18–24″	18–42″	18–36″
Low ornamental grasses	15–30″	15–30″	24–30″
Tall ornamental grasses	3–7′	3–4′	36–42″
Low-spreading shurbs	15–24″	2–5′	36–48″
Small shrubs	18–30″	2–4′	2–3′
Medium shrubs	3–4′	4–8′	4–5′
Tall shrubs	5–7′+	6–10′	6–8′
Small flowering trees	12–18′	14–20′	12–15′
Shade trees	40′+	25–80′	30–45′
Evergreen trees	30′+	15–25′	14–16′

*Mature height and spreads are approximations and will vary according to site conditions and specific plant species.

Figure 6.4 The chart lists the average range of height and spread for the various plant types and their recommended plant spacing.

Grouping Plants: Developing Masses

As noted in the previous chapter, most plant communities in nature consist of colonies of species massed together in various-sized groups. Intermingled within these groups of plants are other groupings of a variety of species, plus an occasional individual plant or specimen. According to Norman K. Booth in *Basic Elements of Landscape Architectural Design* (1983), by using nature as our guide, clustering plants together in groups, we can establish a sense of visual harmony. Grouping allows for consolidation of individual parts into a unified whole. Plant arrangements formed with too many individual plants will appear disjointed, "spotty," or chaotic.

MASSING BY NUMBERS
Unless you intend an individual plant to serve as a "special effect," it's best to limit the introduction of these "loners." When you do use individual plants they should generally be as specimens and strategically placed. In general, realize that in the mixed planting composition plants should, in fact, be massed.

As a rule of thumb, it's a good idea to assemble plants in odd numbers, such as 3, 5, 7, etc. Odd numbers produce more unified compositions because the human eye cannot as easily split or divide odd numbers of things (see Figure 6.5). Odd numbers within each of the subgroups support and reinforce one another (Booth 1983).

Determining the number of plants within a massing will depend on three factors:

▷ First, the number of plants within each massing will be dependent on the size of the bed being developed. The overall size of the planting block or mass should be in proportion to the size of the bed—keeping in mind that too large a massing will cause monotony and one too small will cause chaos. Additionally, you'll want to base the proportion of the massing not only on the relationship to the overall of the planting bed but to the percentage of each plant type used in the overall composition, as well. For example, if the overall composition has greater proportions of perennials than other plant types the scale or proportion of each perennial massing should relate to other perennial massings, not to other plant types.

▷ Second, the type of impact you want to make in the design will determine the size of the mass. For instance, if you introduce a powerful plant like a *Canna* with the intent to create a bold tropical flair, it may be appropriate to make the massing disproportionately larger than other massings, for impact.

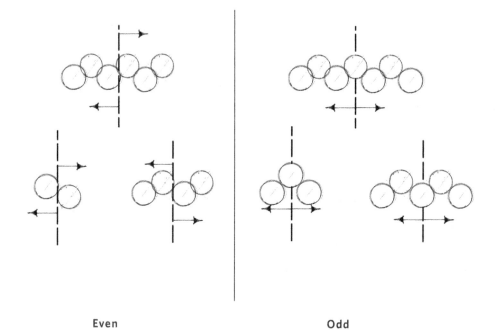

Figure 6.5
The eye tends to split even groups so odd-numbered group plantings are recommended.

Even   Odd

▷ Third, the number of plants in each mass will vary based on the mature size of the plant. As an example, consider a composition with equal proportions of large shrubs and small evergreens: in this case, the number of small evergreens required to match the volume produced by the large deciduous shrubs will be greater. Therefore, a massing of nine *Berberis thunbergii* 'Crimson Pigmy' (Crimson pigmy barberry) would be needed to balance three *Viburnum carlesii* (Fragrant viburnum).

ESTABLISHING PATTERNS AND LINES

Much of the art and science of planting design has to do with establishing patterns and lines on the ground, using massings of various plant types to create volumetric spaces masses and voids. The resultant patterns must be visually interconnected, however. This we accomplish by interlocking and interweaving massings to form a tapestry of living plant material (see Figure 6.6). According to John Ormsbee Simonds, in his book *Landscape Architecture: A Manual of Site Planning and Design* (1983), masses are dynamic: They may direct and concentrate interest inward; they may direct attention to an alternative point in the composition; or they may impel outward motion.

As we've said so often throughout this book, groupings for mixed plantings are best established with drifts or blocks of different plant types. This technique results in bold masses of various plant types that best showcases the aesthetic qualities of the individual plant characteristics. By displaying plants en masse, we minimize the risk of underutilizing a plant's best attribute at the same time we establish unity. Remember, you'll be arranging masses so that the backdrop formed by one plant type accents the foreground planting of another, and vice versa, thereby producing interest using elements of contrast. For example,

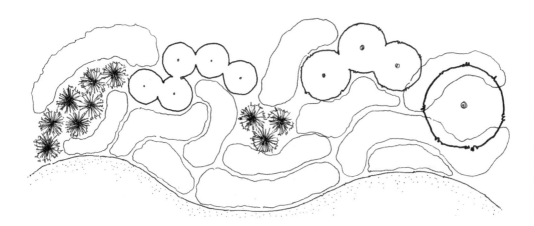

Figure 6.6
Various styles can be used to develop massing shapes that interlock with one another.

evergreens may form the backdrop to deciduous shrubs, grasses may be behind perennials, low evergreens in front of grasses, perennials adjacent to tropicals can all create the desired effect. Also keep in mind these patterns must take advantage of the seasonal attributes of the various plant types. As we've said so often, as one plant is fading, an adjacent massing—to the rear, side, or in front of it—should be coming into season.

Alternating plant types to showcase their seasonal attributes is, however, a complex undertaking. What we are doing, essentially, is to "paint" with living plant materials. In doing so, we must take full advantage of each plant's color, texture, and form as displayed in the various seasons; we must also ensure that the massings transition smoothly from one to another. According to Florence Bell Robinson in *Planting Design* (1940), varying and integrating the projections and recesses of plant masses will help us achieve these objectives.

Groups or masses of plant types should, as mentioned before, be visually connected so that they "feel" unified. Achieving unity requires simplicity of line and form, by the repetition of lines established by the opposing masses and by interlocking forms (see Figure 6.7). To this end, you'll want to juxtapose masses, so that a predominant form becomes apparent throughout the composition, and distribute masses and forms to produce a pattern (Robinson 1940). This not only will serve to literally connect the masses but will alleviate potential maintenance problems. Remember, you want to avoid gaps between masses of plants. Therefore, it's important consider the relationship of plant massings to desired ground-plane patterns, existing patterns in the landscape, and available bed depth.

When plant masses are linked together effectively, an intimate relationship develops between plant types, and the transition between massings is subtle. That means, for example,

Figure 6.7
Edges of plant masses should reinforce one another to establish lines in the composition that "thread" the composition together.

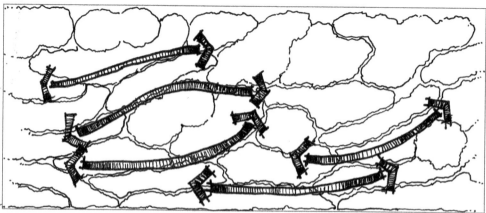

a plant mass may appear simultaneously in front of, behind, or adjacent to another massing, which adds to the contribution of that particular plant, thereby enriching the aesthetic of the composition. Gertrude Jekyll expressed these effects well in her book *Colour in the Flower Garden* (1908):

> I am strongly of the opinion that possession of a quantity of plants . . . does not make a garden; it only makes a collection . . . merely having them, or having them planted unsorted in garden spaces, is only like having a box of paints from the best colorman, or, to go a step further, it is like having portions of these paints set out upon a palette. This does not constitute a picture . . . In practice it is to place every plant or group of plants with such thoughtful care and definite intention that they shall form part of a harmonious whole, and that successive portions, or in some case even details, shall show a series of pictures.

Thus, planting compositions appear more unified when plants are positioned as groups or masses of species together. Jekyll devised a technique to interconnect plant masses by arranging them in long, thin "drifts." This technique, shown in Figure 6.8, effectively leads the observer from one plant drift to another. She designed the drifts to run in front of and behind adjacent drifts to form a unified composition. A particular benefit of this technique, especially with flowering plants, is described by Richard Bisgrove in his book *The Gardens of Gertrude Jekyll* (1992): "The drifts have a practical purpose in that while a considerable

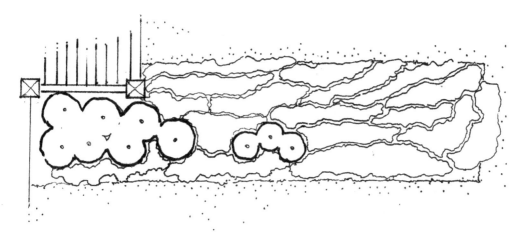

Figure 6.8
An example of a Jekyll plan that illustrates her technique of drifting plant masses.

quantity of each plant is revealed when in flower, its thin trail disappears as it ceases to flower and other plants come into prominence." It is the linearity of each drift, and the overlapping of taller and shorter plantings dissolving the edges, that make drifting such a powerful technique. As the seasonal attributes of one drift start to fade, the resultant void is quickly filled by neighboring drifts whose seasonal attributes are beginning. Using plants with multiple seasonal attributes can further minimize void spaces, as recommended in previous chapters.

It is important that the overlapping be multidimensional. That is, it must occur front to back, side to side, and top to bottom, in order to link all portions of the planting together in a seamless whole:

▷ The degree of overlap should vary throughout the composition. For example, one massing may overlap its adjacent mass by 20 percent, whereas the next may overlap 60 percent (see Figure 6.9).

▷ The width of the overlap should be in proportion to the other masses in the overall composition. Avoid noticeable seams among masses. The more random in appearance the overlap, the more natural the composition will appear.

The forms and patterns the massings assume can vary, depending on the aesthetic of the design, the natural lines of the site (either from existing man-made elements or natural

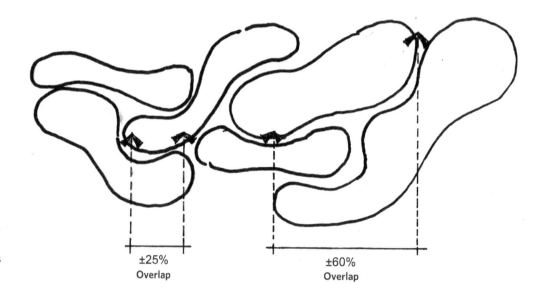

Figure 6.9
Varying the degree of overlap between plant masses creates interest and locks masses together.

±25%
Overlap

±60%
Overlap

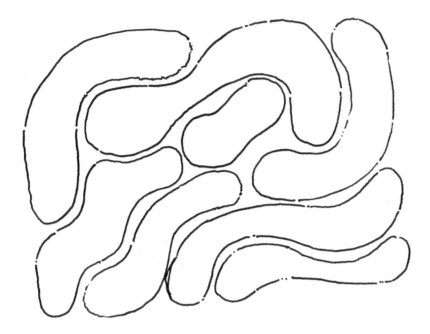

Figure 6.10
Informal curvilinear overlapping of masses "lock" one another together.

landforms), and the composition of plant types. If no patterns exist on the site, you must develop them. This involves the organization of space and the development and repetition of form. Overlapping, interlocking, and drifting will all be used to varying degrees as plant masses take form. Free-form planting masses and drifts are most appropriate for curvilinear, naturalistic, or informal landscapes, where the fluid arrangements of masses overlap and embrace one another (see Figure 6.10). On more formal or geometric sites, patterns should be based on rectilinear masses that interlock and overlap (Nelson 1985).

Landscape architects and designers throughout history have used various patterning techniques for massing plants. Jekyll used thin linear drifts of perennials much as a painter would use long narrow strokes of a paintbrush on a canvas. The Brazilian landscape architect Roberto Burle Marx made famous a style of massing that re-created canvas art on the landscape. He used bold and colorful tropical foliage plants in curvaceous or blocky abstract massings to instill modernistic patterns in the landscape. The landscape architecture firm Oehme van Sweden drew inspiration from Marx, Jekyll, and Japanese garden designers, emphasizing a plant's texture and color by using simple drifts filled with large numbers of perennials and grasses. They added interest to this technique by placing an occasional shrub or evergreen between massings for emphasis.

Calculating Bed Depth

Traditionally, designers have recommended a bed depth of 8 to 12 feet, especially for traditional English mixed borders. Though this precept still stands today as an appropriate depth for mixed borders, one form of a mixed planting bed, modern mixed planting beds need not be confined by this old rule. As mentioned earlier in this chapter, bed depth has a correlative relationship to the number of layers of plant types desired; it is not necessarily restricted to linear borders. That is to say, the greater the number of plant layers desired in a composition, the greater the depth of the planting bed should be. Beyond that, and more specifically, it is the mature size of the plants in each layer, in concert with the types of plants comprising the various layers, that will determine the bed depth (see Figure 6.4, page 131). Generally speaking then, a composition developed with only grasses, perennials, and ground covers will require less depth than one that includes evergreens, shrubs, perennials, and ground covers because, in the latter, collectively, the mature size that each plant type will attain in each successive layer will be greater.

Bed depth is also, understandably, related to the overall height of the composition. The height of the plants in the bed should to be proportional to the bed depth and the overall size of the garden. A small garden or shallow bed can be overwhelmed by the presence of a tall plant. As a general rule, therefore, the depth of a planting bed should correspond approximately to the tallest plant in the composition. Thus, in a planting bed confined to a 4-foot strip between the edge of a building and a walkway, the tallest plant used should not be any taller than 4 feet. Or, if the tallest plant used in a composition is a 6-foot shrub, the planting bed should not be shallower than 6 feet.

These are general rules, however. As a designer, it will be up to you to determine where and when to apply these rules. Your guiding principle is that the overall proportion of the composition, not an individual bed, will be the determining factor. It is important at all times to maintain a global view of the composition, garden, or landscape.

TWO METHODS FOR DETERMINING BED DEPTH

Determining the depth of a planting bed can be achieved using one of two methods. First, bed depth can, from an abstract viewpoint, or at the conceptual stage, be determined by the number of layers desired and the types of plants specified by for each layer. Recall from the previous chapter the five layers: ground, foreground, midground, lower canopy, and background layers (see Figure 5.11, page 113).

As an example, assume a composition includes one plant type for each of those five categories: in this case, a minimum depth of eighteen to thirty feet would be required

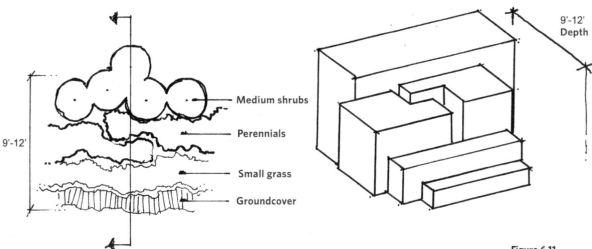

Medium shrubs

Perennials

Small grass

Groundcover

9'-12'

9'-12'
Depth

Figure 6.11
A direct
relationship exists
between the
number of layers,
the plant types,
and the overall
bed depth.

(again, see Figure 6.4, page 131). But what if the mixed planting composition does not contain all five layers? Some may have more, others fewer. There are no limitations, theoretically, to the number of layers a mixed planting can have. Therefore, if space on the site is not a constraint, you could determine the bed depth needed in plan view by first working in elevation to determine how many layers and which plant types you want to use. Then by finding the mature height and spread of the various plant types, you could establish the bed depth needed based on the plant types specified for each layer. This method of determining bed depth is rarely used, however, because, typically, there are space constraints as dictated on the ground plane.

The second method assumes that the bed depth is known. You could determine roughly how many layers to include by working the above process backward. If a bed line has been established and the depth of bed is known, you could use the mature size of the planting types to determine the number of layers. (In the next section you'll learn how various bed lines are determined as part of the site design.) For example, if, through the site design process, you determined that the planting bed was to be 12 feet deep, you would subtract from that number the mature spread of each plant type you planned on using. So, if you were to design the composition with a medium shrub layer (2 to 5 feet), two perennial layers (12 to 24 inches each), a small ornamental grass layer (18 to 24 inches), and a ground cover layer (8 inches minimum), you would have a planting bed that contained five layers with an approximate mature bed depth of 9 to 12 feet (see Figure 6.11).

Later, if you chose, you could go back to the original design and reduce the bed depth in that area to 9 feet to maintain the plantings in certain layers. Alternatively, you could increase the size of the plants in one or more of the layers. There are numerous possibilities. The key is to remember that the process is not linear; more often than not you will go back and forth in the process, refining massings until your composition looks the way you want it to.

Establishing the Bed Line

Mixed planting beds are defined and enclosed by lines—bed lines. We talked at some length in Chapter 3 (page 39) about the importance of line to the design of mixed plantings. Lines in the landscape, as you know, are powerful elements, connoting movement or motion, as well as defining limits. Within the lines that enclose the planting bed are the plant materials that make it a mass. In contrast to the masses are open spaces, which are called *voids*, a term you've seen used throughout this book. These voids, which may be associated with lawns, patios, or walkways, for example, are of equal importance to the bed: One defines the other.

Figure 6.12
Positive space is created by the surrounding and enclosing planting beds.

The strong relationship between the two cannot be overestimated, for it is the quality and shape of mass that determines the quality and impression of the void.

It is the opposing forces of mass and void that give you, as a designer, unlimited opportunities for varying the types of settings to produce special experiences. It will be the voids (also referred to as *negative space*) in your compositions that make the masses (*positive space*) stand out (see Figure 6.12). For instance, large areas of plantings representing mass juxtaposed against small areas of void produce intriguing spatial relationships. Perfect balance of mass and void is difficult to achieve, and depending on your design intent will not always be what you want. In fact, often, the relationship will be more one of perception than actual physical volume of dimensional space. The visual weight of the mass will greatly affect the actual percentage of mass vs. void. Generally speaking, where there is more void or open space, the landscape will tend to take on a more elegant or refined appearance. Of course, the selection of the plants becomes paramount to the success of the composition. Simple plant compositions lend themselves to elegance, whereas more complex planting schemes will direct focus to the plantings themselves. And with greater mass comes a greater risk that the space will feel confined or cluttered.

TYPES OF LINE AND THEIR EFFECTS

An almost infinite variety of lines can used to create landscape beds, each having a unique effect on motion, whether real and perceived. Lines can, according to Clauston (1977), establish a "design speed," generating a momentum that the eye follows through the landscape (see Figure 6.13). Recall from Chapter 3 that lines cause predictable human responses, and every line has its own abstract design connotation. Clearly then, your design intent must be

SLOW

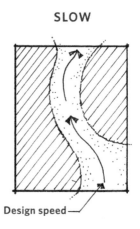

Design speed

FAST

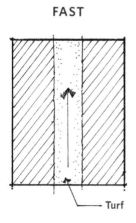

Turf

MODERATE

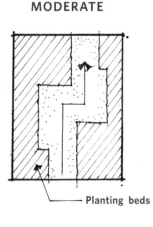

Planting beds

Figure 6.13
The speed for which one perceives and visually travels through the landscape is related to its shape and the direction of the lines.

carefully considered, taking into account the countless effects created by various types of lines. Consider, for example:

A line or its trajectory can be meandering, erratic, looping, curvilinear, or direct (see Figure 3.2, page 40)

Curved lines, as they relate to establishing bed lines, typically require large spaces to accommodate the bold sweeping forms necessary to express curves properly. Therefore, they are appropriate in informal designs. Soft undulating curves with shallow radii should generally be avoided except in special situations.

Straight lines are connected to geometric forms, hence are usually associated with urban or formal settings. These forms, the same found in architecture, should mimic the architecture to bring about unity between buildings and the landscape.

Tangent lines are most applicable where straight and curved lines connect. A tangent is a point in space at which two lines meet or touch. Tangent lines are important to planting design as they provide for a smooth and continuous transition between forms. This is especially true when square or rectangular forms are combined with circular or elliptical forms. The tangent establishes unity and harmony between forms and enables the viewer's eye to follow the edge of the forms without disruption, thereby establishing strong visual relationships in a composition (see Figure 6.14).

Extension lines, from existing elements, forms, or structures in the landscape, impose a framework for further development of a site design. These lines, which can be both real and imaginary, facilitate the linkage of divergent elements and forms. They act as guidelines for the alignment of forms based on tangents, described above. In that, they function much like a grid (discussed later in the chapter) by providing a framework to develop a comprehensive design.

As you begin to consider the types of lines you'll use to delineate planting beds, you'll also want to keep in mind the "viewing speed" conveyed by lines. A mixed planting, by its nature, demands a slow speed so that all of the various plants can be perceived. Bed lines that are curved and sinuous elicit a slow meandering reaction, whereas straight or diagonal lines pull the observer's eye along at a quicker pace. However, as with other guidelines, the design intent may change this and it will be up to the discretion of the designer.

DEFINING BEDS AND ESTABLISHING SPACE

Lines, as just stated, are paramount to the creation of space. They define areas for plants, which in turn defines the voids. For any space to have a significant purpose and form, it must

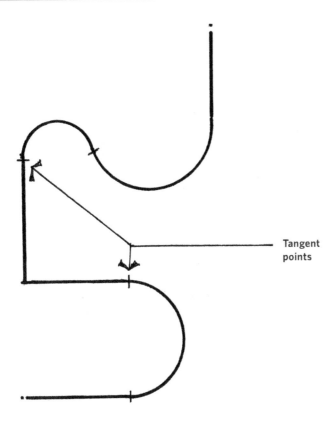

Tangent points

Figure 6.14
Merging lines with differing shapes and configurations should always be done on a tangent to avoid sharp or awkward angles.

have a definitive enclosure. The size, shape, and character of the enclosure determine the quality of the space (Simonds 1983).

The space for a mixed planting bed is defined by the *outer edges* of the bed lines. The addition of plant materials will showcase the character of the space and give it three-dimensional volume. Plants, internal to those edges, are used like walls and architectural components of a building to build "outdoor rooms." In these rooms, "doorways" and "windows" give either physical or visual access into or out of the spaces by varying the placement, height, or relationships between plant materials. Enclosed by walls of plantings, these spaces also can have "floors" surfaced by turf or ground cover, as well as "ceilings" formed by tree canopies. Figure 6.15 shows the walls and ceiling of a space created by plant materials.

The landscape, however, is not always viewed in terms of contained space. More often than not, people experience a landscape by moving from one space to another, in a progression that is transitory and linear. The experience is enhanced when that sequence unfolds as a series of volumetric spaces that vary the relative degree of enclosure Changes can be seen in light, texture, patterns, color, or views.

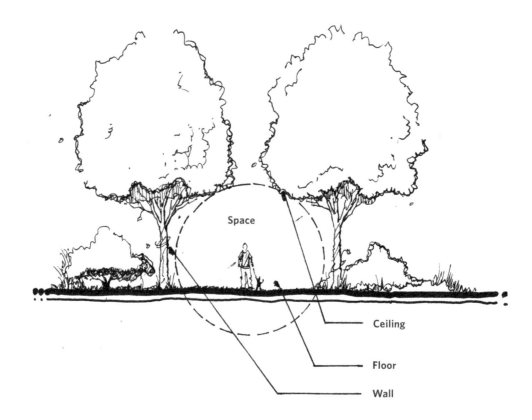

Space

Ceiling

Floor

Wall

Figure 6.15
(ABOVE)
Small trees and shrubs can be used within planting beds to create "walls" and "ceilings."

Figure 6.16
(BELOW)
Transitional spaces, usually linear, are needed to separate landscape rooms.

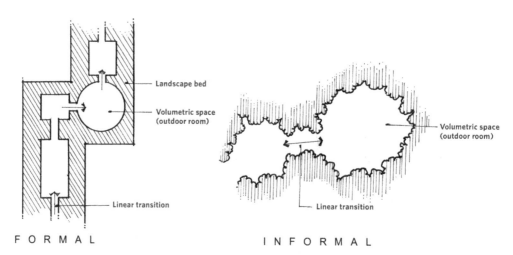

Landscape bed

Volumetric space (outdoor room)

Linear transition

FORMAL

Volumetric space (outdoor room)

Linear transition

INFORMAL

Nick Robinson in *The Planting Design Handbook* (1992), suggests that there are two keys to understanding this progression and the subsequent relationship between spaces. One is the organization between a group of spaces; the other is the character of the spaces between. The beds that establish the edges define this linear progression (see Figure 6.16). The character and experience is established by the plantings contained within.

While it is the relationship between mass and void that establishes the feeling of a space, as described above, it is the linear organization of an edge that creates the experience as a progression of events. And, as just explained, based on whether the beds are defined by lines that are curvilinear, angular, or straight, the speed of the experience will be set. The mixed plantings contained within those lines should reinforce the design speed, building to a climax and varying in interest along the way. Sometimes the design will call for a progression or plantings that are subtle, where the character of the sequence may evolve so slowly as to be almost imperceptible to the viewer. Other times the transition may be highly distinct, for example, leading from a planting theme of bold tropicalism to one of subtle color sequencing and fine-textured foliage. The overriding guideline here is that the experience must be suited to the location and the objective set forth in the design.

Developing a Design Theme

Mixed planting spaces acquire their character from the elements that contain them and that are set within them. Each element can be used to impart some special quality or design feature. It is important to develop a composition that has a common theme or style. A visual theme establishes a commonality among forms and elements within a composition and creates harmony, comprised of similar forms, shapes, or colors that work together to produce a visually ordered formation.

Logically, then, one of the first challenges in designing mixed bed plantings—or any planting, for that matter—is to determine the shape of the bed. As discussed previously, the relationship of bed lines should be based on principles of basic geometry. According to Noman K. Booth and James E. Hiss in *Residential Landscape Architecture: Design Process for the Private Residence* (1991), to achieve visual unity on the ground plane requires the designer to consider geometry of form, desired character of the design, and relationship of bed lines to existing structures or landscape elements. Consistency of form in these bed lines is one of the essential means for establishing unity in the landscape.

But before you can put a single plant in the ground, you must first decide on a theme or a pattern. The theme gives the composition a personality, or character, and establishes a ground plane pattern that will serve as the foundation for the bed lines. Begin by evaluating these factors:

▷ Context of the site

▷ Site topography

▷ Surrounding architecture

▷ Client's aesthetic preference

FORMAL OR INFORMAL?

Initially, all design themes are categorized very broadly, as either formal or informal. Deciding on one or the other will help you to coordinate the layout, ensuring that all component parts of the design relate harmoniously to one another.

Formal Patterns

Formal, symmetrical patterns are abundant in nature—just look at a leaf or the human body. Based as they are on geometrical shapes and axis lines, formal patterns are easily comprehended by humans because they imply order and structure. The elements of a formal plan are usually in equilibrium with a central point or the opposite sides of an axial line. These types of lines and patterns strongly relate to one another through their relationship of either parallel or perpendicular lines to the axis. In traditional formal designs, the principal interest lies in the geometric patterns established on the ground plane. Additionally, it will be paths or vistas or visual corridors that link the various design components into an organized composition.

Though governed by structural plantings—thereby limiting, controlling, and directing vision—formal design patterns offer several interesting opportunities to display mixed plantings. They serve as a framework for compartmentalizing planting units. Patterns should always be balanced, and typically focus on a central axis; depending on the complexity of the design, however, they may also have a cross-axis, as shown in Figure 6.17. Often a formal plan is designed to extend architectural and other landscape elements further into the landscape, or serve to link elements together. Forms in these design patterns are often united by simple hedges or border edgings. In sum, successful formal plans are those where the symmetry of the plan can be understood at a glance (Simonds 1983).

For you, the designer, formal design patterns establish a neutral framework to plant against, providing an ordered setting where plants of high ornamental value can stand out—texture, color, and pattern become more obvious in these designs. Plantings can be allowed to

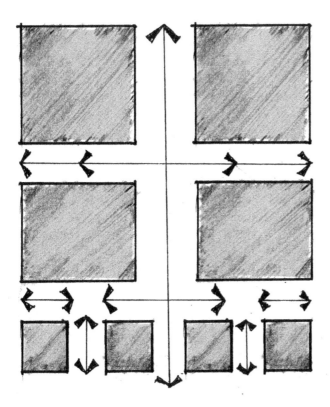

Figure 6.17
Central axes and cross-axes can be used to formally divide and link spaces and elements.

spill over formal edges and cross margins. Adding plantings with irregular forms, contrasting textures, and brilliant colors will emphasize the contrast between the neatness and order of the formal pattern, thereby adding to the interest of the mixed plantings.

Informal Patterns

There are no hard or fixed lines in informal designs, thus they more closely resemble those found in nature. Informal patterns also lack symmetrical balance—they are, by definition, asymmetrical. This gives designers great freedom to incorporate a wide variety of planting elements, which, subsequently, gives the viewer the freedom to interact with the composition more spontaneously.

John Ormsbee Simonds, in his book *Landscape Architecture: A Manual of Site Planning and Design* (1983), describes the human response to informal designs as "probing and exploring a vague and luminous flux of evolving visual impressions." He explains how a person's eye travels through informal compositions, sifting and choosing various elements. Because the

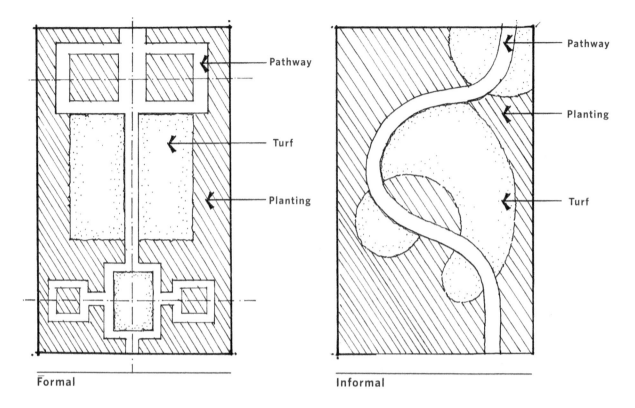

Formal

Informal

Figure 6.18
The contrast can be seen between the formal and informal arrangement of planting beds and differences in transition of spaces.

informal pattern has no real or perceived order, the possible visual impressions are limitless (see Figure 6.18). This differs dramatically from the formal plan where each object or plant is designed to be perceived in relation to the layout of the plan.

GEOMETRY OF FORMS

Chapter 4 outlined the visual dynamics of various geometric forms in elevation and associated them with various plant forms. Here we will evaluate forms on the ground plane, or on a flat surface. A shape on the ground plane imposes a dualism between mass and void. The shape of the void will tend to expand relative to the surrounding bed edges, while the bed edges will tend to push in on the voids at their weakest points (see Figure 5.3, page 105). It is this dynamic that alternately gives a sense of movement and rest within the space.

The patterns that can be produced using this mass-and-void dynamic are limitless. But broken down into their simplest elements, a rather limited number of "base" forms can be discerned, all relating to a geometric form, or shape. Squares, rectangles, triangles, and circles are the fundamental shapes used in virtually every design, and each shape conveys its own unique character. Christopher Alexander in his book, a *Timeless Way of Building* (1979), explains this:

"Of course the patterns vary from place to place, from culture to culture, from age to age; they all are man-made, they all depend on culture. But still, in every age and every place the structure of our world is given to it, essentially, by some collection of patterns, which keep repeating over and over and over again." This pattern repetition is true in garden design as well.

As a designer, it is critical to understand the composition of those forms, their abstractions and combinations, for it is the resultant shape they take that affects people's sense of aesthetics and emotions. By understanding the basic tenants of shape you will be better able to effectively manipulate and combine shapes on the ground plane. Norman Booth and James Hiss in their book, *Residential Landscape Architecture: Design Process for the Private Residence* (1991), detail the inherent characteristics of the square and circle as the primary shapes used to develop design themes. However, the designer must also consider the triangle and rectangle. These aforementioned geometric forms are often used by designers in some abstraction to establish a theme in a composition

Circle

The circle is a perfect form. It is uniformly convex, and from its central point or radius point, exert forces outward equally on all sides (see Figure 5.3, page 105). The circle has two features that affect its use in design: the center point and the circumference. It is the center point of the circle or radius point that is the prominent point of force from which all things radiate (see Figure 6.19). The subconsciously perceived forces exerting outward toward the circle's edges

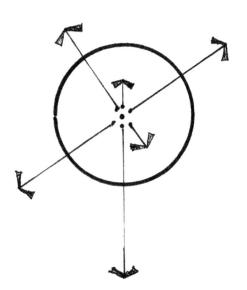

Figure 6.19
A circle's center point (radius point) must be linked in some fashion to all other surrounding forms or elements.

Figure 6.20
Extending the radii and increasing a circle's circumference provides a guide to effectively creating harmonious radial designs.

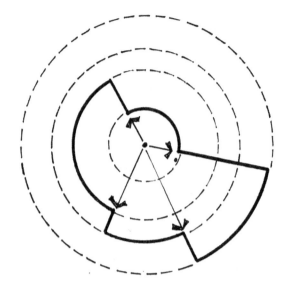

naturally pull a person's eye to the center. Virtually all lines used in a radial design must originate from this point or relate in some fashion to it. Therefore, a harmonious circular design will have radial permutations (defined by lines that are arcs) and relate to the radius point. Lines that do not have a relationship with the center point are to be avoided, as they constitute poor design. It is from an established center point that radii (lines that extend from the radius point) extend outward at various lengths to define the circumference of the circle itself. Additional lines can be extended at various lengths to establish additional radial forms.

A design using repetitive concentric circles or arcs utilizes the radius point to establish the form (see Figure 6.20). Lines and edges that have a relationship to the circle's circumference are more stable looking than ones that don't. Developing lines at various angles from the center point and replicating concentric circles are variations of radial designs that achieve in harmony and rhythm, thus making for a unified design. Radial designs that have lines that relate to one another or a common point are better designs than those that don't, as shown in Figure 6.21.

Because a circle is a pure form, it can be a unifying element. Centrally positioned among disparate elements, it can tie disparate parts into a harmonious whole. Figure 6.22 illustrates how a central circular area of turf can unite a variety of unrelated elements.

Square

The square has a stable balance of forces exerting on it. Outward forces push at the corners as well as the sides, while inward forces push in at the sides (see Figure 6.23).

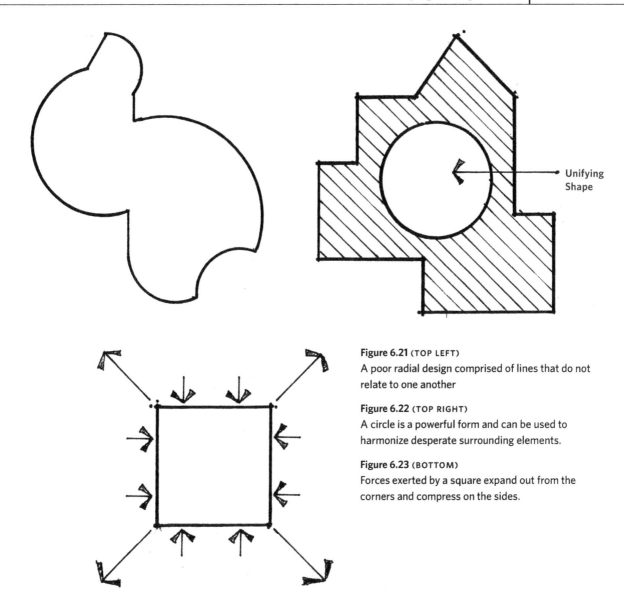

Figure 6.21 (TOP LEFT)
A poor radial design comprised of lines that do not relate to one another

Figure 6.22 (TOP RIGHT)
A circle is a powerful form and can be used to harmonize desperate surrounding elements.

Figure 6.23 (BOTTOM)
Forces exerted by a square expand out from the corners and compress on the sides.

The square is considered a formal form and can be divided into equally shaped halves. The division lines form two central axes parallel to its sides converging at a central center point. Each axis line points outward to one of its four sides (see Figure 6.24). A diagonal axis can be extended from the center point to the corners of the square forming a series of small triangles. These have a lesser degree of formality associated with them and are often more difficult to work with in terms of developing formal axial relationships to other forms.

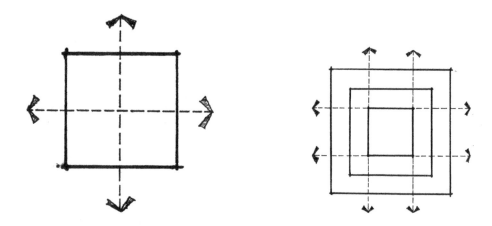

Figure 6.24 (TOP LEFT)
Axis lines originate from a square's central point and equally divide it into smaller components.

Figure 6.25 (TOP RIGHT)
Extending the lines of a square provides a guide for linking additional compositional elements.

Figure 6.26 (BOTTOM)
An extended grid, as illustrated by the plan of the City of Savannah, shows how edges of one shape can be extended to create a network of related spaces and shapes.

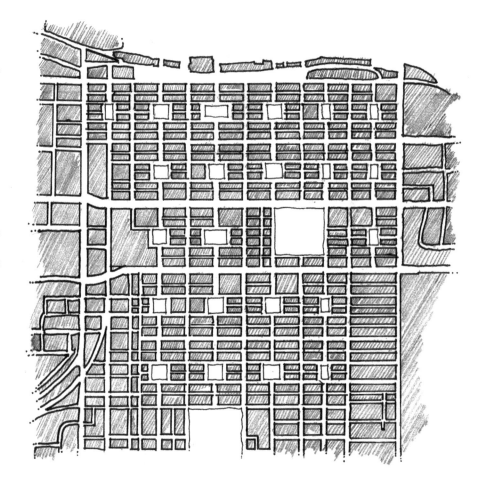

The square form is the core shape for development of a grid system. A grid system based on a square provides a pattern template to guide a design through a theoretically unlimited amount of compositions. Tied to its axis and edges, a square's lines of force extended beyond the shape itself create a framework for modular design (see Figure 6.25). We detail this more on pages 161–173. The proportions established by a single square are conveyed throughout the pattern and ensure proper proportion. The repetition of pattern reinforces rhythm and harmony. Extending a square's shape and manipulating its edges is the most efficient use of form and space. This fact has been illustrated throughout history by the development of grid systems to lay out city streets and blocks (see Figure 6.26).

Triangle

The triangle has forces that are pushing outward toward each of its three corners (see Figure 6.27). The inward pressure is being applied along the three edges but is subordinate to those forces at the corners. Triangles, specifically equilateral triangles, like circles, have a central point from which lines of force radiate. Unlike circles, however, triangles have corners that concentrate their force or directional thrust in specific directions—a strength and weakness when working with triangles.

Triangles offer a dynamic tension not present with squares and circles in plan. Diagonal lines usually form the edges of triangles. These lines exert a powerful directional force to a composition and will direct a person's eye to a place. Lines of force oppose one another and lead outward in differing directions. Additionally, the relationship of lines to one another in the triangle results in a closing space. The lines funnel attention or movement into an apex, which becomes the focus of the space.

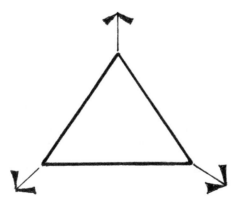

Figure 6.27
Outward forces are exerted by
the corners of a triangle.

The designer must be careful to consider, however, that the space established in third dimension will not read as it does in plan. Triangles will, by their angular nature, create spaces with acute angles that are too slender to make any spatial contribution to the composition. The result is narrow angles of turf, concrete, or planting beds, which are often too difficult to maintain or too weak to stand the test of time. These are essentially awkward "leftover spaces." This negative occurrence must be considered when using triangles, and their effect countered in the design by blending them with other shapes.

Rectangle

The rectangle, unlike the square, has a greater degree of forces pushing inward along the two long sides. This "squeezing of the sides" enhances the rectangular shape, conveying a strong sense of movement in the direction of its long axis (see Figure 6.28). For this reason, focal elements are often positioned at either end of a rectangle's long axis.

Like the square, the rectangle can be divided into equally sized segmented units. The established proportions, which are in relationship to the size of the rectangle itself, drive the placement of other shapes. Because the rectangle has a strong axial connotation, which divides it horizontally and vertically, dividing it into four quadrants will result in smaller-sized rectangles within. It is often these axial bisections that guide the placement of additional forms. These strong axial relationships are best exhibited in formal designs.

COMBINING FORMS

When embarking on the exercise of combining shapes, the primary objective is to bring order to a design. A visually pleasing composition will feature various shapes and patterns that are sensitively combined. Therefore, designers must develop the ability to organize and arrange shapes effectively.

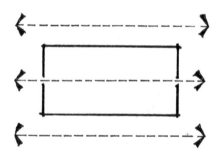

Figure 6.28
The long axis of a rectangle creates the dominate force for its shape.

Design Don't

Avoid sharp corners or acute angles, those less than 45 degrees, in your compositions. The narrow spaces they form result in weak relationships between opposing forms and attract attention to an otherwise wasted space. Moreover, their narrow strips are difficult to link with other forms (see Figure 6.29).

In three-dimensional space, sharp corners and narrow spaces of turf are difficult to maintain and are often trampled and compacted by foot traffic. It is also difficult to grow plants in these areas, or maintain ground cover—plantings tend to grow quickly out of bounds. Plus, sharp corners in hardscape are susceptible to cracking if done with concrete, or difficult to construct if using bricks or pavers.

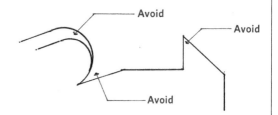

Figure 6.29
Sharp angles and narrow slivers are poor design connections and should be avoided.

The process of combining forms is heavily influenced by the characteristics of the geometric shapes just described, and then fine-tuned by the principles of design—order, rhythm, and harmony. It produces the composition's masses and voids—that is, the planting areas and associated open spaces. As the designer you must consider the effect that one form has on another, including the lines and spaces that are created when forms are combined.

The characteristics of each individual form will, of course, be altered when combined with another. As you begin to combine shapes to develop a composition, you will need to consider six important design principles: dominant space, unity, proportion, mass and void, axis, and connectivity. How you, as the designer, apply these principles will vary based on the particular situation and the design objective and, of course, be informed by your education, experience, and aesthetic sensitivity.

Dominant Space

A dominant space is the core, the heart, of the composition; as such, it is a necessary component of any design. The dominant space typically establishes the central place from which all other elements are developed, as shown in Figure 6.30. Therefore, it should have a common element that relates to the secondary or less important spaces. This common element may be a texture, color, line type, shared line or form, or—in the case of combining forms—the size or shape of the space.

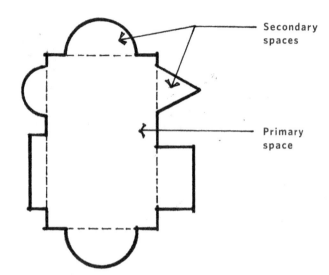

Secondary spaces

Primary space

Figure 6.30
A dominant space established by a pure shape unifies dissimilar elements.

Guidelines for establishing a dominant space include:

▷ Develop it as a simple shape, one readily comprehended in a single field of vision. This will make it more prominent than surrounding spaces.

▷ Make the space a distinct, identifiable form, such as a square or a circle or some other clean geometric form. In general, avoid amorphous or amoebic like forms that often create weak spaces (although there are exceptions).

▷ Develop a hierarchy of lesser dominant spaces in association with the main space (see Figure 6.31).

Unity

Simply, unity in a composition is achieved when all of the elements look as if they belong together, when they are connected by some common element—for example, the repetition of form or an interconnection among forms, such as a linkage to an axis as, shown in Figure 6.32. One way to introduce unity is to repeat a shape in different sizes, thereby creating a rhythm. Another way is to vary the size of the shapes. In either case, it is the commonality of the elements that results in visual unity.

Proportion

Proportion, said Lynch (1989), is the relation of parts, and is of central importance in any design. Proportion is often subtle or hidden—that is, it's not necessarily obvious—and is

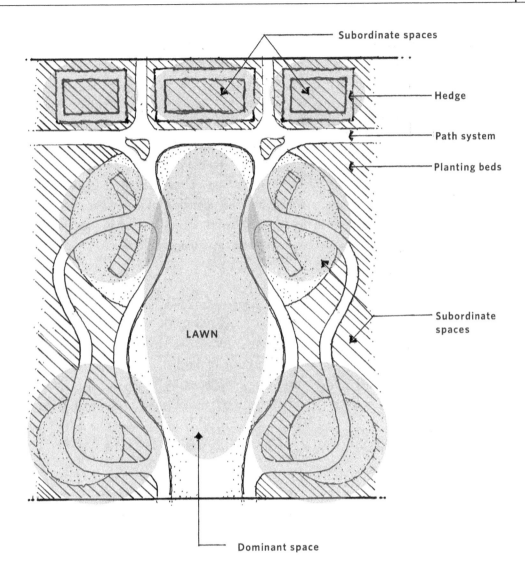

Subordinate spaces

Hedge

Path system

Planting beds

Subordinate spaces

LAWN

Dominant space

Figure 6.31
(TOP) A dominant central shape provides a strong organization framework for different shaped ancillary spaces.

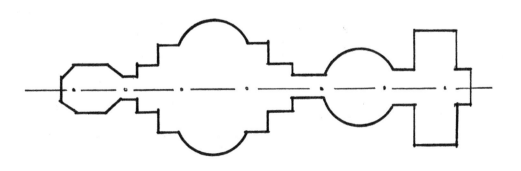

Figure 6.32
(BOTTOM) An axis line used as an organizational element to link elements and to create a unified succession of spaces.

exemplified in the geometric progression of sizes of shapes. Known ratios, such as the Golden Mean (see Figure 5.4, page 106), set out specific ratios for width to length and can be used to establish pleasing proportions among various form types.

Achieving a pleasing proportion in a composition is based on the relationship of the parts to the whole. Specifically, the size of a form should relate proportionately to the size of the area that contains the form. For example, assume a topiary is set within a planting bed or next to a building or other structure: In this case, the topiary must be sized in proportion to its surroundings. Determining the exact size of an object is more of an art than a science. Large forms set in a proportionately smaller composition will create visual dominance, and thus become the focal point of the space. The designer will need to exercise his or her judgment against the design objects to determine the appropriate relationship between spaces and objects.

Mass and Void

As explained earlier in the chapter, when developing masses and voids, you must balance the amount of bed space (mass) with that of open space (void). The edges of each respective space (planting bed edges) will determine the resultant space of the other. The outline on the ground plane establishes the form, which is made up of the bed lines that define the space between the masses. It is also possible to reverse this relationship, which can have a dramatic effect on the quality of the space. Figure 6.33 illustrates how it is the masses that define the spaces.

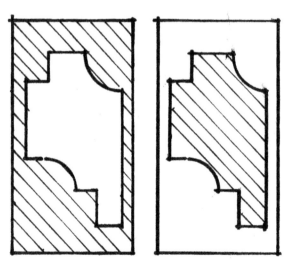

Figure 6.33
The quality of a space is influenced by the relationship of mass and void.

In *Landscape Architecture: A Manual of Site Planning and Design* (1983), Simonds had this to say about creating mass-and-void relationships: "[They must be] planned in opposition to each other and to the landscape . . . so that as one moves through or about them, one experiences an evolving composition of opposing elements, a resolution of tensions, and a sense of dynamic repose."

The form you choose (square, circle, etc.) will establish the framework for this relationship. You will need a strong central form to establish a strong space. And vital to this process is to evaluate the spaces on how people will *experience* them, not merely how they look on paper in a plan. To that end, follow these guidelines:

▷ Place yourself into the spaces as you create them.

▷ Think in three dimensions, arranging forms to account for the transition and progression of spaces.

▷ Realize that the plantings within mass areas impose tension; the voids impart a sense of repose.

Axis

Using an axis as the base from which to combine forms is the single most powerful approach to organizing space. It imposes discipline, hence is often used in creating formal designs, though it can be effective in informal plans as well. An axis is a linear organizing element that connects two or more points or spaces, or links one form to another. In plan view, all forms relate in some fashion to the axis, either directly or implicitly (see Figure 6.32, page 157). Any form impinging on, adjacent to, leading toward, or ending on must have a formal relationship to the axis. The subsequent relationship of that form will have a compositional link to the axis (Simonds 1983).

Utilizing the axis approach in a landscape often subjugates the forms of spaces to one main axis or a series of secondary axes. The terminal or intermediate cross-axis of one arterial axis may function as the terminal or intermediate axis of another. The complex street grid of Washington, D.C., illustrates this principle (see Figure 6.34). When combining forms to establish multiple axial relationships, the result is a formal and efficient layout of primary, intermediate, and terminal spaces. Subsequently, the mass-and-void relationships give rise to a series of interconnected garden rooms. The formal gardens of the Arts and Crafts movement in England epitomize the use of the axial arrangement of forms to organize garden rooms, as shown in Figure 6.35.

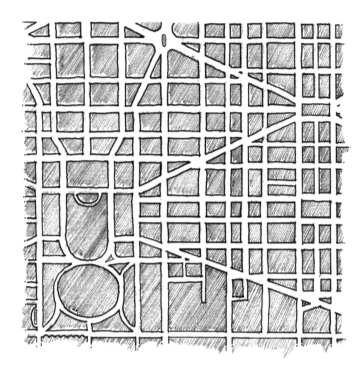

Figure 6.34 (TOP)
A plan of Washington, D.C., illustrates how axis lines are used to organize the street grid.

Figure 6.35 (BOTTOM)
The plan of Folly Farm illustrates how axes are used to organize garden rooms and provide a linkage to the architecture.

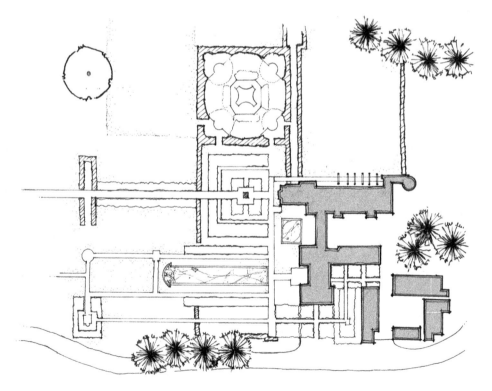

Connectivity

When forms are placed randomly in the landscape—that is, the various elements or forms lack a strong mass-and-void relationship—generally, the result will be a chaotic landscape. That is why the last principle we'll discuss, connectivity, is so vital to a successful planting composition: It establishes a physical link among the elements, to make a unified whole or a procession of interconnected spaces.

Two good methods to achieve connectivity among forms are: (1) group or mass elements together using a line or axis; and (2) one form touching another in some harmonious manner. Establishing a solid mass-and-void relationship can often be accomplished by connecting or linking spaces through a series of beds.

Using a Grid

A coherent design generally follows one, and sometimes two, of six basic formular approaches: rectilinear, rectilinear-45, radial, arc-and-tangent, irregular, or curvilinear (Linn 1993). (Rarely will more than two of these six forms work together to build a harmonious theme.) Using a grid system based on these six geometric arrangements helps ensure that a coherent rhythm and proper scale are followed throughout the design.

The rhythm, scale, and proportions set forth in the development of a grid pattern are not arbitrary. With few exceptions, the gird pattern is based on a form or proportion of some element or group of elements that exist on the site being developed. These existing elements establish what are called *lines of force* (see Figure 6.36), identifying prominent points, edges, elements, doors, windows, significant architectural or landscape features, or corners on the site, and extending them outward help to determine these lines (see Figure 6.37, page 163). This, in turn, will determine the framework for the grid pattern, from which to connect site elements together (see Figure 6.38, page 164).

Often these lines of force determine axis lines or edge lines and guide the articulation of masses and voids. Lines of force can also establish view corridors, open-space corridors, path systems, or other "lines" in the design that will have some significance or prominence in the final composition.

The grid patterns and possible design themes and their characteristics discussed in the following subsections are intended only as a guide, to give you, the designer, a starting point giving form to a design. They do not, by any means, represent the only possible solutions or form-based techniques, so do not let them inhibit your creative thinking.

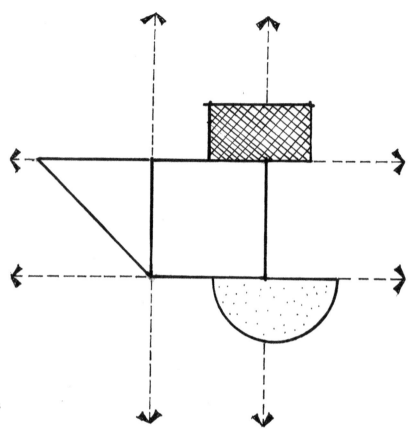

Figure 6.36
Extending edges or axes provide
guidelines for assembling compositions
of forms.

RECTILINEAR

A rectilinear design uses vertical and horizontal lines on a grid that intersect perpendicularly and thus have a 90-degree relationship to one another. This theme is most commonly associated with formal designs, though it can be used for informal designs as well, as shown in Figure 6.39, page 165.

When using a rectilinear design, consider these points:

▷ Rectilinear designs make the most efficient use of space, so they are often used for small and constricted sites.

▷ Flat sites are ideal for rectilinear designs because the level topography enables people to perceive the order and purity of the spaces.

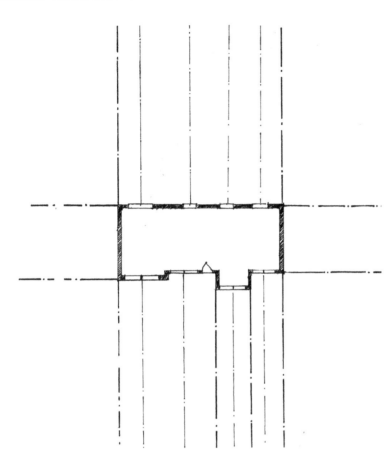

Figure 6.37
Extending the lines of major elements of a building begin to establish a proportional framework for landscape development.

▷ Rectilinear designs are commonly associated with urban sites or when a strong link is desired with the architecture of a building. Often, lines of force from key elements in the architecture are extended and serve as axial organizational lines in the development of a concept.

▷ Formal designs are most successful when large powerful forms are used to delineate spaces, and smaller elements are minimized.

RECTILINEAR-45

A rectilinear-45 design is so called because it introduces 45-degree lines to a rectilinear pattern on a grid (see Figure 6.40, page 166). Essentially composed of diagonal and straight lines, rectilinear-45 design is similar to the rectangular theme except the entire grid is rotated 45

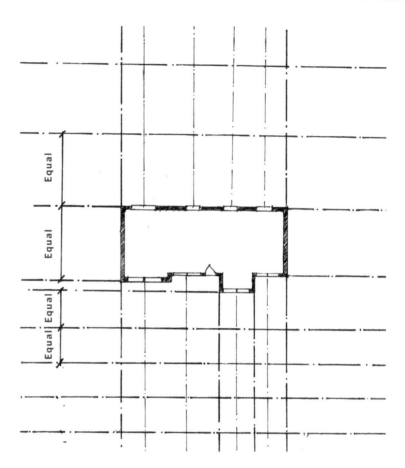

Figure 6.38
A completed grid based on the proportions of the house.

degrees. All of the characteristics of diagonal lines, discussed earlier, apply. This form results in an active and dynamic theme, as the diagonal lines imply speed—the viewer's eye is led quickly from one area of the composition to another. Establishing smooth transitions from one portion of the composition to another becomes important. Avoid acute angles for the reasons identified earlier. When using a rectangular-45 design, consider these points:

▷ Rectangular-45 design themes are especially beneficial when imposed on long narrow sites, for when the diagonal line is located along the longest possible long axis, it gives the impression of a much larger space (see Figure 6.41, page 166).

▷ Diagonal lines in rectilinear-45 designs can be combined with focal points to establish strong visual statements.

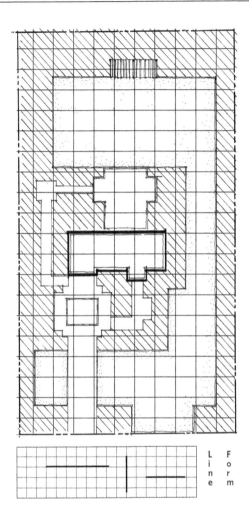

L   F
i   o
n   r
e   m
Line Form

Figure 6.39
A rectilinear grid establishes the design theme
and forms the basis to establish relationships
between landscape beds, paved, and turf areas.

RADIAL

The radial design approach uses concentric circles that radiate from a central point (radius point) with multidirectional straight lines to form the grid (see Figure 6.42, page 167).

When using a radial design, consider these points:

▷ This design approach is best utilized when there is a strong central element or feature that serves as a focal point, such as a piece of sculpture or a fountain.

▷ The key to radial designs is that everything must emanate from the central point. Variety is achieved by varying the lengths of the radii that extend from the center and their associated portions or arcs of circles.

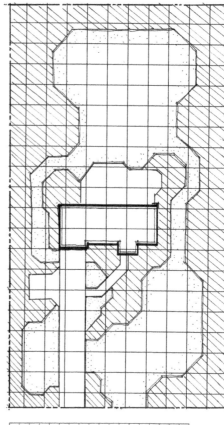

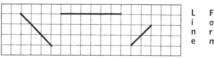

Figure 6.40 (TOP)
A rectilinear
45-degree grid establishes the design theme and
the foundation on which to establish relationships
between landscape beds, paved, and turf areas.

Figure 6.41 (BOTTOM)
A diagonal line cut across a shape will increase the
apparent size of the space and make it more
dynamic.

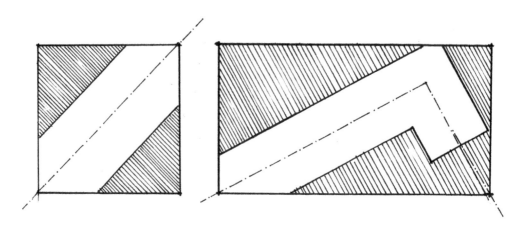

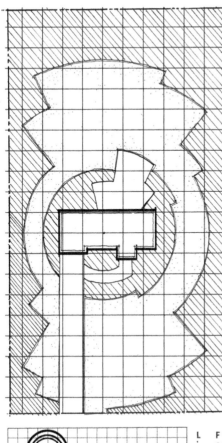

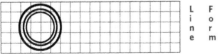

L   F
i   o
n   r
e   m

Line   Form

Figure 6.42
A circular design theme establishes a radial pattern to develop landscape beds, paved, and turf areas.

ARC-AND-TANGENT

An arc-and-tangent approach utilizes both straight and curved lines, combining horizontal, vertical, and 45-degrees lines with quarter-, half-, three-quarter, and whole circles on a grid (see Figure 6.43). The straight lines add a formal element and are softened by the curved intersection of the two. Often, the final form of the arc-and-tangent concept derives from the straight grid patterns of rectangular designs. That said, take care not to simply round the corners of 90-degree intersecting lines; rather, use the arc-and-tangent principle to develop spaces that are the semblance of circles and squares and rectangles, as shown in Figure 6.44, page 169.

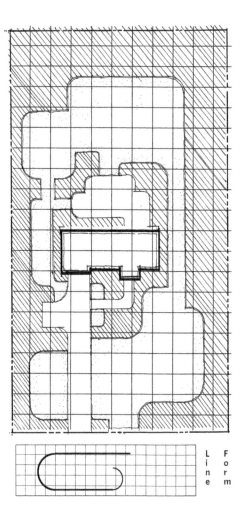

Figure 6.43
An arc-and-tangent design theme is used to develop
the forms of landscape beds, paved, and turf areas.

When using an arch-and-tangent design, consider that:

▷ Arc-and-tangent designs lend an air of formality, but softened somewhat. They are usually best suited for urban (rectangular or square) sites or for those projects that have a
theme requiring a more understated flair than that resulting from a strict rectilinear
design theme.

IRREGULAR

An irregular design approach contains vertical, horizontal, 45-degree-angle, and multidirectional straight lines on a grid (see Figure 6.45, page 170). There are no curved lines in an irreg-

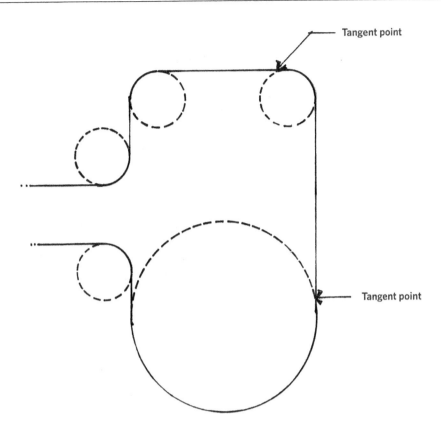

Tangent point

Tangent point

Figure 6.44
Merging square and circular shapes should always be completed with a clean tangent point.

ular approach, and the straight lines used can be of any angle and intersect another at obtuse angles.

When using an irregular design, consider these points:

▷ Irregular designs are often associated with more dynamic and modern compositions intended to produce dynamic tension. The forces of each opposing line conflict, thus creating great visual excitement.

▷ Irregular designs have the highest probability of failing because they may lack rhythm. Too many varying angles and line directions can too quickly tire the eye. Thus, caution should be used in their design.

▷ It is important in irregular designs to include a strong central open area, or void, to spatially organize and link the varying lines to a common element.

Figure 6.45
An irregular design theme establishes the basis for
landscape beds, paved, and turf area forms.

CURVILINEAR

Curvilinear designs use compound curves on a square grid—there are no straight lines (see
Figure 6.46). These designs are made up primarily of—or portions of—circles that overlap, or,
for concentric circles, that radiate around a common radius point.

When considering a curvilinear design, consider these points:

▷ Best suited for large landscapes, the curvilinear approach is most commonly associated
with "natural," informal designs.

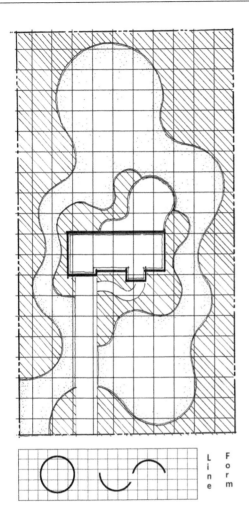

L   F
i   o
n   r
e   m

Figure 6.46
A curvilinear design theme establishes the form to develop landscape beds, paved, and turf areas.

▷ The sweeping nature of curvilinear designs imposes movement in the composition, slowly pulling or leading the viewer's eye through the design. Thus, these designs tend to impart a pastoral, relaxing feeling.

▷ It is important in curvilinear designs to use gracious and bold curves with large radii. Avoid weak and sloppy curves, such as those shown in Figure 6.47, as these lack rhythm.

▷ Make the lines connecting one curve to another seamless—meaning they transition smoothly from one to another, as shown in Figure 6.48. Try to make intersecting lines

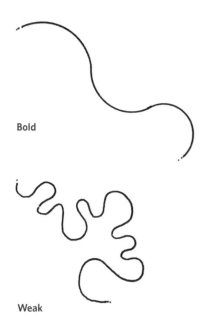

Bold

Weak

Figure 6.47 (TOP LEFT)
Bold sweeping curves are better than
shallow or tight ones.

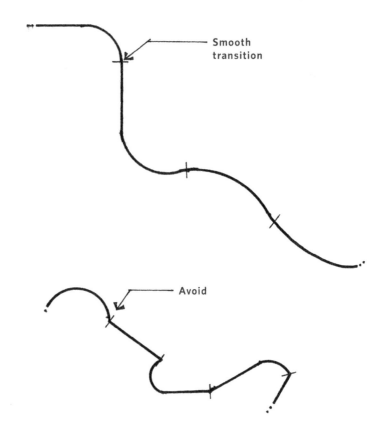

Smooth
transition

Avoid

Figure 6.48 (TOP RIGHT)
Smooth transitions should be made when connecting differing line types.

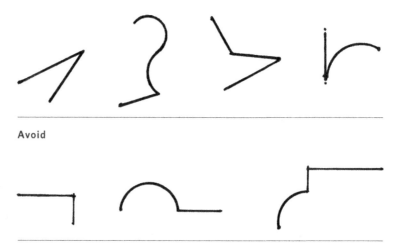

Avoid

Desirable

Figure 6.49 (BOTTOM)
Sharp angles should be avoided in the
establishment of bed lines or pavement.

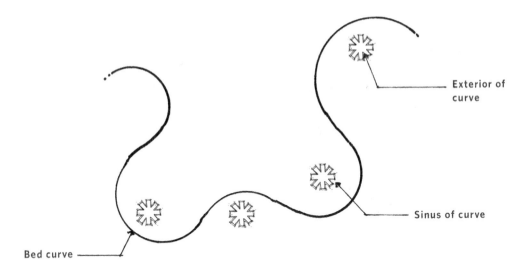

Exterior of
curve

Figure 6.50
Bays and recesses
of curves often
demand strong
visual elements
within.

Sinus of curve

Bed curve

meet as close to 90 degrees as possible, and avoid sharp corners or intersections (see Figure 6.49).

▷ Accentuate curvilinear designs by pairing them with rolling landforms. And on curvilinear designs imposed on flat grades, add strong points of interest to the deep hollows or exterior curves to showcase the important portions of the curves (see Figure 6.50).

GRID DESIGN SUMMARY

The key to designing on a grid is to ensure it has a proportional relationship to the site, or relates to the predominant size or structural elements on the site. Thus, a small site will need a tighter or smaller grid than a larger site. In a grid, multiples of a shape or repetition of scale of predominant architectural elements will bring visual rhythm and harmony to a site or site elements—usually the site architecture (see Figures 6.37 and 6.39, pages 163 and 165, respectively).

Conclusion

Once the proportions of the site are translated into a particular thematic grid, the design can develop into an overall composition that identifies landscape beds and open areas for turf, paving, etc. The shapes and their permutations should be an abstraction of a grid, not necessarily a strict interpretation of it. The theme grid or pattern should be used as merely a guideline as a point of departure. Establishing a theme based on a grid will help the designer develop stronger visual relationships, ensure design harmony and rhythm, and result in an overall coordinated design. Now it's time to develop the plantings for the beds themselves. The next chapter will outline a process to develop planting compositions.

7 | Composing and Structuring a Mixed Bed

TO EFFECTIVELY DESIGN A MIXED PLANTING, a designer must layer plantings—front to back, back to front, side to side, top to bottom. When layering plants, it's important to remember the five classifications of plant materials: ground, foreground, midground, lower canopy, and background (see Figure 5.11, page 113). It's also essential to keep in mind the roles different plantings play in a mixed composition:

▷ Structure plantings provide stability.

▷ Mass plantings provide bulk.

▷ Theme and accent plants give emphasis.

▷ Plants that bloom, have foliage effects, and contrast, serve as infill material between the more important plantings (Ortloff and Raymore 1951).

In any successful scheme there must be a balance and harmony of all of these interests.

Layering as Part of the Planning Process

Planning for a mixed bed requires a thoughtful approach to building layers of plants. Remember that at the early stages, you will not be concerned with specific plants, but rather with general plant characteristics. Gradually, you will begin specifying individual plant attributes. You can visualize the process as a series of overlays, with each additional layer specifying greater levels of plant characteristics.

As you identify more detailed plant characteristics, you will also be narrowing down the number of potential plants that fit the criteria. A typical process for specifying the characteristics of a particular composition may include:

Layer 1 Identify plants by type—shrub, grass, perennial, etc.

Layer 2 List the desired height or size of the plant.

Layer 3 Specify the desired ornamental characteristics (e.g. fruit, flowers, foliage, etc.).

Layer 4 Identify the time of year or season you want those characteristics to appear.

Layer 5 Identify cultural conditions.

Your final specification list will be so detailed that you'll find only a few plants will fit your performance criteria.

Locating the Plants

Once you have specified the plant characteristics, the next challenge is to start locating them in the composition. Where should you place them? How do you determine their locations? How should the various plant types relate to one another? What function will each plant or massing serve in the composition? How will it support its neighbor while playing its individual role in the composition? These questions will be answered by following four steps in order:

1   Identify the locations and massings of the structure plants.

2   Add theme plants, to establish the character of the composition.

3   Insert accents or focal points, to add interest and provide contrast.

4   Fill the remaining voids.

Of course, this outline is an oversimplification—each of these steps involves in-depth consideration. The following sections take you through the process, in detail.

Identify Locations of Structure Plants

As you're well aware by now, any planting composition must have a structure of some kind, provided either by the plantings themselves or by hardscape elements such as walls, fences, or buildings. For the purposes of this book, we discuss structure as provided by plantings; hardscape elements used for this purpose are not covered here.

Structure plants are the backbone of any planting, large or small. Recall from earlier chapters that many structure plants are evergreens, or those having a tight form so that during the winter months they maintain interest in the composition. Providing as they do the framework of the composition, structure plants also serve as the points of departure for other planting types (theme, specimen, massing, and infill) that follow.

Plant Deconstruction

Deconstruction in the context of plant design is a technique that can be used to give you a better understanding of how a composition will function. Like peeling away the layers on an onion, you unveil the various layers one at a time. The purpose of this exercise is twofold: first, to ensure that each successive layer could stand on its own, as an individual composition; second, that the removal of any layer would not ruin the effect of the composition.

In spite of the fact that this process will result in more open space as each consecutive layer is removed, each layer should maintain a balance between texture, color, form, height variation, etc. regardless of the number of layers present. You must also balance the seasonal succession of each layer; and equally distribute color, texture, and form—within each individual layer as well as collectively throughout the composition. Figure 7.1 illustrates a four-layer composition being deconstructed.

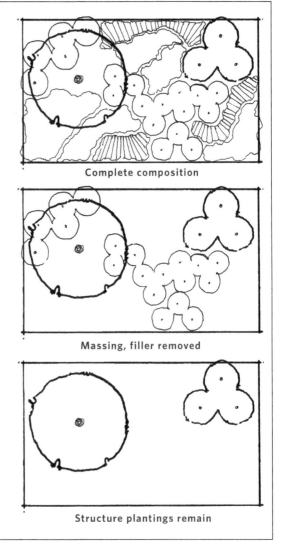

Complete composition

Massing, filler removed

Structure plantings remain

Figure 7.1
Each successive layer of a complete composition (infill and shrub) is removed to reveal the structure planting that comprises the foundation of a composition. In any given composition each layer must satisfy the rules of composition and be able to stand alone.

To decide which types of plants are appropriate to use as structure plants depends on a number of factors:

- ▷ The scale of the landscape or garden (e.g., a one-acre lot vs. a ten-acre lot, or a campus landscape vs. a residential landscape)

- ▷ The function and purpose of the planting

- ▷ The desired aesthetic

In addition, you will need to determine whether these plantings will establish structure as *architecture*, for *compositional balance*, or for *successional balance*. We will discuss each in turn.

STRUCTURE PLANTINGS AS ARCHITECTURE

When used as architecture, structure plantings become the "building blocks" in a composition; they establish space, punctuate, screen, or enframe spaces in the landscape. As such, they provide a framework for the composition, which you, the designer, will use to establish open and closed landscape cells (Jakobson 1977) or as we will term them bays and voids. As the composition develops, you will design outdoor rooms in larger compositions, and bays in smaller compositions. These spaces provide the areas for successional plantings to be developed (see Figure 7.2).

When you place structure plants you will consider three variables for enclosing space: *ground plane*, *vertical plane*, and *overhead plane*. These may be altered or combined in an infinite variety of ways, depending on the desired effect. Large and dense plants are mainly trees, although larger shrubs may also be used to form building like walls, partitions, and ceilings, as well as create windows and doors that serve as portals to other landscape features (see Figures 7.3 and 7.4). As the viewer moves through or passes by the spaces, the architectural plants begin to reveal themselves. And how each enclosure is perceived will vary with the relative height of the plantings, their spacing, and density, according to Norman Booth in *Basic Elements of Landscape Architectural Design* (1983). How the viewer experiences the quality of the space is dependent on the types and levels of the plantings that are between the spaces.

Plants of any size can be used to define space, but they must be in proportion to the size of the landscape or garden. Trees of various sizes generally dominate for this purpose, due to their size and mass. Their architectural framework is evident in their mature trunks, their branching structure, and their foliage. Trees are most effective when they form vertical walls or overhead ceilings, where they define edges—similar to the exterior walls of a building. Smaller plant materials are used to reinforce them. In particular, shrubs can delineate smaller compartments within those spaces—similar to the interior walls of a house. Plants serving as walls are shown in Figure 7.5, page 182.

Tree trunks naturally function as building columns. Their presence implies an edge, separating one area from another. (Note, we say "implies an edge" because a person's view is not restricted by the trunk columns, but tends to go beyond them. This is beneficial in the mixed planting design because it allows for greater compositional depth.) The degree of separation or enclosure will vary, of course, depending on the size of the trunks, the density of the grouping (if so used), and the pattern of arrangement (Booth 1983).

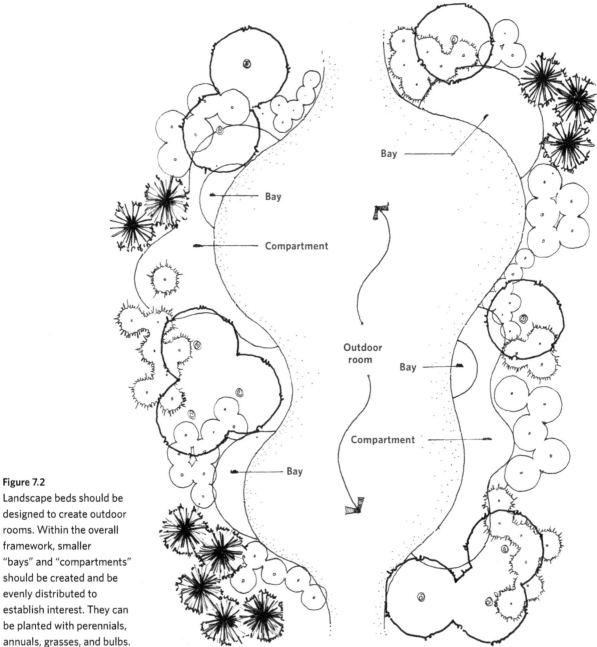

Figure 7.2
Landscape beds should be designed to create outdoor rooms. Within the overall framework, smaller "bays" and "compartments" should be created and be evenly distributed to establish interest. They can be planted with perennials, annuals, grasses, and bulbs.

Bay

Compartment

Bay

Bay

Compartment

Outdoor room

Bay

Plane

Vertical

Overhead plane

Ground   Plane

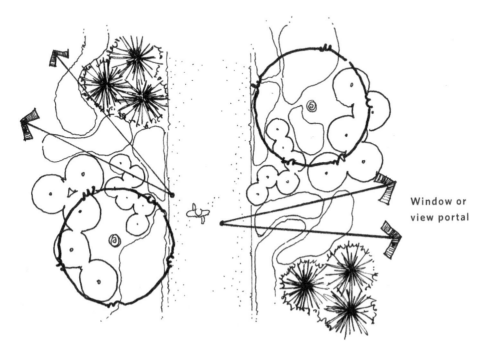

Window or
view portal

Figure 7.3 (ABOVE)
Plantings, used
like architectural
building
components, can
define outdoor
"rooms."

Figure 7.4 (BELOW)
Within each
room, planting
components can
be used to
channel or frame
views out toward
the larger
landscape like
windows in a
building.

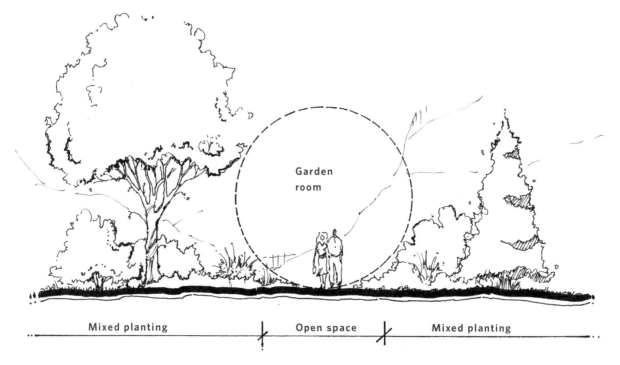

Garden
room

Mixed planting | Open space | Mixed planting

Figure 7.5
The size of the space desired will determine the types of plants needed to enclose or create the "garden room." Bigger, more open rooms will require that large plant materials be used (trees) vs. smaller rooms, which will be created by smaller plant materials (small trees and shrubs).

Trees, thanks to their foliar mass, also add a sense of space for which the quality of that space will be based in part on the type of tree used. Larger trees are effective in forming ceilings that define the upper limits of a space. The higher the canopy, the greater the depth that can be achieved in a composition. Smaller trees, with their lower levels of enclosure, are effective as individual highlights within a mixed planting. Evergreen trees function more like solid walls than transparent screens.

STRUCTURE PLANTINGS TO ACHIEVE SUCCESSIONAL BALANCE

Structural plants also play a role in building succession. That is, evergreens, trees, and shrubs can be used not only for their characteristic forms, but also for the additional attributes they exhibit as the seasons change. It is not only important that structural plantings be evenly distributed and visually weighted throughout the composition—they must be balanced so that their seasonal displays emerge over a varied and extended period of time.

For example, if you are thinking of specifying deciduous shrubs for use as a structural element you should consider the impact those plants will have when they are devoid of foliage. What effect will a twiggy framework have on the overall composition? And which of those plants bear fruit? What type of fruit set will it have? How heavy will the fruit set be? When will the fruit make the most impact? Will it flower? And don't forget to factor in the foliage color, both during the spring when leaves emerge as well as during the autumn when the leaves turn color before they drop.

Evergreen plantings that do not change much can be relied on to maintain their shape, texture, and foliage color, thus providing a consistent look to the composition. But because evergreens have a heavier visual weight than deciduous shrubs you will need to balance their use as structural element with other types of structural plantings.

In sum, when choosing structural plants for successional balance, be sure to include a mixture of types so that in spring, winter, fall, and summer your composition show-cases a prominent ornamental quality of each structure plant in turn, thus achieving ongo-ing interest. These characteristics should, of course, be coordinated with the other plant types.

STRUCTURE PLANTINGS TO ACHIEVE COMPOSITIONAL BALANCE

The way to achieve compositional balance with structural plantings is to evenly distribute the visual weight of the plants you have chosen throughout the composition. Generally, this is easier to accomplish when you use more than one plant type—in fact, it's a good idea to incorporate a wide variety of forms and plant types throughout the composition.

At the same time, however, you must carefully assess the visual weight of the individual forms against their cumulative distribution throughout the entire composition (see Figure 7.6). Generally, this means balancing large trees with other large trees, deciduous shrubs with other equally weighted deciduous shrubs, etc. That said, it's also possible to offset the balance to good effect, for example by juxtaposing a tree with several shrubs or several shrubs with an evergreen. This is very effective in larger compositions, as it creates greater variety, thereby reducing the risk of monotony (see Figure 7.7, page 185).

A good approach to achieving compositional balance is to locate larger, weightier plant materials at the beginning of the design, then begin to incorporate lesser-weighted materials with each successive layer. This technique assures an even distribution of materials.

Figure 7.6
Balance is achieved in the background, midground, and foreground using a variety of plant types with characteristics that possess equal visual weight.

Add Theme Plants

Theme plantings used repetitively in a composition can evoke a certain mood. They affect what is perceived and felt in a garden. Thus, as you start the design process and are considering the mood you want to establish, you will be thinking about which plants will help you achieve it. Let's say you've decided on a tropical theme; chances are you might consider plants such as *Canna*, *Yucca*, *Phormium*, *Acanthus*, *Hydrangea*, or other bold-leaved or colorful foliage type plants. To complete the design and balance the composition, you'll also want to pair these plants with others having more neutral qualities, such as small-leaved or fine-textured evergreens.

The effects created by a unique theme plant give you the opportunity to develop a style, a mood, that is representative of a time, place, culture, or emotional state, and that can produce an immediate but lasting impression on the viewer. You may choose a theme plant for the uniqueness or boldness of its fall foliage, the color or combination of colors of its flowers, its form, or its texture. Or you may choose a plant simply for the overall sensation it produces, which is so hard to put into words—tropical, bold, soft, elegant, powerful, picturesque, cottage-y, colorful, cool, hot, airy, and on and on—for no two people will express in the same

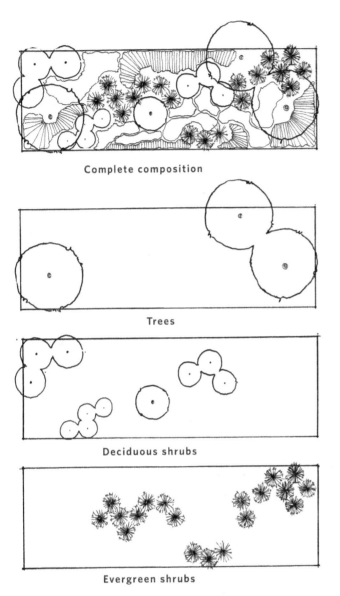

Complete composition

Trees

Deciduous shrubs

Evergreen shrubs

Figure 7.7
Within a single planting, various plant types with differing visual weights are used in balance with one another to create a harmonious composition. Each layer must stand as an independent composition. By "peeling" away the various layers (plant types) each separate composition reveals the balance achieved.

way the effect a beautiful mixed planting has on them. But it hardly matters what words are used to describe the effects of a theme plant—what is important to you, the designer, is to take advantage of the highly distinct characteristics the cause such intense and varied responses.

Needless to say, then, the plants best used to create a theme are those of strong character, whether in color, form, or texture. But, remember, these plants will not stand alone, so you must factor in how they will "get along" with their neighbors. Contrast with harmony is the objective. Once the theme plants have been set, other plants you choose will play supporting roles. In essence, theme plants are focal points and must be carefully located and used in moderation.

Using a theme to develop a plant palette is invaluable to a designer. Once you have chosen your theme you have the inspiration and framework for expanding your design. The theme also serves as a sort of discipline, in that it minimizes the number of plants that will work to carry out your theme.

According to Nick Robinson in *The Planting Design Handbook* (1992), theme plantings can generally be divided into three basic groups, based on the visual characteristics of plants, on taxonomic relationships, or on native habitat or plant communities. It's also important to point out that *theme plantings* differ from *theme plants* in terms of the impression they make.

▷ Theme plantings establish a unified composition, in that we associate plants with their environment—for example, wetland, stream edge, woodland—for they have adapted to specific microclimatic conditions.

▷ A theme plant is an individual, with a unique characteristic. It is used to provide a contrast and, often, as noted at the beginning of this section, is used repetitively throughout a composition to bring about the desired effect.

A closer look at various plant habitats will help to understand theme plantings and theme plants.

TYPES OF THEME PLANTINGS

Marsh, Wetland, Pond Edge

Plants in these environments are accustomed to living in wet or moist airless soil, for they live in water, at the water's edge, or in permanently wet ground, hence tend to have lush foliage with flowers that are usually subordinate to the foliage. For this reason, water necessarily is a major element in any design or composition where these plants will be used. The degree of moisture will determine the types of plants that are appropriate for any given area. In this habitat theme, the plant mix typically will comprise a large proportion of herbaceous materials, a few shrubs, and even fewer trees. Evergreen species in these environments are generally quite rare. In terms of the mixed planting, this theme has limited opportunities for creating a multiseasonal effect; rather, plants in these environments usually reach their crescendo during the spring season.

Woodland

Woodland gardens are generally considered "wild," hence their designs are often inspir by nature. Moderate to dense shade and soil rich in humus are the conditions necess for woodland plantings to thrive. An incredible diversity of plant materials is naturally s'd for this environment, from the forest canopy to the midlayer of deciduous trees and everens to the ground layer with herbaceous plants, spring bulbs, and ephemerals. However, n' of the beauty of woodland gardens comes from the foliage types and plant mass as ole, for other than early-season spring bulbs, broad swaths of color are much more diffic achieve in this setting. Therefore, where color is concerned, the design goal is to strat lly locate accent flowers throughout the composition and throughout the season.

Note that it is difficult to re-create woodland conditions, so before dec on this setting as your design theme, consider carefully the location of the proposed ing. Light in particular is an issue, ranging from full light to partial to full or deep shade is factor will be a major determinant in your selection of a plant palette. The deeper de, the fewer numbers of species of plants will be appropriate.

Meadow

Natural meadow communities are complex systems and take year imes decades, to establish themselves. Often grown on nutrient-starved soils, the pl dependent on the specific soil type and microclimate of the geographical area. Man ants self-seed and compete against each other for space, so the resultant plant co is based to a great degree on natural selection and survival of the fittest. The "su nts in meadows are typically grasses and perennials, with some shrubs interspers ng root on the edges between plant communities.

From a design theme standpoint, therefore, meadows ixed planting opportunities. However, zones of meadow plantings can often be in into larger mixed planting compositions.

Coastal

Plantings along coastal areas are, of course, greatly o alt-laden winds and sandy, dry soils lacking in nutrients. Plants in these commu be low-growing with deep root systems, thereby limiting plant selection for oses. Nevertheless, coastal plantings do present unique opportunities to inst tings. And even though confined to the aforementioned low-growers, a wid nt types are available for this theme setting; occasionally, a taller shrub can b it must be of sturdier stock to

...hstand the harsh seaside environment. Taller trees and palms are not advised, except for ...e that provide good shelter, thereby creating microclimates for smaller plantings.

Moving inland a bit, the harsh conditions give way to a more Mediterranean type of cli...e, and so the choice of plant materials and types greatly expands. Plants suitable for suc...as typically can tolerate long, hot summers with little water because their structural mec...sms have built-in systems to reduce evapotranspiration. Plants in this category often take ...ramatic sculptural forms and have colorful leaf structures; for example, plants with large ...leaves, fanning palms, and spiny cacti, among others, can be combined to create bold image...adding floriferous deciduous trees and shrubs to the mix will give a dramatic contrast to ...xotic forms and silvery-gray and glaucous-blue foliage that is resistant to drought.

THEME PLANTS

Grasses

Grasses ca...xcitement to a composition, thanks to the wide range of sizes, textures, and forms. That ...of the reasons they are an excellent theme plant choice. Whether it is the feathery foli... *Nasella tenuissima* (Mexican feather grass), the bold foliage of *Cortaderia selloana* 'Pum...arf pampas grass), or the stiff upright form of *Calamagrostis x acutiflora* 'Karl Foerster' ...erster feather reed grass), grasses used repetitively throughout a planting can add a ...e, carefree "beachy" feeling to a composition.

Tropicals

The use of tropi...as a theme has become something of a recent trend, due to their capability to imp...ic character to a composition. Favored for the ornamental value of their foliage, the e...characteristics of tropicals vary from boldly dramatic foliage textures to richly colo...But a little goes a long way with these plants, as it does not take many of them to in...g of "tropicalism" in a setting.

However, the...f these plants is mostly apparent during high summer only, so using tropical planti...me has its limitations; certainly, it will not "carry" the composition throughout th...equently, it is important to link tropicals with a secondary theme, so that when ...onger dominant, the secondary theme takes over.

Shrubs

Shrubs, as you know b...in a wide variety of forms, textures, foliage, and flower color, making them a m...onent than other plant types. They generally "hold their own" year-round. Thus, ...l theme plants. Their size diversity, in particular, makes them useful in small or large compositions since they can be positioned in the front or in the back of the composition based on their pattern of growth. For example, inserting a *Berberis thunbergii* 'Crimson Pigmy' or *Spirea bumalda* 'Gold Flame' would provide a dramatic foliar contrast and serve as striking theme plants when placed at intervals in front of a composition.

A word of caution is in order, however: In spite of their great value design-wise, it's best to incorporate shrubs that can "carry" multiple seasons. There are many shrubs that look spectacular when in flower but turn dull or lack solid form during the remainder of the year. Avoid these types of shrubs. In fact, for theme purposes, it's a good idea *not* to use shrubs that depend on flowers. For example, choose some of the evergreen shrubs, those with powerful or dominant forms. Architectural shrubs such as clipped box, columnar junipers, or arborvitae add an air of formality. Or consider a strong formal shape contrasted against more informal shapes and loose perennial plantings. Such forms used repetitively go a long way toward developing a sense of unity and a strong theme.

FOLIAGE AS THEME

We've talked before about the great value of using foliage due to its longer-lasting effects, as compared with flowers. When it comes to using foliage as a theme, however, keep in mind that it will not dominate a composition in the same way that flowers would, so base your foliage choices on color or bold texture.

Recall from Chapter 4 the vast array of foliar effects that are possible, from solid to variegated leaf patterns and from fine to bold textures. Any of these foliar characteristics can be used to create a theme, for foliage colors and variegation patterns carry a great deal of visual weight and are very effective in establishing a distinctive mood. A variety of effects can be achieved by using foliage:

Foliage color The benefit of choosing plants with foliar color as theme plants is that you can then incorporate plants with other colored parts to support them, such as flowers, stems, or twigs. Doing so reinforces the theme and helps to establish unity through repetition of color.

Foliage texture Using foliage texture as a theme is a bit complex. Effectively using a plant with a certain texture, whether fine, medium, or coarse, depends on the texture of its neighboring plants to achieve the desired impact. Typically, only the coarsest or finest of textured plants will work well as theme plants—bold in the far view and fine in the near view.

COLOR AS THEME

There is a difference between using plants with color as theme plants and having a color-themed garden. A color-themed garden will use multiples of a particular color (both foliage and flowers) throughout (perhaps in the hot or cool color ranges, or pastels), making the color theme easily identifiable by viewers. A monochromatic or narrow color-ranged theme sends a clear message. Vita Sackville-West's White Garden at Sissinghurst, and the red border at Hidcote Manor Garden—both in England—are two of the most famous examples of color-themed gardens. Sometimes a color-themed garden may last for only one season, then turn to another color as the season changes, accomplished with floral displays vs. foliage, which as we've said so often, is more constant throughout the seasons.

Insert Accents or Focal Points

A specimen or accent plant is one that has a single or several outstanding characteristics that make it stand out among its neighbors—such as highly contrasting foliage, a striking form, brightly colored and interestingly shaped flowers, or dominant fruits. Accent or specimen plants, as noted earlier in the book, are the exclamation points in mixed plantings, hence should be used sparingly. Each should be chosen and placed for a specific purpose in the composition; they should never be used unless having an intentional purpose or for special effect (see color plates, Figure 7.8). Remember, when overused, these plants cause visual clutter and, consequently, reduce their own impact.

Though closely related, accent and specimen plants differ slightly in their use:

Specimen plants are used as focal points, thus generally are inserted as "loners"—hence the term *specimen*, which in this context means an individual. As a designer, you must plan carefully the placement of a specimen plant to generate a particular effect—to showcase a special area of the composition—based on your design objective, which usually, at least in part, is to stop the viewer's eye. You will accomplish this by contrasting the plant's special attribute or characteristics against that of neighboring plantings. The rule of thumb here is: no more than one specimen plant in any one field of view.

Accent plantings, like specimen plants, possess high ornamental value, but they are not considered as distinct, thus are less powerful for design purposes than specimen plants. Rather, accent plants are used in conjunction with a series of other planting within a vignette to highlight or "accent" another plant (or plants) or hardscape feature. Accent plants can be used either singly or as a massing to direct attention to an object, such as a piece of sculpture, or special area, such as an entryway, but most often they are used in multiples throughout the composition.

Figure 7.9
Surrounding feature plants with neutral evergreens allows the dominant characteristics of the feature plant (hibiscus) to stand out more effectively.

USE TECHNIQUES

The setting for specimen or accent plants is all-important. Surrounding or backdrop plantings to accent or specimen plants must be comparatively neutral so that their contrast is notable. Examples of effective ways to place these "standout" plants include:

▷ Surround them with evergreens (see Figure 7.9).

▷ Locate them among plant massings with nondescript or neutral characteristics (see Figure 7.10).

▷ Place them among plants with contrasting attributes (see color plates, Figure 7.11).

▷ Set them in larger masses of a single plant type for contrast (see Figure 7.12, page 193).

In the last example, even plants that are not normally visually dominant can become powerful accents when carefully paired with plants with opposing characteristics (Robinson 1992).

Figure 7.10
Bold foliage plants set within large areas of nondescript groundcovers can be used to highlight feature plants.

Note that some specimen or accent plants serve their purpose *only* when they appear in groups, otherwise their impact is completely lost. Usually it is a plant's unique form that qualifies them in this category of use. The best way to display a unique form is in a simple base planting or ground cover, as shown in Figure 7.13, page 194. Textural and color relationships among the specimens and ground plane plantings must support the form and provide contrast. The specimen or accent plantings then can "rise above" the ground cover, which essentially serves as a foil so that the specimen plants have their day in the sun, as it were. This technique can be further developed by placing the individuals within the group far enough apart so that each plant stand alones yet remains part of the group (see color plates, Figure 7.14, page 195).

Another technique for using accent plants is to let one or a few individuals to "escape" from a larger adjacent plant massing, as shown in Figure 7.15. By doing this you can differentiate plants that are more commonplace, that have less noticeable forms or ornamental characteristics. Two other design effects emerge, as well: First, the isolated plant draws attention to the adjacent mass, especially when it is in high season; second, it allows the same plant to be displayed two ways—en masse and as a stand-alone specimen thus, highlighting

Figure 7.12
Setting a single plant with an outstanding characteristic in a massing of a contrasting material, such as this *Araucaria* in a sea of *Stipa*, is an effective way to dramatically feature a single plant.

different characteristics of the same plant directly adjacent to one another. The size of the composition will be a factor in which technique you choose. In smaller compositions, one specimen plant generally will suffice; in larger compositions, it may be appropriate to have several, but, again, they should be far enough away from each other so that they are not seen in the same field of view. In looser, more cottage-garden-type compositions or collectors' gardens, multiple accent or specimens may be used, but with restraint, so as not to introduce confusion.

Figure 7.13
Massing a variety of sizes of a single dramatic plant, such as these *Agave* in a simple ground cover, is a technique that dramatizes a plant's unique form.

TIMING AND LOCATION

Specimen and accent plants will be positioned at different stages during the design process, depending on the intent of your design:

▷ In the beginning of the design process, as you develop the planting beds around fixed elements in the landscape, you will find that certain points warrant greater attention than others (doorways, corners of buildings, entrances, etc.). These points are fairly easy to distinguish early in the design process. Other plantings (massings, infill, etc.) should later be positioned adjacent to the specimen plants accordingly.

▷ When a planting bed in the landscape is freestanding—it does not have a fixed relationship to structural or architectural elements—the specimen plant may be located at any time during the design process. The purpose of the specimen plant is to build interest and break up the long, undulating lines of other massings. In an informal design, specimen plantings can emphasize a form in the landscape, such as at the deep bay or sinus of a curve in a bed line or at the crest of a bed line (see Figure 6.50, page 173). They can

Figure 7.15
Allowing a single plant to "escape" from the "mother mass" into a simple adjacent groundcover is a technique that can be used to highlight a plant's effect in mass and singularly effectively dramatizing the plant.

also be used to attract attention for some other reason. In a formal design, specimen plants can be used to conclude a terminal axis. Without these points of interest, a composition can be monotonous and become dull. The role of the specimen plant, in this case, is to stop or direct eye movement.

▷ Accent plants can also be situated later in the process, after the structure and massing drifts have been installed. Remember, accent plantings are usually associated with another planting type. Thus, to define an accent plant is not necessarily easy since a plant's ability to punctuate depends largely on the other plants with which it is associated (Ortloff and Raymore 1951). Gertrude Jekyll, for example, believed that a mauve-colored flower was not its best unless it was accented with a creamy yellow flower. Therefore, the location of the mauve flowers drove the placement of the creamy yellow accent. Or, consider a plant with a conical form, which can be a powerful accent to a massing of rounded shrubs. Here, too, the placement of the conical shrub is dependent on its relationship to the rounded shrub massing.

Infill or Filler Plantings

Infill plantings play a subordinate but nonetheless important role in the mixed planting composition. They are termed *filler* because they fill in the voids created by structural massings and accent and theme plants (see color plates, Figure 7.16). Their purpose is:

▷ As temporary space fillers, until more permanent materials grow and reach maturity.

▷ As permanent infill materials, occupying the bays created by the specimen, theme, and mass plantings.

▷ As caretaker plants, discouraging weeds, conserving moisture, and reducing maintenance.

TEMPORARY INFILL

As John Brookes noted in *The Book of Garden Design* (1991), infill plantings "can be used as stopgaps between permanent shrubs and trees." Annuals, tender and rapidly spreading (but not invasive) perennials, tropicals, biennials, and seasonal bulbs are excellent temporary fillers because they will grow quickly and establish over a season. Temporary infill plantings are especially important in the front layers of the composition where open spaces are more noticeable. Low-growing ground-cover types are particularly useful for filling gaps or awkwardly shaped spots.

The added benefit of using temporary fillers is that they enable you to continually experiment with a variety of plant types and aesthetic combinations while surrounding plants grow. The disadvantage of this type of planting is that it is highly labor- and maintenance-intensive. Soil needs to be prepared and plants need to be installed and removed several times in a season, depending on the desired effect. Therefore, you will want to reserve this type of infilling for gardens that have dedicated staff to provide the necessary upkeep.

PERMANENT INFILL

Permanent infill plantings are "co-stars" in the overall composition. They help to develop smaller "planting vignettes" in the bays of the composition. As discussed in the next section, the interrelationships of mass plantings introduce bays where "other events" will take place, to spark interest across and throughout the bed (see Figure 7.17). The bays contain fillers that are often planted with materials that have more colorful seasonal attributes, such as perennials, tropicals, or annuals. The opportunity to exploit these seasonal attributes is created by permanent and structural massings, specimens, and accent plantings—usually shrubs, trees, or ornamental grasses with neutral or limited ornamental value.

The success, or failure, of permanent infill plantings is directly linked to the surrounding types of materials used for the massings—they must complement one another through

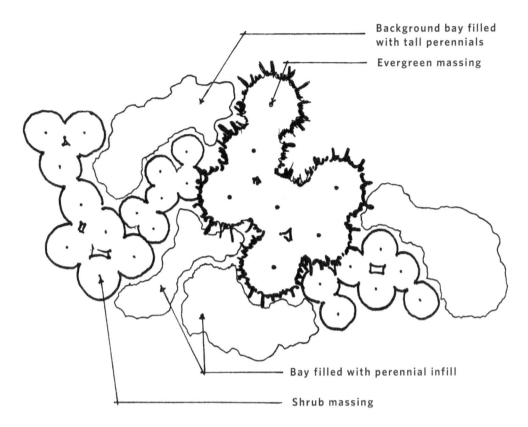

Background bay filled with tall perennials

Evergreen massing

Bay filled with perennial infill

Shrub massing

Figure 7.17
Structural plantings, such as various types of shrub masses, can be used to create "bays" that can then be filled with plants having seasonal attributes such as perennials, annuals, tropicals, or bulbs.

accent and contrast. If, say, the surrounding massing materials have multiple or extravagant ornamental characteristics, the associated filler material should have neutral qualities and vice versa.

Understanding the Importance of Massing to the Planting Composition

A planting composition should be comprised predominantly of massings (five or more plants of the same species or cultivars). Why? Because plant materials used in broad sweeping masses provide a sense of harmony. The lines of the plantings flow into one another, linking diverse elements and carrying the eye smoothly from one segment of the composition to another. The shapes and forms created by a massing can be used in turn to form smaller bays that contain infill plantings, as explained in the previous section.

Masses should be arranged of different plant types and species of different sizes, and be spaced at various distances to create a mixture of bay sizes; and the open spaces must be proportionate and balanced throughout the composition. Too much massing with too few bays for other plant types precludes a truly mixed composition. Likewise, too little mass and too many bays result in a composition with not enough visual weight to carry it through the seasons. Here's what H. Stuart Ortloff and Henry B. Raymore had to say about masses in the book *Color and Design for Every Garden* (1951): "A pleasing composition presents a mass effect rather than a collection of separate ideas." The idea is to use massings to frame, enclose, and strengthen composition vignettes, in which the accent and theme plantings provide the necessary points of interest. Well-arranged masses are designed to become a single planting unit, highlighted by a pattern or texture or the color of foliage or flowers.

Ortloff and Raymore recommend plants good for massing as those species that:

▷ Have a solid foliage mass throughout the growing season.

▷ Are rounded in form (which facilitates their ability to merge well).

▷ Make a strong connection to the ground.

▷ Have a solid form, so that when the foliage is absent in the winter the plants still look attractive.

To arrange these groups effectively, follow a few basic guidelines (which, as usual are open to your interpretation as the designer): patterns of light against dark, interweaving of spaces, and contrast of texture and form. Brian Hackett, in his book *Planting Design* (1979), used the analogy of a jigsaw puzzle to describe how plant masses should interlock. The outline of each group is a part of an adjoining group. When combined, they make a complete picture, as shown in Figure 7.18.

The point is, you will want to arrange plant groupings in interconnecting and overlapping drifts. The best way to illustrate this is to contrast the massing styles of Gertrude Jekyll and Roberto Burle Marx.

Jekyll's style of arranging masses was to "drift" perennials, but with a definitive beginning and ending to each drift. In this way she directed the masses to flow from one end of the composition to the other. The drifts were shaped such that the "head" of one drift was slightly enlarged, from which it narrowed to the "tail" section, which then trailed out to merge with the next massing (see Figure 7.19, page 200). By following Jekyll's technique you, too, can ensure a smooth transition between and among groups—you will be creating a design rhythm, which we've talked about so often in this book as being vitally important to the success of a mixed

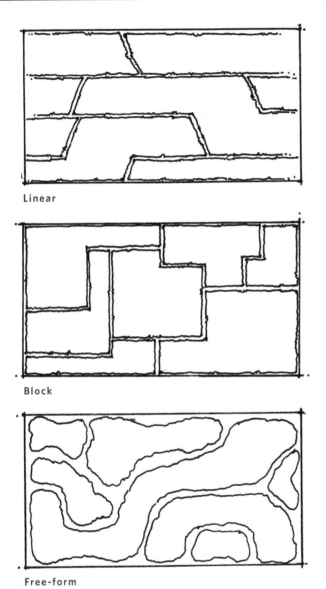

Linear

Block

Free-form

Figure 7.18
A variety of pattern forms can be used to develop planting masses that interlock and overlap.

planting. In addition, this technique causes drifts to interlock much like fingers clasped together. This interweaving also serves to unify the composition.

On occasion, however, you may want to let the drifts give way, to appear to run in to smaller masses or even specimen or theme plants. This will change the pace of the rhythm, for further interest (Bisgrove 1992).

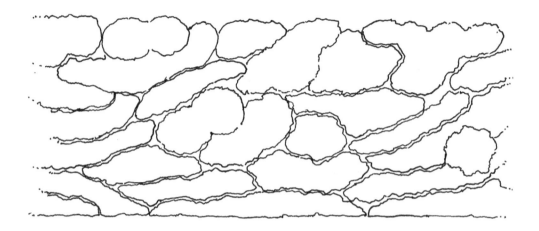

Figure 7.19 (TOP)
Drifting was a technique that Gertrude Jekyll used for designing plant massings.

Figure 7.20 (BOTTOM)
The bold style of Marx's compositions contained planting masses that assumed forms of large "biomorphic shapes."

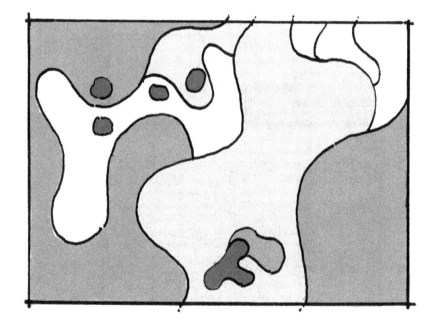

Roberto Burle Marx took a somewhat different approach: He massed tropical plants, rather than drifting perennials. His forms might be compared to the work of a modernist painter who groups blocks of patterns and shapes. Marx preferred to repeat species and to group similar kinds of plants in large monochrome blocks to emphasize their common elements—to make simple bold statements, reminiscent of the colors and culture of his home country, Brazil (see Figure 7.20). According to Marta Iris Montero in *Roberto Burle Marx: The Lyrical Landscape* (2001), the shapes appeared as "undulating biomorphic shapes," often at the expense of creating space. In addition to Marx's bold use of repetition, his style is notable for the way he contrasted color or texture and his ability to isolate and contrast a single specimen in a massing of plants.

Today, designers borrow the massing techniques of both designers. But regardless of the technique you use, remember that the masses must overlap in form and their layers of plant types. Rarely should you have, for example, three of the same plant types (e.g., three species of perennials in a row) layered next to one another. A perennial may be in front of a grass, which may be in front of a tropical, which may be in front of an evergreen, etc.

Ideally, massing groups should take on an irregular form; the arrangement should be neither compact nor clumpy. Again, according to Florence Bell Robinson in *Planting Design* (1940), these masses should be composed of plants of various sizes, characteristics, and types, with some crowding together, others spreading out, some overhanging, and others lying below.

The number of plants per massing will be dependent on the overall size of the composition and the desired effect. Generally, in most landscapes, masses consisting of five to fifteen plants per massing are typical. The theory is that using fewer plants per mass or multiples of single plants results in a spotty composition. For larger landscapes and those designs that emphasize a particular characteristic of a plant, larger quantities of plants per massing can be used. These variations are shown in Figure 7.21. The designs of Oehme van Sweden depict this; they typically

Large massing

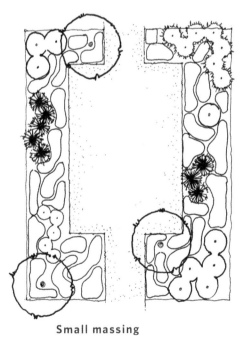

Small massing

Figure 7.21
In these examples, the overall composition (bed framework and structure plantings) are identical; however, the size of the infill massings are varied.

include quantities of thirty to seventy plants per massing drift, making for a dramatic and bold statement (see Figure 7.22).

Other massing guidelines to follow:

▷ Vary the proportion of mass groupings from one group to another; avoid pairing similar-sized groups.

▷ Base the size of each massing on its relationship to the others, as well as to the overall size of the composition. For example, a composition developed for a townhouse yard would require masses much smaller than one developed for a three- to five-acre single-family lot. The masses in the townhouse garden might include one to five plants per mass, whereas the plants in the single-family lot would range in number from seven to fifteen-plus.

▷ Vary the size and shape of the mass, and alternate different plant types, to achieve variety and contrast in massings. A perennial mass may be slightly smaller than an adjacent shrub mass, which might be significantly larger than an adjacent mass of ornamental grasses.

Figure 7.22
The planting techniques of Oehme van Sweden use a variety of methods to mass and display plants in a composition.

Factoring in Maintenance

It may not be the most interesting aspect of the landscape design profession, and it may even seem a hindrance to creativity; nevertheless, a major determining factor—some might say the driving force—in the success of a mixed planting is the level of maintenance that will be required to ensure it continues to look beautiful and serve its objective. When designers fail to take maintenance into account when developing their plant mix, the composition is destined to deteriorate in a very short time.

We are working with a dynamic artistic medium; plants grow and change over time and require care and attention, some more than others. Staking, deadheading, cutting back, and pruning are all maintenance activities that need to take place at one level or another, regardless of the mix of plant types.

The amount of maintenance planning will, necessarily, vary from client to client and from landscape to landscape. For example, when working for a residential client, a major determinant will be the level of horticultural expertise the client has, as well as the amount of time he or she has and is willing to commit to maintenance operations. You must then align these two factors with the plants you select.

If your client is a public entity, such as a college campus or corporation, you will have to ascertain whether the resources, in both staff and time, will be committed to the project, then work closely with the people who will be doing the actual work to maintain the landscape. Do they have the horticultural expertise to safeguard your design for the long term? Are they an in-house crew or outside professionals? Will they be dedicated to the project, or will they be expected to add this work to an already heavy labor load? The answers to these and other project-specific questions will be vital to your design process. They will have a major influence on plant types you specify and how they will be arranged.

DETERMINING THE MIX

Compositional mixes fall into three broad categories:

▷ Public landscape

▷ Landscape beds

▷ Garden beds

This classification is drawn primarily to help you choose a plant mix that's right for the situation based on level of maintenance. Some will include the complete spectrum of plant types, while others may include only a few.

Mix-Maintenance Formula

These percentages are to be used in determining your plant mixes, based on type of composition and commitment to the level of required maintenance. For a point of departure the assumption is made here that the composition suggested will be appropriate for a general-purpose landscape bed. The following compositional mix is suggested: approximately 15 percent trees, 35 to 40 percent shrubs (25 percent evergreen and 10 to 15 percent deciduous), 10 to 15 percent grasses, 10 to 15 percent perennials, and 10 percent ground covers. The use of annuals and climbers will be completely dependent on the site and the client, and so will vary from project to project. In more well-maintained landscapes, you would increase the percentage of perennials, as well as factor in more annuals and tropicals. In public landscapes, you would increase the percentages of trees and shrubs, respectively. Again, the desired aesthetic and the level of maintenance required will determine the mix percentages.

Public Landscapes

Landscapes designed for the public realm may include, but are not limited to, roadside or high-way plantings, urban landscapes, buffer plantings along residential or commercial develop-ments, some college campuses, and areas along the peripheries of large estates. When you develop mixed plantings for a public landscape, you must always assume that there will be no landscape maintenance. Yes, this is an extreme position to take, but all too often maintenance is so variable in these landscapes that it is imprudent to assume anything else. Your best-laid plans will be hindered by limited budgets and understaffed or uneducated crews, and not enough resources, all of which can spell doom for your design. Because of poor planning and a lack of understanding of the maintenance requirements, public landscapes often fall into disrepair after a short time after installation.

To prevent this happening to your work, in landscapes destined for the public realm, it's best to design them simply, using bold drifts of only the hardiest and most durable of plants. It is critical that you exercise restraint. Choose only the most proven of plants, those that can withstand the harshest of conditions—which may mean sacrificing more exciting species or the newest and hottest cultivars on the market. Durability must be your guide. Generally, then, the mix of these compositions comprises mainly trees, durable deciduous and evergreen shrubs, and hardy ground covers. Large masses of one plant type, often numbering in the tens to thirties or forties are the norm. And in very large landscapes, such as along highway or roadsides, it is not unusual to see massing quantities number in the hundreds. Occasionally, you can add an ornamental grass and hardy perennial as accent or theme plants, but limit them and choose them based on the ability of the stewards to provide that extra level of maintenance they'll need (see Figure 1.10 on page 13 and Figure 3.26 on color plates).

Do not misunderstand here, however: Limiting plant types does not mean sacrificing year-round interest in these landscapes. It simply means you must choose plants with variation and dependable seasonal attributes.

Landscape Beds

Landscape beds may appear in corporate headquarters, public gardens, high-end residential community entrances, residential properties or estates, college campuses, or other areas that are regularly maintained by a commercial contractor, gardener or horticulturist, dedicated in-house staff, or educated or committed homeowner. These plantings are more refined than those in public landscapes. Though they may be intended as private gardens, landscape beds also are designed to instill a gardenlike environment in a nongarden setting, which may be viewed by the public.

As a designer of landscape beds, you will layer greater numbers of plant types than you would for a public landscape, though species durability still should be a driving factor. Annuals and tropicals are often included, but are treated as annual rotations, usually in designated blocks at key points of interest in the front of compositions where they can be easily maintained. Plants in landscape beds are massed but in smaller drifts than those in public landscapes, and in fewer numbers—from a minimum of three to somewhere in the teens.

Garden Beds

The primary objective of a garden bed is to showcase a wide variety of plants (often a collection) for the most dramatic of horticultural displays. Mixed plantings designed as garden beds are the most intensively developed compositions. Usually associated with private gardens (residential or commercial) or public gardens (botanic gardens, arboreta, or civic gardens), they are the most complex in their arrangement, often including every plant type available with a broad array of species under each plant type category (see color plates, Figure 1.1). They are maintained either professionally by an experienced gardener or, in the case of residential properties, by serious amateur gardeners or horticulturists. Typically, the commitment, resources, and expertise for maintenance are readily available.

These compositions are highly dynamic; they are constantly changing and being adjusted to heighten their aesthetic appeal. They often contain the most cutting-edge plant types and cultivars, some of which may not be the most durable or long-lasting in their displays. They may also include multiple rotations of various plant types, especially annuals, tropicals, and bulbs, to continually heighten the effects and extend the length of peak display.

Conclusion

Thus, both maintenance and aesthetics factor into determining the appropriate type of planting mix or bed type that should be developed. Landscapes compositions with more trees, shrubs, ground covers, and grasses require less maintenance than those that include perennials, annuals, and tropicals in the mix. Larger amounts of perennials will create a different tone than those with more annuals and tropicals or those with shrubs used as the predominant material. It will be up to you and your client to find the ideal mix based on these two factors.

8 | Specifying Plants by Their Characteristics

BY NOW YOU'RE WELL AWARE that the process of planting design is not linear—anything but. In most cases, in fact, you will find you must step back at various stages to reevaluate previous decisions you've made regarding a plant's height, type, display characteristics, and relationship to other elements in the composition. That's one of the reasons we caution against specifying plants in other than general terms until you are satisfied with your preliminary design intent. Only then can you begin to refine elements of your design. As the process evolves, each decision you make will be more definitive, until you arrive at a final set of criteria to select the plants you will use. Even then, for those who will stay involved with the design after completion, you will continue to refine, modify, and make adjustments to these criteria during the actual planting, until well after the plants have been installed, even into the maintenance period, for the simple reason that we are working with a dynamic medium—plants grow and change over time.

Specifying Characteristics

Once you have all of the criteria in hand for the plants desired for use in the composition (aesthetic and cultural), it is relatively easy to select the right plants, from reference books, plant lists, or your own knowledge of plant materials. We will cover cultural and horticultural criteria of plant specification in Chapter 9, page 238.

Every aspect of each plant's makeup comes into play now—height, form, color, texture, and seasonal attributes. It's incumbent upon you, as the designer, to assure that the characteristics of each plant will "fit in" the composition whether by complementing, contrasting, or accenting neighboring plants; each must contribute to the composition as a whole. In the following subsections you will be presented with a logical sequence for doing just that. We begin by identifying the most enduring plant characteristics or attributes, and work down to the more temporal or seasonal attributes. This sequence is only one approach, however. You will ultimately develop your own preferred method for specifying characteristics, based on your personal creative style, your experiences, and the project at hand.

PLANT TYPES

We've said it so many times throughout the book: A successful mixed planting is one in which seasonal interest is successional—as one plant fades, another nearby begins to "show off." The key to accomplishing this is to include as many different plant types as possible, given the desires of the client, the environmental conditions of the site, and maintenance considerations.

Identifying plant types and deciding how to arrange them generally takes place early in the design process, at the abstract compositional and elevational study stage. As the process evolves the designer must transition to plan view, deciding how to arrange the plant and plant masses on the ground plane. Recall that, with the exception of structural plantings (massing drifts and individual structural plants), plant types should alternate—be adjacent to and in front of or behind one another. The strengths of one plant should be used to offset or accent another.

GENERAL GUIDELINES FOR PLACING PLANT TYPES

- ▷ Locate structural plant materials first, ensuring even distribution throughout.

- ▷ When maintenance will be minimal, use small trees, shrubs, evergreens, ground covers, and grasses as the primary compositional mix. Add perennials, bulbs, climbers, annuals, tenders, and tropicals to the composition, in that order, with increasing levels of available maintenance.

- ▷ Ensure that at least 20 to 30 percent of the composition is made up of evergreen materials.

- ▷ Balance and distribute deciduous and evergreen shrubs evenly throughout the composition.

- ▷ Use other plant types to mask voids created by perennials, annuals, tropicals, and bulbs that die back.

- ▷ Ensure that background plantings contain a high percentage of structural plantings. Generally speaking, small trees, shrubs, evergreens, and larger grasses will dominate the deeper background plantings.

- ▷ Install finer levels of detail in the front of the bed.

- ▷ Keep in mind that masses in the rear of the bed will tend to be larger than those in the front.

Throughout the process of locating plant types, keep in mind that you are seeking a balance among all the plant types. Ultimately, it is the design objective that determines the final plant mix.

It is important that you work in both plan and elevation views simultaneously, so that you can more accurately visualize the final form of the composition (see Figure 8.1). Ultimately this visualization technique will become innate.

HEIGHT

The objective of layering in a mixed planting composition is to vary the vertical arrangement of plants in the horizontal plane, and vice versa, as shown in Figure 8.2. Blocks drawn in elevation are the three-dimensional representation of elements in the plan view and illustrate the

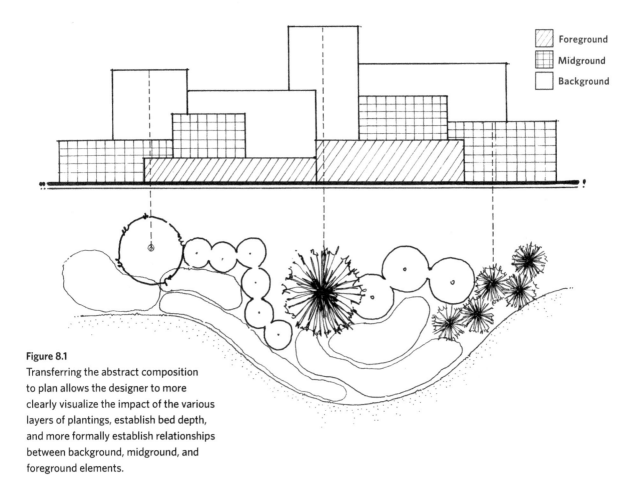

Foreground

Midground

Background

Figure 8.1
Transferring the abstract composition to plan allows the designer to more clearly visualize the impact of the various layers of plantings, establish bed depth, and more formally establish relationships between background, midground, and foreground elements.

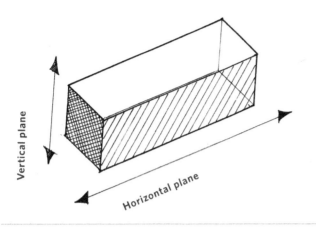

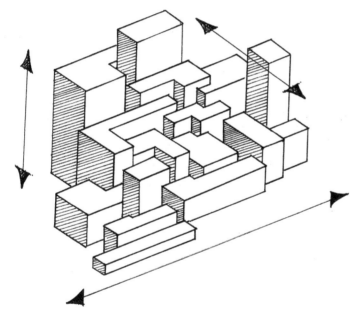

Figure 8.2
The most intriguing compositions are those that develop complex interrelationships between boxes (plant masses). The objective is to vary the height in the vertical plane, and vary depth across the composition in the horizontal plane.

relationship of various heights of one plant group to another. This is a technique that will help you to visualize and layer plant heights effectively, to create interest, even intrigue, in both directions.

Remember the layering procedure from Chapter 5: We started with the background and worked forward to the foreground plantings. As shown in Figure 5.11, page 113, each layer has a height range associated with it. When specifying individual heights of plants, you must stipulate a height range, not a layer. However, the layer concept helps to visualize the desired result. Keep in mind these height ranges:

Ground coverings 3 to 12 inches

Low plants 12 to 24 inches

Medium plants 2 to 4 feet

Tall plants 4 to 6 feet

Background plants 6 feet and taller

Again, it is best to locate background planting layers first, proceeding to block out the intermediate layers until you arrive at the foreground plantings. That said, placing deciduous and evergreen trees are an exception: You should locate them separately and in plan view. Therefore, locate and identify them only by their plant type (evergreen tree, flowering tree, or shade tree), as shown in Figure 8.3. The issue of height is, of course, complicated by the simple fact that plants grow, so their height varies throughout the year, which dramatically affects the appearance of the composition over the course of the growing season. Plant types such as perennials, grasses, annuals, and tropicals cannot necessarily be defined by a single plant height. Thus, the height of these plants must be treated as variable, until the final mature height is achieved. And they should be distributed so that not too many of these plants are in close proximity to one another to avoid creating too many early season "holes" in the composition. It's a good idea generally, based on design intent, to arrange the plant types that surround these variable growers to camouflage, mask, and or support them during their growth period or the early part of the growing season.

GENERAL GUIDELINES FOR SPECIFYING PLANT HEIGHTS

▷ Plan the depth of the plant bed to be roughly equivalent to the height of the tallest plant in the composition.

▷ Arrange plants to generally graduate in height from the front of the composition to the back with intermittent variability (see Figure 5.9, page 110).

▷ Create vertical interest by including a variety of plant heights and distribute plants freely throughout a composition.

▷ Locate some taller plants (mainly herbaceous, tropical, and grasses) near the front of the composition to break things up and provide interest through contrast.

▷ In island beds, locate the tallest plants in the center.

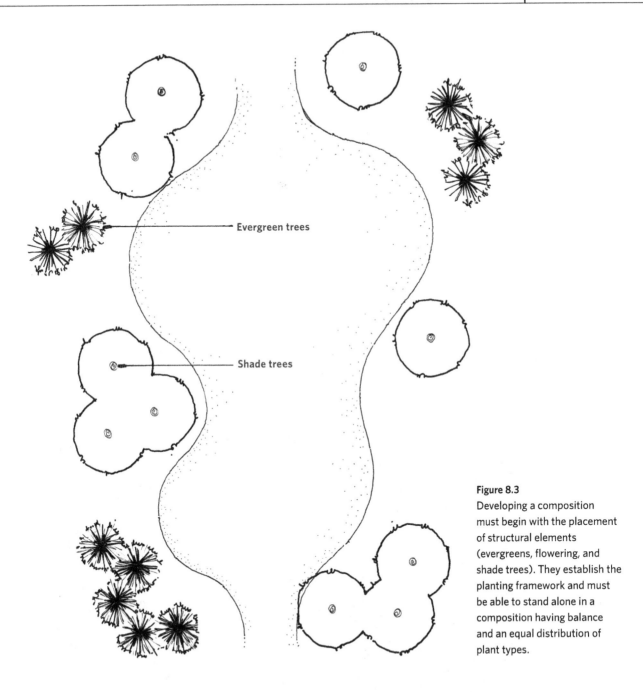

Evergreen trees

Shade trees

Figure 8.3
Developing a composition
must begin with the placement
of structural elements
(evergreens, flowering, and
shade trees). They establish the
planting framework and must
be able to stand alone in a
composition having balance
and an equal distribution of
plant types.

Remember that larger compositions can accommodate a wider range and freer distribution of plant heights than smaller gardens or compositions. But in all cases, your ultimate objective is, according to William R. Nelson in *Planting Design* (1985), to develop well-spaced variations in plant heights.

FORM

Form is vitally important to the success of a mixed composition. In periods of reduced light, when viewing from a distance, or when foliage and flowering plants are dormant, it will be the plant forms that dominate the appearance of the composition. A mixed planting composed of only one plant form is monotonous and uninteresting even if the shape used is dramatic. The key design principle for successfully combining shapes is to aim for harmonious contrast. This can be achieved by developing compositions with varying forms while repeating the use of a single neutral plant form throughout the composition as the dominate form.

A limited number of plants can be said to possess strong forms, and those that do are best used selectively for interest—just a few in any one field of view to avoid visual clutter (see Figure 8.4). The majority of plants grow in rather amorphous ways, and so are best reserved for bulk massing as harmonizers.

Figure 8.4
A composition with large numbers of plants with strong forms must be balanced with plants with neutral forms or visual clutter will ensue.

An effective way to begin thinking about the placement of plant forms is to consider the overall mass or volume of each plant and how, or whether, it can be balanced by a void. According to Lucy Gent in *Great Planting* (1995), remember that the voids are as important as masses in creating the overall composition. Strive for a balance of the two.

GENERAL GUIDELINES FOR PLACING PLANT FORMS

▷ Balance a variety of form types and their relative visual weight throughout the composition, to achieve harmony.

▷ Develop the majority of the composition using neutral forms, such as rounded or horizontally growing plants.

▷ Repeat a strongly shaped form at regular intervals in a composition. This establishes rhythm, which will provide the designer with an opportunity to develop the remainder of the composition as a "wilder" appearance.

▷ Avoid placing too many dramatically shaped plants close together, to prevent the composition from becoming visually unstable.

▷ Establish a focal point in a composition by isolating a dramatic plant form among more neutral shapes.

▷ Avoid pairing unique forms unless the intent is to flank a landscape element (doorway, bench, etc). The eye splits pairs; in a mixed composition, groupings should always be comprised of odd numbers (see Figure 6.5, page 132).

The level of contrast and harmony is a matter of taste, coupled with design intent. To achieve a higher degree of visual excitement, use more contrasting plant forms; for a composition that is more subdued, work with more plants of similar forms, and introduce contrast and variety through the use of texture or color.

TEXTURE
It is the leaves of most plants that give them their distinct texture—specifically, the shape and size of the leaves and the quality of the light on their surface or between them (Nelson 1985). However, texture, especially in a garden designed for year-round interest, also may be derived from a plant's form, or even its parts. Cumulatively, it is the size and shape of a plant's textural units—leaves, twigs, stems—that give a plant its "textural value" (see Figure 4.10, page 83). Textural differences are relative and become apparent in plants only when they are surrounded with plants that have dissimilar characteristics.

Though there are numerous fine textural delineations, simply, textures can be categorized as *fine* (e.g., grasses, various ferns, *Ilex crenata*, *Nandina domestica*, or *Buxus* spp.), *medium* (*Viburnum carlesii*, *Privet* spp., *Euonymus* spp.), and *coarse* (*Gunnera* spp., *Hosta* spp., *Hydrangea quercifolia*).

As you are refining a design, you will assign a desired texture classification to each planting type: for example F = fine, M = medium, and C = coarse. You will, naturally, vary textures and, in general, evenly distribute them throughout the composition. The extent of distribution will be based in part on the effect you are trying to create, whether high visual interest, variety, emphasis, sequence, or repetition.

GENERAL GUIDELINES FOR USING TEXTURE

▷ Use texture to add accents—for example, set a large-foliage plant among a sea of small-foliage plants.

▷ Create a background against which to set a distinctive element or contrast a special plant.

▷ Emphasize depth or reduce its effect.

▷ Achieve unity through the continuation of one type of texture.

▷ Vary the distribution of textural classifications to create variety.

Keep in mind that textural effects in a composition depend on the distance the observer is from the composition, due to the fact that only light and shadow are perceived at greater distances; thus, the greater the distance from the planting, the more you will need coarse-textured foliage or contrast between textures. Aim to strike a balance; too much contrast causes unrest. Coarse-textured plants give off a high degree of visual energy and so must be balanced with fine- and medium-textured varieties, enough so that differences are discernable.

When "going to extremes" with textural differences, do so for impact only—that is, limit the effect to select areas within the planting composition. And don't forget: Color and form can be used in lieu of fine-textured plants to achieve balance with coarse-textured plants. But this is more difficult to achieve and requires more finely tuned design skills. Generally speaking, when you use more fine-textured plants the result will be a more unified composition.

COLOR

As recommended throughout this book, you should avoid giving too much importance to color, especially flower color, in your designs, due to the relative short bloom periods of most flowering plants. However, if it's necessary to meet a design objective or the wishes of the client and a composition must include numerous species of flowers and flowering plants, then you must turn your attention to achieving color harmony.

To that end, you must consider the color effects generated by *all* plant parts—foliage color, flower color, fruit color, and the textural or reflective surface quality of the foliage—for they all influence the value and intensity of surrounding colors. And when you incorporate plants that have colorful plant parts, as opposed to just colorful flowers, you will find it easier to achieve durability in your color displays.

The first step in deciding where to place color in the composition is to determine where the design needs focus or accent. Then you can begin to choose the individual color traits that will help you accomplish the design objective, whether it's to make a single plant stand out among surrounding plants, provide an accent to an adjacent plant, or simply to replicate a pattern or theme (Nelson 1985). Needless to say, a wide range of color effects are possible, but depend on the particular plant types.

GENERAL GUIDELINES FOR USING COLOR

▷ Factor all aspects of color: the tint or shade, the intensity, the various hues, and the value of the surface—glossy, bright, or dull.

▷ Evaluate what the impact of the plant will be when it is not displaying color—remember, color is temporary.

▷ Decide on a theme to guide your selection and placement of plant colors. Will it be monochromatic, analogous, complementary, or riotous (see the section on color in Chapter 3, page 45).

▷ Consider colorful plants in relation to surrounding plant materials. If a plant is strong in form and texture, color will raise the energy value—perhaps too much, and disrupt the harmony of the composition. The weaker the visual energy of the color, the larger its area of coverage should be, and vice versa.

▷ Avoid spotty assemblages of color.

▷ Distribute color displays evenly across the seasons. No one season should be more colorful than another.

▷ Factor in the maintenance implications of color. Generally, flowering plants require more upkeep.

Ideally, a composition should be able to stand on its own without color; then, color can be used to enhance an already beautiful planting.

Planning for Succession

The first step in planning for succession in a mixed planting is to decide whether a peak or high point of successional interest is, in fact, desired; and, if so, when. This may seem contradictory to the notion of the mixed planting where the objective is to have a continual sequence of display events. However, within that continuum there may still be crescendos of interest followed by less powerful displays. For example, this approach would be appropriate if you were designing a composition for a summer residence or a fall retreat. The design objective might be to showcase more plants in a client's favorite season such as spring, summer, or fall. Or, in a larger garden, you might design compartments for peak displays at different times of the year. (Smaller gardens generally do not afford this luxury and are often best designed for continual interest rather than for one or two peak periods a season.)

Regardless of the type or size of garden, period of interest, or organizational design technique, you should always map out evergreens first because they set the rhythm that everything else will "keep time to." Evergreens do not fall under any seasonal category because they provide ongoing interest in the garden year-round. They are the stabilizing forces, in that they form the basic compositional framework. Their height and mass define the basis from which all other plantings will be integrated; thus they should be evenly distributed or balanced in the composition (see Figure 8.5). You must also place them based on any function they will serve: Will they screen, buffer, provide a physical barrier, enframe, or accent other elements in a landscape? Once you have the evergreens in place, you will need to determine which of two approaches you will take to develop succession, based on the level of maintenance the composition will receive:

Hands-on approach This approach, as you can guess, is for those compositions that will receive attentive maintenance and active gardening—they will be studied and tweaked over time to maintain continuous threads of succession. The design will be modified in response to a number of factors, some controlled by the gardener or designer, others not. Understandably, this method is generally associated only with the most intensively managed landscapes. Here, design is equal to gardening, done on a continuum as plants respond to environmental conditions and change with the seasons. Modifications are made in response to these changes, many of which cannot be anticipated or designed for. Sadly, from a designer's standpoint, the opportunity to work in this way happens rarely; it is a luxury.

Hands-off approach In most cases, you probably will not be given the opportunity to continue your involvement in the compositions you design. You will fully plan and produce the plantings, then have to leave the maintenance to others.

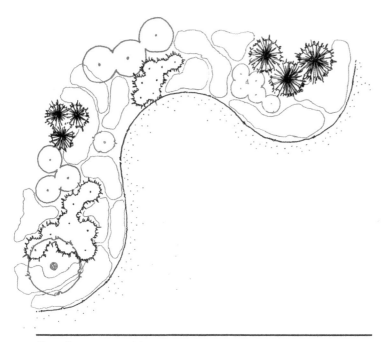

Complete composition

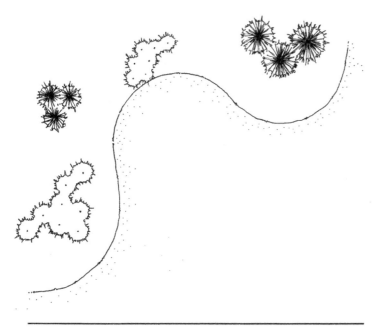

Evergreens

Figure 8.5
A variety of evergreen types and forms should be evenly distributed throughout the composition to establish a solid multidimensional framework.

Regardless of whether your long-term involvement will be hands on or off, your goal for any composition is to plan for seasonal changes, which means choreographing the "dance" of flowers, leaf and stem textures, color, etc., to ensure an ongoing display of floral and textural events. Your success will depend on the proper distribution of plant types throughout the composition, so that there is never a concentration of events in any one section of the planting at any one time. Succession planning, then, requires a controlled and pragmatic process.

This process begins by viewing the growing year as six periods:

> ▷ Winter

> ▷ Early spring

> ▷ Late spring

> ▷ Early summer

> ▷ Late summer

> ▷ Fall

During each of these periods a unique range of plant materials flourish, giving each period a distinct character. Understanding the plants for each of these seasons will enable you to maximize the potential of each growing period.

WINTER

Plant structure and form are the dominant characteristics during the winter period, for the disposition of plant types based on these two aspects is clearly evident during the winter months, in the absence of foliage. Structure is most important for the winter scene, and plants having strong structures should be dispersed evenly throughout the composition.

In the winter composition, evergreens and conifers are the "heavyweights." They stimulate visual interest, stabilize the garden, and "furnish" otherwise empty spaces. Their dark green foliage can contrast dramatically, for example, against the dried golden foliage of ornamental grasses. Beautifully shaped trees and shrubs will take center stage in the cold months, as they fill the voids left by perennials, annuals, and tropicals. Bark texture and color, often set off by evergreens, becomes amplified on plants such as *Lagerstromea*, *Betula*, *Acer grisium*, *Cornus sericea*, and many others.

Often, winter plantings also serve as reminders of the previous season's displays, in the form of seed heads, berries, and fruits. These residual plant parts also play a prominent role on the winter stage. And late winter flowering plants such as *Hamamaelis*, *Corylopsis*, and *Helleborus foetidis* are welcomed visual treats. Minor bulbs such as *Galanthus*, *Cyclamen*, and *Crocus* begin to make their appearance, a welcome sign that spring is just around the corner. But their dainty size requires that they be planted close to the edges, where they can be seen.

EARLY SPRING

In late February and early March the "early risers" begin to appear along with the increasing amounts of daylight and subtly rising temperatures. Mother Nature has turned on the growing switch. The emphasis of early spring is on those plants covering the ground plane, so these are typically best positioned in the front of the composition or under tree or shrub canopies. The structural elements of the winter garden are still very much in play during the early spring months. In fact, to a certain extent, they become more exaggerated: Deciduous trees and shrubs take on an eerie haze as their leaf and flower buds begin to swell. The garden, however, is still pretty much devoid of foliage.

The flowers of early-spring bulbs tend to be more diminutive and more sophisticated in their structure than those that bloom later—such as the early perennials and major bulbous types. Plantings, such as *Narcissus*, *Tulipa*, and *Muscari*, start to emerge as the ground begins to "green up" with leafy structures poking up from the soil. Other later-blooming bulbous plants also begin to send up their spiky green shoots, but will hold off flowering until later. Make a note to place these bulbous "late bloomers" carefully, as their foliage remains long after the show is over and can become an eyesore as it competes with other plantings for attention.

Evergreens are still giving full value at this time of the year, and are still a dominant feature in the landscape. While they are not necessarily elements of great interest, they do form excellent backgrounds against which to contrast other plant types. Evergreen perennials, such as *Helleborus* spp. with its chartreuse flowers, add another color dimension. And the evergreenlike variegated foliage of *Arum italicum* and *Cyclamen hederifolium* introduce ground-level interest, as they hover brightly over the bare brown earth. Contrasting well against these evergreen foliage plants are the welcome flowers of *Galanthus* or *Chionodoxa*.

Early-flowering shrubs including *Forsythia*, *Abeliophyllum*, and *Chaenomeles* now burst into action. Still devoid of foliage, their forms are accentuated by solid masses of color—yellow, white, and red, respectively. Be aware, however, that many shrubs in this category do not display seasonal attributes other than their flowers and so should be used judiciously if even at all in the mixed bed, as they consume valuable space. Spectacular early-flowering trees such as *Cercis* and *Amelanchier* spp. also should be used sporadically for interest and be widely distributed through the composition.

Most of the flowering plants that "awaken" at this time of the year disappear by the time summer arrives and, therefore, should be treated mainly as underplantings for other plant types.

LATE SPRING

In late spring the subtlety of the winter garden disappears. Brown twigs give way to unfurling lime-green leaf structures. The stars of this prime-time spring show begin to pop in bold bursts of color—trees such as *Prunus*, *Malus*, and *Cornus* come on strong.

Underneath their canopies a variety of plant types begin to leaf out or poke above the soil. Plants with colorful shoots such as those of the *Paeonia* provide unique points of interest. It is still not possible at this time to develop coherent color schemes, but pairings and small groupings of plants that combine flowers with crisp, new, colorful foliage make excellent accents to evergreen plantings.

Only the flowers of bulbous plants rival the colorful burst of the spring blooms of shrubs and trees. The continual flowering of late-season *Narcissus*, *Tulipa*, and some of the early *Alliums* light the ground with their bright colors, often shown to best effect in large, massed drifts.

But all too soon, this abundance of color comes to an end—this is the shortest season—reminding us of the need for restraint in designing with flowers and to incorporate other ways to include color throughout the seasons. Plants such as *Weigela*, *Syringa*, and *Deutzia* among others should be left out of the mix, as they have few ornamental characteristics once their brief flowering period has come to and end and they are left to consume valuable bed space, which is better reserved for the later-flowering species and those with multiple attributes.

EARLY SUMMER

After a brief transition period following the explosion of spring color, a succession of early-summer-flowering plant types takes the stage. This season marks the beginning of the longest-running display of flowering shrubs, when, seemingly all at once, *Spireas*, *Viburnums*, *Ceanothus*, and *Cytisus* come on together. As with spring-flowering shrubs, these should be used judiciously and, with the exception of *Viburnums*, *Aronia*, *Nandina*, multiflora and Meidland roses, and a few others, be planted in limited numbers. Instead, multidimensional shrubs should be the focus and be placed to provide accent. These should not consume too much bed space, however; there must be enough room to showcase ornamental or seasonal plants. Shrubs used en masse are appropriate for larger compositions and landscapes as bulk filler plantings but in smaller garden settings should be used in a limited capacity and judiciously.

Foliage never looks fresher than it does in the early part of summer. Gold foliage plants such as *Spirea* 'Gold Flame' are best juxtaposed against steel-blue-, pink-, or purple-colored plants or plant parts. These shrubs' foliage, however, tends to burn and look shabby in later parts of the season and should be associated with other plants that either mask or detract attention from them.

During this period, bedding is in transition, from spring to summer replacements. If you are going to use bedding plants in the composition to minimize gaps, be sure to consider biennials that have an early-season display, such as poppies, lupins, foxgloves, or *Alliums*, among others, as well as early summer perennials. Avoid overusing and carefully place annuals or tropicals with support plantings, as they are small at this stage and create voids.

This is the season, too, when perennials begin to "wake up." Though beautiful, many of the early-season perennials are short-blooming and do not last long—two good reasons to select perennials carefully. Moreover, early-flowering perennials do not produce a lot of foliar growth and their mature height remains relatively low. On the plus side, however, many of these plants respond well to shearing after flowering and often push a second flush of growth, and even flower for a second and third period. With this is mind, keep an eye toward positioning them in the front to middle regions of the composition, and show a decided preference for those species that perform well and have staying power.

As early summer turns into midsummer, many of the perennials come into full bloom, giving you, the designer, a full color and shape palette to work with. *Hemerocallis*, *Salvia*, hardy geranium, *Verbascum*, *Alchemilla*, and *Nepeta*, among others, perform at peak levels now; annuals, too, are at their peak, even late bulbs such as some of the *Alliums* rise to tower over lower plantings. Don't get carried away, though: Resist the urge to "overmass," to put too many of these plantings together. When their colors fade, you'll be left with wide, gaping voids. The watchword for these plantings (perennial color) is *restraint*.

LATE SUMMER

Despite the common belief that the high heat of late summer spells demise for the mixed planting, in fact this can be a zenith season, for it is at this time when everything has reached its ultimate: colors are brilliant, textures bold, leaves replete, and stems as high as they will go. And generally speaking, most things that flower later flower longer.

Late summer also marks the climax for border flowers. Many of the perennials are borne on taller plants, best positioned toward the rear of the composition. This is also "showtime" for some of the more durable and long-running shrubs, such as *Potentilla*, *Daphne*, *Buddleia*, *Hydrangea*, and some of the newer cultivars of shrub roses. Many of the early-flowering shrubs are now beginning to set fruit or berry.

Using a Time Grid to Define Succession

The time grid is a design tool you can use during the later stages of the design process to help you plan for the even distribution of seasonal interest throughout the six periods: winter, early spring, late spring, early summer, late summer, and fall. Using the seasonal interest chart given in Chapter 2, Figure 2.1 (page 21), the idea is to draw a matrix on which you itemize when each of the plants you have specified for a composition will be at peak performance and to identify seasonal occurrences such as flower color (bulbs, annuals, and perennials); foliage (color and texture); stem or twig color, berries, etc. Figure 8.6 gives an example of a completed time grid.

5	5	4	4	4	6	6	6	4	4	6	6	2	2
5	2	2	4	6	6	3	5	5	5	6	6	2	2
5	2	2	6	6	3	3	3	2	5	4	4	1	1
3	3	3	5	5	1	1	4	2	2	4	1	1	2
3	1	1	5	2	1	1	4	4	1	6	6	4	2
4	4	1	2	2	3	3	3	1	1	3	3	4	2

KEY:
1= Early spring   3= Early summer   5= Fall
2= Late spring   4= Late summer   6= Winter

G	G	B/V	B/V	B/V	G	G	G	Y	Y	G	G	Y	Y
G	R	R	B/V	G	G	W	R	R	R	G	G	Y	Y
G	R	R	G	G	W	W	W	O	R	R	R	P	P
B/V	B/V	B/V	O	O	B/V	B/V	O	O	O	R	P	P	R
B/V	P	P	O	Y	B/V	B/V	O	O	W	G	G	Y	R
Y	Y	P	Y	Y	P	P	P	W	W	P	P	Y	R

KEY:
B/V= Blue/violet   O= Orange   R= Red   Y= Yellow
G= Green   P= Pink   W= White

M	M	F	F	F	M	M	M	M	M	F	F	M	M
M	C	C	F	M	M	C	M	M	M	F	F	M	M
M	C	C	M	M	C	C	C	F	M	M	M	C	C
F	F	F	M	M	M	M	F	F	F	M	C	C	M
F	M	M	M	F	M	M	F	F	C	F	F	F	M
F	F	M	F	F	M	M	M	C	C	M	M	F	M

KEY:
F=Fine   M=Medium   C=Coarse

You can use the time grid to organize the distribution of plants for the various interest periods using one of two graphical techniques, one representational, the other more abstract. These techniques can also be used to develop color distributions and compositions (see in Figure 8.7), assign texture distributions (see Figure 8.8), locate structure plantings, and define winter interest distributions. Here's the process:

1. Divide your grid into 1-foot-square increments to represent the configuration of the landscape bed under design (see Figure 8.9). You'll use this to map out the approximate range and distribution of various desired attributes of seasonal interest throughout the composition.

Figure 8.6 (TOP)
Imposing a distribution grid over a planting area is a technique that can be used to "map out" the succession of seasonal events across the six periods of interest—the objective is to evenly distribute seasonal interest across the composition and among the seasons.

Figure 8.7 (CENTER)
The distribution grid can be used to develop color associations and interest but must be carefully coordinated with the time grid so that the period of color (flowers, foliage, etc.) and associations are correctly sequenced.

Figure 8.8 (BOTTOM)
The distribution grid can also be used to develop textural associations for a composition.

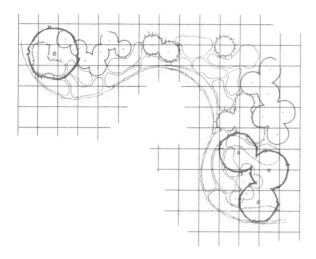

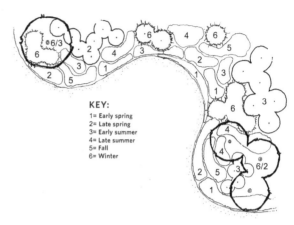

KEY:
1= Early spring
2= Late spring
3= Early summer
4= Late summer
5= Fall
6= Winter

2   Label each square to represent a period of bloom from one of the six periods of interest. The number of grid squares blocked out for a particular season should be roughly equivalent to the area where you will locate a massing of a particular plant to be "on" during that period.

3   Once you have identified the season of interest, begin specifying the desired characteristics of the plant located in each position. Generally, early-blooming plants are located toward the front of the composition, and under larger plantings; late-summer- and fall-blooming plantings are located toward the middle and rear of the composition.

Figure 8.9 (TOP LEFT)
The abstract distribution grid is imposed over an actual planting composition. Each grid square will be used to identify the desired period of interest, color, and texture, as shown in Figures 8.6–8.8.

Figure 8.10 (TOP RIGHT)
The representational method assigns seasonal interest, color, and texture to a specific plant or massing *after* the composition is developed.

The representational method can be used only after you have determined the general plant layout, the configuration of masses, and plant types. Then:

1   Assign each plant type or massing zone to an interest period (see Figure 8.10).

2   Add the other layers of design specifications (plant type, height, color, texture, dominant characteristic for the chosen season) to the grid.

Both methods will help you to visualize the distribution of seasonal interest, enabling you to see quickly any gaps in your design. Then you can begin to make adjustments based on your findings, to ensure even seasonal distribution patterns that meet the intent of the design. Finally, you can begin the plant selection process—identifying the best plant species and varieties to meet the period of interest and plant attributes desired.

Late summer is also when ornamental grasses, tropicals, and annuals become dominant. Annuals and tropicals produce an abundance of attributes—billowing foliage and dense and profuse flowers—from now until first frost. As the season progresses and flowers begin to fade, those plants with hardy and showy foliage begin to take on greater prominence. As this happens, a more tropical look begins to emerge, and form and texture play a more important role. Plants such as *Phormium*, *Canna*, *Eucalyptus*, *Musa*, *Arundo*, *Cordyline*, and other foliage-based plants make for impressive visual treats; and hardier types such as the ornamental grasses now capture attention. And because ornamental grasses come in a variety of sizes, you can find appropriate spots for them throughout the composition, which when used repeatedly can be an effective way to create a theme or add harmony. And for theme or specimen plants during this season, there is a wide variety of grasses with colored or variegated foliage to choose from, among them *Pennesetum setaceum* 'Rrubrum', *Arundo donax* 'Versicolor', *Hakonechloa macra* 'Aureola', and others.

FALL

Fall is Mother Nature's last burst of glory before flowers and foliage disappear, leaving the structure plantings and faded grasses to hold interest in the composition over the winter months. Fall foliage colors can match and even surpass those of the most colorful of flowers. The quality of light, the cold weather, and the scent of the changing season enhance the scene. Berries and seed heads glow and take prominence both before and after the foliage has turned, setting the stage for early winter displays. Evergreens now begin to play a more prominent role with their dark green palette; and late-flowering plants such as *Asters*, *Anemones*, *Dendranthema*, and *Helianthus* add bright spots of contrast.

As the season wanes, the mixed planting takes on a golden hue. Grasses reach their ultimate heights and shapes and often tower over other plant types. Now more than ever, textures dominate. These effects on the composition must be given ample consideration during the design process, as they last for several months, into the deepest of winter.

And so the planting cycle begins again, each season offering myriad design opportunities for the mixed composition.

Creating a Memorable Impression

Everyone who has ever visited a professionally designed garden or landscape can recall planting arrangements they saw that made them stop in their tracks. What was it they found so captivating? Perhaps it was the contrast of form or texture, the harmonious relationship of the colors, or the soothing overall impression created by the composition. For each person, it is different.

How you achieve this will be done at several design levels, which we've talked about throughout the book: in the form of color contrasts or accents, textures, forms, or visual weight. And you will harmonize all these elements so that in spite of its numerous individual components, the composition will come together as a whole.

At the initial stages, you will concern yourself with the overall impression of the composition, progressively addressing the development of plant vignettes within the composition. A number of design tenants can be used as a guide to the assemblage of these vignettes. These are described in the following subsections.

VARIETY

Variety, as you know, is the foundation of a mixed planting composition; it is what sustains interest year-round. However, though easy to achieve variety can be challenging to control. Restraint is necessary, to avoid chaos, but not so much that the result is a boring composition. Beyond this general guideline, your options as a designer are very broad when it comes to the application of variety.

Height and Depth

Varying the height and depth of plants serves both functional and aesthetic purposes. From an aesthetic standpoint, interest is created through interconnectedness of the foreground, midground, and background plantings. The objective is to stagger, overlap, and interlock planting heights, both vertically and horizontally—for example, by placing a tall plant toward the front of a composition for interest. Staggering the height from front to back naturally establishes depth. This technique also can be used to build smaller "rooms" or bays for other combinations of plant types, further creating interest.

GUIDELINES FOR USING HEIGHT FOR VARIETY

▷ Consider how plants evolve over the season. Specifically, perennials, grasses, tropicals, and annuals affect the composition as they change—early voids later turn into masses.

▷ Instill variety in an apparent random but planned fashion; avoid obvious stair-step patterns.

▷ Juxtapose large plants and small plants for drama.

▷ Install taller, airy plants in the foreground to break up larger masses and create depth.

▷ Place a taller plant occasionally within a mass of lower plantings or in the front of a composition, for emphasis.

▷ Use smaller evergreens as "facer" plants to mask lower portions of taller leggy perennials and shrubs.

▷ Alternate layers of plant types to produce interesting depth patterns.

▷ Showcase plant parts (seed pods, flower plumes of perennials or grasses) in contrast against something lower.

Texture

Foliage texture is the primary means to manipulate light, shade, and shadow patterns in a composition and to impact its depth. Distance is an important factor here, as details of texture get lost the farther away they are. Therefore, to achieve variety in the far view you will need to impose more dramatic textural differences. And light is essential to the design, as the quality and amount of light and will either be reflected or absorbed, depending on the surface coating of the leaves.

GUIDELINES FOR USING TEXTURE FOR VARIETY

▷ Create a rhythm of varying patterns by balancing textural variation throughout the composition.

▷ Establish depth by undulating the positions of coarsely textured plants in the fore-, mid-, and background of the composition.

▷ Increase the illusion of depth by placing finely textured plants in front of more coarsely textured plants.

▷ Use leaf surface quality (e.g., glossy or dull) in contrast to add another textural quality.

Form

As we've said so often, a plant's form is its longest-lasting quality. A composition that functions on form alone can be successful. Thus, introducing a variety of forms throughout a composition is critical to the mixed planting design. Tension and opposition are key concepts when pairing one form with another for variety. For example, juxtaposing vertical with horizontal forms (the two most extreme form types) will produce high degrees of contrast, and so these should be balanced with more neutral, rounded or spreading, forms.

GUIDELINES FOR USING FORM FOR VARIETY

▷ Make a dramatic statement in a composition by incorporating upright conifers. Used selectively, conifers contrast the more amorphous plant types.

▷ Use upright or spiky forms to break up larger masses of mounding forms.

▷ Remember that early-flowering perennial forms are low and rounded, while their late summer and early autumn flowering relatives are usually taller, position them in the composition accordingly.

Color

Color is a transient element; therefore it should be used only to accent, not to build a composition. Color variety is also an optional design feature; it is not required. Color variety can be achieved simply by using a number of colors or by varying the ways and areas where color is presented—on foliage, twigs and stems, flowers, etc.

GUIDELINES FOR USING COLOR FOR VARIETY

▷ Consider using a variety of plant parts to achieve color effects.

▷ Spread color throughout the composition; never concentrate it in one place.

▷ When a particular color scheme is desired, sacrifice color variety.

HARMONY AND RHYTHM

As noted, all parts of a composition must unite to produce the design intent. This requires congruity among the elements of a design. Each group of plants must play a part, yet they must be at all times subordinate to the desired effect of the whole. Therefore, an important goal in developing compositions is to provide an organizing element or elements that pull together the other components—the smaller vignettes located throughout the composition.

The most common and effective way to achieve harmony and rhythm is through the use of repetition—of texture, form, or color—to establish a cadence that makes viewing a composition pleasurable. Patterns may also be used to establish harmony and rhythm, by the direction, size, or shape of the vignettes or plant masses within a composition. Generally, you will want to use a combination of these techniques to create a sense of harmony and rhythm in your mixed planting designs.

The following subsections delve further into the ways you can use the various elements within a planting composition to achieve harmonious and rhythmic compositions.

Texture

Textures harmonize when they are relatively uniform across a composition or are repeated at regular intervals. That said, a slight textural alteration repeated throughout the composition can establish a pattern of variation without sacrificing harmony. But too many will be disruptive, so tread carefully.

Finely foliaged plants are best situated at closer distances for this purpose, where plant parts reflect and absorb light equally, resulting in an even surface quality. In larger areas, greater textural differences are more successful. But regardless of the distance of the viewer to the composition or the size of the area, one type of texture should predominate.

GUIDELINES FOR USING TEXTURE TO CREATE HARMONY AND RHYTHM

▷   Distribute a texture, regardless of its type (coarse, medium, or fine), evenly throughout a composition, to create harmony.

▷   Repeat finely textured plants to create a soothing ambiance.

▷   Place coarse-textured plants at greater distances from the observer, to unify.

▷   Plant smaller areas with simple and less distinct textural differences.

Forms

When it comes to using individual forms to instill harmony or rhythm, it's important to keep in mind that they become less noticeable when several plants, regardless of their form, are placed together in a group or mass. More neutral forms, those that are rounded, oval, or horizontal, used en masse or individually, are the best harmonizers, as they demand less attention. More distinct forms can serve this purpose only when used in a repetitive fashion—for example, a disparate composition containing a series of plants with strong forms repeated at regular or syncopated intervals.

GUIDELINES FOR USING FORM TO CREATE HARMONY AND RHYTHM

▷ Limit the number of differing forms in any one composition.

▷ Use neutral forms for the bulk of the composition.

▷ Use bright color combinations (reds, oranges, or riotous color schemes) to subdue strong form differences.

▷ Remember: The simpler the color palette, the more important the form of a plant.

Color

Color can add an important dimension to any planting composition, but it is the value of the color that produces a harmonizing image, according to David Lauer in *Design Basics* (1985). To use a number of colors harmoniously requires that their values have only small variations of light and dark; likewise, color schemes that incorporate analogous hues also tend to harmonize naturally, as their level of contrast is minimal and the progression from one color to another is gradual (see Chapter 3, page 50). Closely related values are calming and tend to harmonize more effectively than loud and bright contrasts in color, even when used in a repetitive fashion.

GUIDELINES FOR USING COLOR TO CREATE HARMONY AND RHYTHM

▷ The most harmonious color compositions are those that use a limited range of colors. A good rule of thumb is to limit the use of color to only three hues.

▷ Consider using a single color repetitively throughout a composition, to unify (monochromatic scheme).

▷ Blend and graduate colors in subtle steps.

CONTRAST

Contrast is a primary ingredient in creating interest in a composition. The value of any one individual form, texture, or color can be emphasized through contrast. Not enough contrast results in a boring composition; too much results in confusion. By bringing contrasting elements into close proximity, the differences appear greater. Sharply contrasting one element against another dramatizes the most distinctive quality of each.

Both strong and weak elements (form, texture, and color) attract more attention when in contrast than in combination, but to introduce contrasting elements effectively you must understand the nature of the features to be accentuated. For example, a sharp blue flower can only be properly contrasted with a yellow one. The impact of this opposition draws the eye because of the differences between the two colors.

Below is a more detailed discussion on how the various elements in a planting composition can be used to achieve contrast.

Height and Depth

Variances in height and depth are what direct the eye through the composition—foreground, midground, and background. Introducing height and depth differences creates pockets of light and shadow, which in turn accent and highlight plant characteristics—texture, form, and color.

GUIDELINES FOR USING HEIGHT AND DEPTH TO INTRODUCE CONTRAST

▷ Interlock plant masses of various heights between the foreground, midground, and background.

▷ Vary the heights of plants across the length of the composition, as well as from the front to the back.

▷ Avoid dramatic changes in height from one plant group to another, unless emphasis is desired.

Texture

Texture is related structurally to form and size, and visually to color. Additionally, the amount and angle of light are important considerations, as much of the impact of textural contrast comes from variances of light and shadow.

The variation in density or size of textural units can be used to highlight key features. Very strong textures—smooth, shiny, rough—when contrasted against one another in equal amounts serve to emphasize opposing textural differences; each will attract more attention than if used alone or with others like it. Contrasting textural relationships can be used to divide space, to break up larger parts of a composition into smaller planting units.

GUIDELINES FOR USING TEXTURE TO INTRODUCE CONTRAST IN FORM AND STRUCTURE

▷ Use foliage texture, along with a plant's winter structure, as the primary textural elements to create contrast in a composition.

▷ Contrast bold specimen plants with fine-textured plants for greater interest.

▷ Use coarse textures carefully in small spaces as they decrease the apparent size of the space.

GUIDELINES FOR USING TEXTURE TO INTRODUCE CONTRAST IN COLOR

▷ Use subtle color combinations (whites and grays, pinks, pastels, and pale greens) and monochromatic color schemes to enhance the differences in texture.

▷ Introduce smooth textures with glossy surfaces to attract attention, and rough textures to hold attention for longer periods.

▷ Use rough textures to make colors more intense.

Form

William R. Nelson stated in *Planting Design* (1985) that a plant's form can either "be an accent or a decoy since it is the design quality that first attracts the eye. The accent form would draw the eye to a point of interest. As a decoy, form can be used to divert the eye from an area or feature that is unattractive." This can be accomplished only if the form in question contrasts with those that surround it. David A. Lauer called this "emphasis by contrast" in *Design Basics* (1985).

Additionally, contrasting one form against another serves to highlight or emphasize the difference between the two and the uniqueness of both. For example, pairing a triangular or pyramidal form with a rounded form of equal size serves to make the triangle appear more angular, and the round form more compact.

GUIDELINES FOR USING FORM TO INTRODUCE CONTRAST

▷ Compose the bulk of a composition using neutral forms (specifically, rounded), to allow for greater contrast when differing forms are used.

▷ Use abrupt form contrasts for emphasis.

▷ Limit strong contrasts in forms to special points of interest for greater effect.

▷ Equalize the visual energy among contrasting forms throughout the entire composition.

▷ Avoid using too many different forms, to prevent visual confusion.

Color

Color contrast depends on a "distinguishable difference between two parts of the same color dimension," according to Michael E. Doyle in *Color Drawing* (1981). High-value contrasts are those opposite on the color wheel or those that are complementary. For example, when a bright red flower is combined with bright green foliage of equal magnitude, both appear more intense. Low-value contrasts are those colors next to one another on the color wheel or analogous.

The degree of color contrast used in a composition—whether subtle or strong—will, of course, depend on your objective, as the designer, to create a mood or emotional impact. Subsequently, your color choices will be affected by ever-changing light conditions, day to day and season to season, as well as by movement through the composition, from shade to sun and back again, because the human eye needs time to adjust for the changing light conditions. The effect of light on color and color contrasts can be dramatic. Even highly distinct color contrasts when viewed in bright light may appear washed out and yellowish (in which case a darker color scheme may be more appropriate); conversely, in too little light, color contrasts may be hard to discern at all.

Distance, too, is a major factor here. At great distances, all of a composition's colors will tend to meld together and read as one large color mass. If that is the intent, fine; but if the objective is to clearly define spatial areas and introduce depth, then strong color contrasts must be made.

GUIDELINES FOR USING COLOR TO INTRODUCE CONTRAST

▷ Avoid using dark color contrasts in low light situations.

▷ Use greater contrasts of color to emphasize form.

▷ Use dark foreground colors contrasted against lighter background colors to create a flat composition; conversely, use light foreground colors against dark background colors to project the foreground element forward.

▷ Introduce contrast carefully, to prevent overuse resulting in a chaotic impression.

Keeping It Simple

Inevitably, beginner designers want to include large numbers of plants and fussy details in their compositions. With experience, however, all designers realize the wisdom of simplicity, for it is usually the simple designs, those that incorporate the most durable and hardiest materials that are the best and last the longest. It's easy to understand why. Designs that use fewer and more durable materials can endure the rigors of time, weather, abuse, and inadequate upkeep. And remember, in most cases, you won't have control over maintenance practices.

Simple designs typically do not reflect current trends. Instead, rely on the most timeless and proven design philosophies:

▷ Use a limited number of species.

▷ Select only the most durable species, those requiring the least amount of maintenance.

▷ Mass those plants in the simplest of forms.

You do not sacrifice artistry by limiting the palette or simplifying the design. Quite the opposite.

9 | Understanding the Planting Environment

DESIGNING WITH PLANTS is not only about effectively choosing and combining plants for aesthetic and functional purposes, but also about choosing plants that are culturally compatible with their environment. Each and every plant species has an ideal habitat. Some thrive in continuous moisture, while others require small amounts of water only periodically. Some flourish in extreme heat, others in cold. To be able to properly identify the plant types you will use in any mixed composition, you must have a thorough knowledge of the environmental factors inherent in the location of the composition. Simply put, the plants you choose for any composition must be compatible with their environment or they will not survive for long. The most beautifully designed planting will fail if you do not first account for the science of horticulture.

Soil type is a primary concern. You must consider texture, structure and depth, moisture capacity, drainage, and nutrient content. Close behind soil in importance is climate, which is closely tied to plant hardiness; then you must factor in exposure to light and solar radiation, which also affect a plant's performance in a composition. We'll look into each of these vital issues in turn.

Understanding Soils

The success of every planting composition is dependent on the soil it's placed in. No planting can ever achieve the desired effect or look its best unless the plants chosen for it are matched to the soil types present on the site. Therefore, before setting out to specify plants for any composition, you must have a clear understanding of the different soils on the site and the effect they will have on the plants' performance. Without that knowledge, you will not be able to pick the most suitable plant types and the success of your design will be at risk.

SOIL TEXTURE AND STRUCTURE

Soil is composed of inorganic materials (various-sized particles of rock, sand, silt, and clay), organic materials (decaying plant and animal life), water, air, and microorganisms. The composition of the inorganic materials will determine which minerals and other essential elements are available to the plants. The organic materials, in part, determine the water-holding capacity and aeration of the soil, as well as contribute mineral nutrients to the plants.

Soil Modification

The characteristic traits of any given soil will determine the level of nutrients and moisture that are readily available to plants. In many instances it may be necessary to modify or amend existing soil characteristics, but it is always wise to first take a "baseline reading" of the soil on the site where you will be working.

Cultivating the soil is a way to ensure that ideal soil conditions are present. Various materials can be added to the soil, either at the time of planting, by working it into the soil, or by surface application after the planting operations have taken place. The method you choose will depend on the condition of the existing soil and the type of amendment required. The objective is to improve soil fertility and structure, to allow for a faster establishment of the plants, to increase long-term plant health, and to reduce plant maintenance.

In many cases, however, it may be impractical to amend the soil. On isolated or large sites, for example, the cost of soil amendment may be too high. In these conditions, it's always best to install plants that meet the conditions of the existing soil types. In fact, this should be your rule of thumb for choosing all plants. Soil modifications should be undertaken only when necessary; they should never be a requirement for success.

Soil texture and structure are based on how the various particles are arranged within the soil and the percentages of the inorganic materials. The amounts of the three types of inorganic materials (sand, silt, and clay) determine the availability of air, water, and nutrients. The largest particles are classified as sand, those in between as silt, and the smallest as clay. According to Russell J. Baige in *The Herbaceous Perennial Garden* (1992), relatively speaking, you can think of a clay-sized particle as the size of a lettuce seed and a sand particle as the size of a seven-and-a-half-inch-diameter balloon.

Soil aggregation, how those particles are combined, is a determinant in nutrient availability. The greater the degree of aggregation, the greater the number and larger the size of spaces between particles (*pore spaces*), which allow for air and water exchange between plant roots and the soil. Sufficient pore space is essential, and soils devoid of pore space are considered compacted. They are virtually dead in that they cannot support plant life for any sustained period. This condition is fairly common in highly trafficked or urban areas.

Organic matter plays a major role in soil aggregation, as it increases microbial activity, which breaks down various elements in the soil and makes them available to plants. Root growth is enhanced because the organic matter helps to increase air space and water-holding capacity. Thus, the texture of the soil influences the pore space, which in turn influences the amount of soil and water being held in the soil.

Texture also influences the nutrient-holding capacity of the soils. Soils that have more clay particles have smaller pore spaces and tend to hold water and nutrients more tightly than sandy or loamy soils, those containing a mix of all three aggregate types, making them less available to plants.

pH

The pH of a soil is a measure of its acidity or alkalinity. This measure directly affects nutrient availability and so must be a key determinant in the selection of plant materials. Therefore, it is imperative to learn a soil's pH level *before* choosing plants or modifying soils on the site for planting. The pH level is measured on a scale from 0 to 14: a pH of 7 is considered neutral; lower numbers indicate increasing acidity, higher numbers increasing levels of alkalinity. Each plant requires a specific level of soil pH to thrive. Those located inappropriately, based on this factor, will produce less vigorous growth or exhibit symptoms of nutrient deficiency due to their inability to absorb nutrients from the soil.

Soil pH can, to a certain extent, be adjusted: It can be raised with the addition of lime or lowered with the addition of sulfur. It is preferable, however, to specify plants that are appropriate to the existing soil pH level.

NUTRIENTS

Needless to say, nutrients, which provide nourishment for plants, are vital to their health and appearance. There are fourteen essential elements known to be necessary for optimum plant growth. Six of the fourteen are used by plants in relatively large quantities and are known as macronutrients. These elements, which are available in varying levels in most soils, are taken into the plant through its roots. Plant nutrients are divided into two categories: primary and secondary elements.

The primary nutrient—sometimes referred to as the macronutrient category—includes nitrogen (N), phosphorus (P), and potassium (K); calcium, magnesium, and sulfur are generally available in large quantities in most soils. Nutrients in the secondary and micronutrient categories include iron, manganese, copper, zinc, boron, molybdenum, chlorine, and cobalt, and are typically present in smaller amounts—if necessary, these nutrients can be increased quite easily by adjusting soil pH levels or by adding organic matter.

Nutrient availability depends on the soil type, as nutrients are for the most part held on the surface of the soil particles and released when the plant roots make contact with the particles. Clay soils naturally hold more nutrients than sandy soils because of their

> ### Soil Testing
>
> To determine the appropriate plants for a particular location and increase the chances of success, it's a good idea to always test the soil you will be working with before you begin planting. Supply several representative soil samples to a testing laboratory specializing in this type of procedure. At a minimum, test soil pH, organic matter content, primary nutrient levels, and soluble salts. Armed with this information, you will be able to narrow down the plant selection to a specific range of plants that are appropriate to the existing site conditions.

greater water-holding capacity. Sandy soils leach faster and thus have less nutrient-holding capability.

Exposure to the Elements

Exposure to the elements or climate is the second most important factor when considering what plants to choose for a composition. The elements that affect the climate and various microclimatic conditions include many variables that fall under the categories of temperature, rainfall, wind, and intensity of light. As with soils, to be successful in the selection of plants requires an understanding and acknowledgment of all these variables for the particular geographic region the project is located. Within regions there will be site-specific variables that affect regional averages or conditions. Microclimatic differences such as thermal pockets (of heat and frost), damaging winds, radiant heat, or varying moisture levels all come into play. Each specific situation will have consequences on the selection of plants and will ultimately influence what will or will not grow in any particular area.

TEMPERATURE

Temperature most directly influences the rate of a plant's growing process. The first consideration must, therefore, be whether a plant species can withstand the temperature ranges likely to occur in a particular region. Plants will tend to grow at faster rates when located in areas where the temperatures are at the higher limits of their natural tolerance.

The United States Department of Agriculture has developed a Hardiness Zone Map based on the average minimal night temperature throughout the continent that helps to predict the adaptability of plants to a particular climatic region. Each zone represents a geographic range where the high and low temperatures fall within a consistent known range. This in turn can be used to identify the plants that are able to survive in each particular location. However, within each range there will be variations. For example, the temperature will generally be higher on the sunny side of walls—those facing south and southwest—and near unshaded paved areas as the hard surfaces absorb radiant energy. South-facing slopes will also warm up and have higher temperatures than slopes facing other directions because they are exposed to the direct rays of the sun.

RAINFALL

Rainfall also influences the performance of plants. Each plant will have a range of moisture (minimum and maximum) that it will need to thrive. Water and moisture are important because they enable a plant to take up nutrients from the soil. Soil moisture dissolves the mineral nutrients so that roots can absorb them for utilization for growing. Some plants need consistent soil moisture, some can tolerate wide swings in moisture levels, while others prefer dry, water-starved soils. As with temperatures, the amount of average rainfall will vary from region to region and location to location within each region. For example, a plant that may grow well in the Southeast region of Zone 9, which is the moist part of the zone, may not perform well in the drier conditions of the southwestern portion of that zone.

The specific location in a composition may also affect the amount of rainfall that a plant may receive. Plants on leeward sides of mountains or structures or under the canopy of trees or large shrubs will reduce the amount of effective rainfall. Modern irrigation systems can completely negate any concern over lack of water, but excessive rainfall cannot be accounted for. Thus, water and humidity levels must also be factored when selecting plants.

WIND

After temperature and water, wind has more influence than any other factor. Its impact, while potentially having the ability to damage plants by bending and breaking limbs and shoots, is greatest on a plant's evapotranspiration system. Winds blowing over leaves have the same effect as wind blowing over wet clothes: They dry the surface out. This effect is often referred to as *desiccation*, in that wind draws moisture out of the foliage faster than roots can replenish it. This can have a damaging effect—especially on evergreens. It will be important to consider from where the predominant winds on a particular site come, and what their frequency and velocity are. Winds from an open field can be quite strong, but even those that have been redirected, channeled, or compressed, such as on the leeward sides of buildings or walls, can be tough as well. The increased velocities can distort plants, warp or bend stems or trunks, or continually dry foliage.

In the Shade of a Tree

Trees present a unique set of challenges as they mature. Problems tend to develop after a tree achieves a relative stage of maturity. As a tree canopy matures and expands, it casts shade in ever-widening circles over the plants beneath them and requires greater amounts of water and nutrients. As a result, the growth of those now-shaded plants may be suppressed, in particular if they require full sun. In some cases, the plantings may have to be removed and replaced with plantings better adapted to shady and dry conditions.

INTENSITY OF LIGHT

As with all other factors, the intensity of light will affect where certain plants can grow. Too much sun on plants that are not accustomed to it can create severe damage; scorching the leaves or even the bark. Conversely, a plant in a shady area that demands higher levels of sunlight will distort itself or stretch to try to get as much light as possible.

Plants are affected not only by the type of light they receive but by when it comes and for how long. Depending on where the plants originate (across the globe or microclimatically within any one region), they naturally require certain periods of light to perform well—that is, produce solid compact masses of foliage or flower, if at all. Exposure to various levels of light is commonly classified into four categories—full sun, partial shade, shade, and deep shade. This is usually determined by how many hours of sunlight will be exposed to a plant or area. A specific range of plants will be appropriate for each setting. It will be important to know light levels of a site and work within the range of plants that are suited for each light level. To a certain extent, light levels may be modified slightly within any one composition by the inclusion of shade casting materials such as trees, shrubs, or large perennials or grasses, or by the removal of trees or limbs to increase light levels.

Accounting for Growth Behavior

Placed in their proper environment, plants often grow vigorously—some even aggressively. In the short term, this may be seen as an advantage with respect to plant establishment, especially on reclamation sites, naturalized sites, or for large-scale plantings where substantial mass is required. But it can quickly become a designer's nightmare in densely planted mixed compositions.

Within each geographic region and each plant type there are a handful of plants that may be considered aggressive growers. They make effective ground covers for larger, more open areas, but when used in a mixed planting, they have the potential to overtake weaker, neighboring plants. From a design standpoint, use of these plants will require careful placement—which in general means they should be located in areas that either contain their growth, such as a raised planter or bed contained by the edges of pavement, or among other equally aggressive plants that will help to keep their growth in check. From a maintenance standpoint, these plants can be controlled in a variety of ways—by pruning, pulling, weeding, thinning, and dividing. We will discuss more on that in Chapter 10, page 252. But, don't forget, often the appropriate level of maintenance to keep such plants in check is not available.

When it comes to siting these fast-growing species—such as some of the shade-casting shrubs or trees, rambling vines, and herbaceous spreaders—they must be given sufficient free space to grow without affecting adjacent plants; or, as noted above, they must be paired with "regulating" neighbors of equal vigor. Certain bamboo species, *Phalaris*, *Tanacetum*, *Aegopodium*, and the shrub species *Sambucus*, and a variety of other species as well, should generally be avoided in the mixed composition due to their aggressive nature. Only by following these guidelines will it be possible to minimize their aggressive growth pattern.

All that said, however, you may find yourself required to produce a composition that must have "instant impact." In this situation, fast-growing plants may be sited close together, to quickly produce a massing. But the time and resources must be available later to thin out, prune, and replant overcrowded areas. Left unchecked, the ramifications of such a planting will be seen quickly: Plants outgrow their bounds; overtake one another; or become leggy, sickly, or even die due to the high level of competition—a competition that is man-made.

Plants, including aggressive plants, multiply and replicate in a number of ways, by self-seeding, stolons, rhizomes, or runners. It's important to understand each of these mechanisms, as this information will help you choose plants for your mixed compositions.

SELF-SEEDING

Many species propagate themselves efficiently through a self-seeding process. So effective is this process that these species can potentially be the bane of any gardener from a maintenance standpoint. Here's how it works: The dried flower parts, when allowed to desiccate and remain on the plant, eventually disperse their seeds. Many plants such as *Buddleia*, *Echinacea*, *Spartium*, *Verbena bonariensis*, the Norway maple, and a host of others are prolific self-seeders and can quickly colonize an area within a few years.

In certain situations, these self-starters are beneficial, especially in those areas planted to naturalize. And in gardens that are intensively managed, certain self-sowing species are welcome guests, often sprouting and adding beauty in places not originally envisioned by the designer. These self-seeders also can add an attractive air of informality or wildness to a composition. However, for each welcome guest, there are usually more that are not wanted and that must be carefully "edited" and weeded out. Otherwise, the composition may relinquish its species diversification over time, due the continual multiplication of these aggressively seeding species.

STOLONS

A stolon is a horizontal branch from the base of a plant that produces new plants from buds at its tip or nodes. In this way, stolons progressively expand their area of coverage, "crawling" over low-lying objects and quickly covering them like a blanket. Stoloniferous growth is most often associated with plants such as *Hedra*, *Vinca*, and *Rubus*, which are effective as ground covers because of their ability to spread quickly and form a dense matting.

Plants that spread by stolons may be desirable where a large area of low-maintenance plantings is required. However, for contained areas or those areas requiring a specified area of coverage, plants that spread by stolons may not be the best choice as regular upkeep may be necessary to curtail their spread.

RHIZOMES

A rhizome is an elongate, usually horizontal subterranean plant stem, often thickened by deposits of reserve food material, which produces shoots above and roots below. Rhizomes expand laterally via underground stems that are born on an established part of the plant. Spreading outward, rhizomatous plants often form large dense colonies, and new plants may appear at great distances from the parent plant. Plants in the wild such as *Sambucus*, *Aronia melonocarpa*, and various species of bamboo illustrate this type of colonization. Both herbaceous and woody plants spread by this mode—some more aggressively than others.

Controlling the more aggressive types of rhizomes can be difficult, as removal, either through pulling or pruning, often leaves small pieces of rhizome behind in the ground, to start the growth process all over again.

RUNNERS

A runner is an elongated horizontal root arising from the base of a plant and growing parallel to the ground to form new plants. Plants that spread by this means exhibit similar characteristics to those that propagate by stolons or rhizomes. Runners can form dense mats of coverage that extend to large areas when left unchecked. True runners are found only on herbaceous plants, such as *Phlox stolonifera* and *Tiarella*.

In certain cases, such as with *Phlox stolonifera*, it may be desirable to locate two or more plant types together, to act as companions, as this allows for greater seasonal variation. But exercise caution with these plants and make sure that you pair them properly; otherwise, one will overpower the other.

Giving Plants Room to Grow

We've mentioned in a number of contexts throughout the book the importance of factoring in the ultimate mature size of the plants you select for your mixed compositions. That factor is critical for plant-spacing purposes, as you might imagine. And because spacing requirements naturally vary from plant to plant and landscape to landscape, this issue becomes something of a mathematical calculation. You must factor in the client's time frames to the equation, as well. For example, how quickly does the client want a mature-looking landscape? Too often, sorry to say. In this regard, designers are prevented from following horticultural best practices due to the constraints of a given project. Thus, determining the appropriate spacing for the various plant types presents a common challenge where no one rule or guideline dominates.

WHAT IS MATURE SIZE?

Answering this question is part of the challenge for planting design in general, for the full size of any plant will differ based on the environmental and soil conditions of the site where it will take root. The range of sizes generally assumed for a plant is based on *averages* among growing regions. And these ranges cannot possibly take into account local or regional variances in microclimatic conditions. This is where your knowledge and experience again come into play: It is incumbent upon you, the designer, to know each plant's mature size and growth rate for the region in which you will be working. Ultimately, you are responsible for making sensible judgments about plant spacing and patterns. What will help you make these decisions is the planning process.

During the design process you must account for the average mature growth of the plants you've chosen, as well as consider the other variables mentioned; doing so will show you, before you plant, whether you need to adjust the spacing, closer or farther apart (see Figure 6.4, page 131). You may, for example, realize you need to space the plants closer together at the time of installation because your client—typically, a homeowner with a shorter time horizon or a developer who wants to promote and market a project—wants an almost-immediate "mature" landscape effect. Though you will be meeting the needs of your client, you will also have to deal with the probable resultant adverse horticultural effects of this decision—usually, overcrowding, resulting in contorted, gangly, or leggy-looking plants. This overcrowding, in turn, increases the potential for disease. Maintenance now becomes the issue.

Ideally, of course, your projects will have longer time frames—such as college campuses, corporate headquarters, or public agencies that develop parks, open spaces, or roadside plantings. For such institutional clients, you will typically be able to space plants properly, allowing them to achieve their full growth without conflicting with other plants.

PLANTING THE MIXED BED

Because so many different plant types are being used and all have their own growth rate, properly planning the mixed bed in advance can be particularly challenging. For example, perennials and grasses may take two to three years to reach their mature size, whereas shrubs take much longer—depending on the species, anywhere from five to ten years. Using the culturally correct planting technique may leave large gaps between plants in the short term, exposing bare mulch areas to drying winds and invasive weeds. Overplanting, on the other hand, will necessitate thinning or cutting back after several years to minimize overcrowding and competition for plant nutrients.

To give plants time to mature together soundly, you may find it necessary to install "temporary plantings" in the composition. Taking this interim step means "filling in the gaps" with other plants to reduce the amount of bare bed space, then removing them as they begin to invade the permanent plantings, or as the permanent plants themselves fill out. Annuals, tender perennials, biennials, and seasonal bulbs may be planted in this way to provide an immediate effect. Particularly useful are those plants that have short life spans. Not only do they serve to improve the aesthetic on an immediate basis, but they also help to suppress unwanted growth, such as weeds. Temporary plantings are generally only practical, however, when the time and resources are available to remove or thin them out when it's time to do so.

Unfortunately, there are no hard-and-fast rules for figuring out plant-spacing requirements. But there are some guidelines you can follow based on three distinct objectives—two of a horticultural nature, the other aesthetically based:

▷ The first horticultural objective is to provide adequate space for a plant's relative mature spread. Essentially, the plant is allowed sufficient space to mature to a moderate stage before it touches another neighboring plant. As the plant continues to grow, the branching pattern of the neighboring plants intertwine with it to form a solid growing mass. This, as we have referred to earlier, is how "massing" of plants is achieved.

▷ The second horticultural objective is to provide enough space for a plant to establish a complete mature spread pattern independent of other plantings. Plants are positioned to never touch—there will always be space between them allowing the individual characteristics of each to be displayed.

▷ The aesthetically based objective is usually client- or design-driven, specifically determined by the time frame during which the composition is expected to *appear* mature. In these situations, plants are planted close together with the intent being that a solid mass will form in a relatively short period of time. This is especially useful when, as just described above, a temporary planting is being installed as a stopgap measure, or when the client wants a composition to take immediate effect.

These approaches can and often do conflict with one another. As already noted, plant spacing based on mature growth patterns often results in a composition that appears spotty in the short term, with noticeable gaps between plants; and planting close together for immediate effect usually results in overcrowding, and requires more maintenance. Sometimes a combination of the two is needed. What's a designer to do?

As a starting point, you can use a plant's height as well as its type to estimate the mature spread. A fast-growing ground cover, for example, needs to be spaced differently from a fast-growing medium shrub. A plant's mode of spread also affects the time it takes to mature and cover a defined area. With these points in mind, and in full recognition that every situation will be different, you can use the Plant Spacing Guidelines chart at right as a general guide. Note the following about the chart:

▷ It is organized by plant type and size (lowest- and smallest-growing to largest material) and, generally, from fastest- to slowest-growing. Smaller materials knit the fastest; the largest materials take more time to mature.

▷ The spacing noted provides for a relatively close-knit appearance within five to eight years—but variations in each category must be assumed.

▷ Plant species type, soil conditions, and environmental conditions also affect the vigor of spread, as already mentioned. Within each category, less vigorous species and those planted in less than ideal environmental conditions should be spaced more closely together.

You can modify this Plant Spacing Guidelines chart according to the desired time frame for achieving a specified level of maturity in your composition. Again, the general rule of thumb is that when the design objective is to produce an "instant landscape," you will decrease spacing. When you have more time or are planning for longer time-horizon project types, you will

Plant Spacing Guidelines

PLANT TYPE	SPACING (ON CENTER: O.C.)
Ground covers	6–12"
Annuals	8–15"
Compact herbaceous plants	12–18"
Upright and vigorous herbaceous plants	15–30"
Low ornamental grasses	24–30"
Tall ornamental grasses	36–42"
Low-spreading shrubs	36–48"
Small shrubs	2–3'
Medium shrubs	4–5'
Tall shrubs	6–8'
Small flowering trees	12–15'
Shade trees	30–45'
Evergreen trees	14–16'

increase spacing. The first category typically includes projects such as model homes, plant or garden shows, or private residences; the second category includes public parks, grand estates, corporate headquarters, or college campuses.

Exploiting Plant Genetics

Plant genetics determine growth rates and patterns and expected life span. These, of course, vary widely from plant type to plant type and species to species. In a mixed composition you will seek to exploit these genetic variations to achieve the objectives of each project you work on. For planning purposes, then, it is imperative that you fully understand the growth characteristics of each plant type during every stage of its life cycle, as well as throughout the growing season.

Conclusion

To properly plan for the future, which is a major component of the planting design process, you must learn as much as you can about how a plant grows and responds to various environmental factors. Professional experience, books, and databases can provide a baseline of this information, but there will always be unknowns on every project. Site-specific conditions will affect stated averages one way or another—for example, plants located in the direct line of strong winds, or in nutrient-deficient soils, or in areas with too much sun or any other less-than-ideal conditions. In more intensively managed landscapes, plant growth rates can be controlled to a certain degree by improving the soil, fertilizing, or pruning; but, remember, this level of upkeep is a luxury. Maintenance can, in fact, break any average, and so must be addressed with the client before any plant selection takes place.

10 | Completing the Process: Selecting the Plants

FINALLY, IT IS TIME TO SELECT THE PLANTS you will include in your composition, ensuring that they meet both the aesthetic requirements of the design and the cultural requirements of the site, as well as consider the maintenance requirements. You've analyzed the site, studied the design framework in terms of the aesthetics, and chosen a design character or theme—you're now in a position to identify the plants that meet these criteria. By waiting until the end of the process to select the plants, you remove any bias you might have for or against a particular plant. This enables you to focus pragmatically on the design objectives and cultural requirements. You also now have the flexibility to continue to modify the plant characteristics based on the aesthetic and functional criteria.

Selecting Plants

At this point, the functional and cultural criteria are set; they will not change on a given site. However, during the selection process you probably will return to the original design composition to modify the aesthetic criteria. You want to leave yourself open to options, by trying out various plants that might be appropriate for each area of the planting composition. Perhaps another, possibly more pleasing, aesthetic characteristic than you originally anticipated will make itself known to you. It's rarely a good idea to identify only one plant for a particular area. Rather, based on the aesthetic criteria, your goal should be to narrow the selection to a few plants that match those characteristics.

The following lists highlight some of the essential criteria that you should identify for each plant or planting area before you make your final selection:

PLANT CHARACTERISTIC

Plant type (perennial, shrub, small tree, etc.)

Plant form

Mature height and spread

Texture

Evergreen or deciduous

FUNCTIONAL CRITERIA

Structural plant   Focal point

Theme plant   Screen

Filler plant

AESTHETIC CRITERIA

Foliage type   Berries or fruit

Foliage color   Fall color

Flower color   Seasonal interest

Ornamental bark, twigs, stems

CULTURAL CRITERIA

Soil pH   Hardiness zone

Soil type (clay, sand, loam, etc.)   Water availability and soil moisture

Soil quality (drainage, organic   Sun and wind exposure
matter, nutrient content, etc.)

Add to these lists as you go, incorporating your personal knowledge and information gleaned from reference books that provide tables or charts on various conditions, functions, and aesthetic qualities. Keep in mind that these criteria will be added gradually as the design process evolves. For example, when working in abstract elevation during the early stages of the planning process, you will be concerned only with the plant characteristics—the plant's type, form, mature height and spread, etc. In plan view, you will then begin to add functional and aesthetic criteria. (At this point, it is imperative to have a drawing that includes the entire area of the composition under design, to illustrate the overall context in which plant decisions will be made.)

Based on your short list of criteria, you will overlay the cultural requirements to narrow further the possibilities: this will lead to just a few choice plants that meet the criteria. Then, when it comes time to make the final selection of species and cultivar, you can refer to nursery catalogs to ensure that the plants you have chosen are available.

Resist the urge to use the latest and greatest cultivars, as they generally have not yet been tested in the landscape. For long-lasting effect, favor those that are the most durable, hardy, and proven.

As your design skills develop, you will broaden your palette of plant materials, and skip or merge steps in the process. As you are better able to visualize your compositions in plan view, you may, for example, work in elevation only for the more specialized areas. And your increasing experience and knowledge of plants and regions also confers upon you the right to narrow your palette based on personal preferences or taste.

Maintaining the Composition

The long-term vitality and beauty of the mixed plantings you design are contingent upon your knowledge of which plant combinations will be compatible throughout the lifetime of the composition. From the beginning of the design process, you must understand how growth and maintenance issues will affect each and every plant type and plant association in the composition.

We've emphasized throughout the book the absolute necessity of factoring in maintenance considerations from the earliest stages of design. This is a critical component to the success of your work. As you know by now, a composition that is destined to receive minimal care after installation will be dramatically different from one designed to receive regular care. But between those two extremes are a number of subsets. For example, does "regular" mean daily, weekly, biweekly, or monthly? Unfortunately, there is much to say about this topic that is beyond the scope of this book, therefore, this discussion is limited to the most important areas of maintenance to consider during the design stage.

The first point is that some type of regular maintenance will be needed regardless of the complexity of the design and the makeup of plant types in the composition, though frequency and levels will be different. Perennials decline if not divided, or they spread out and begin to take over less-vigorous neighboring plants. Shrubs grow thick with woody growth, sucker and spread, or die back. Trees rise and spread their canopy, and their lower limbs may become intertwined with shrubbery. Weeds take advantage of small openings in the ground layer and spread among other plants. Lawns infiltrate bed edges.

To counter these and other evolving changes, a regimen of care appropriate to the compositional mix will have to be instituted, to include one or more of the following: weeding, cultivating, mulching, pruning and training, staking, deadheading, and division.

WEEDING

A critical component in bed care is weeding—the removal of undesirable plants that compete for plant nutrients, water, and root space. Weeds also may harbor undesirable insects and diseases.

Weeds can very quickly establish themselves. They then take over a planting—to the detriment of the other plantings—which they kill or maim (especially perennials and groundcovers), eventually leaving gaps in the composition. For all these reasons, as well as the simple fact that weeds are generally considered an eyesore, a regular weeding program should be established, especially during plant establishment and the first few years in the life of a composition. Weeding can be done by hand or with herbicides, or the plants can be suppressed with mulches.

CULTIVATING

Cultivation is a method of controlling small, recently emerged grassy and broad-leaved weeds, and is generally undertaken for more intensively planted compositions, especially where a number of herbaceous materials have been used. This form of maintenance is usually reserved for gardens, as opposed to landscape-type beds.

The goal of cultivation is to turn the weeds under or loosen them before they have a chance to establish their root systems or before they set seed. This breaks up the crust of the soil, enhancing aeration and providing for greater water penetration. Generally, cultivation must be done every several weeks, or as necessary based on the number of recently sprouted weeds and the type of composition.

MULCHING

Mulching is an alternative approach to cultivation used to suppress weeds and to reduce the loss of water from bare soil. Mulch also moderates soil temperature, preserves surface soil structure, adds nutrients to the soil, and prevents mud-splattering on foliage and flowers. The best mulches are those that are biodegradable and can be absorbed into the soil after the first full year or during the succeeding year. Mulches in this category include composted leaf mold, mushroom manure, pine straw, or double-shredded hardwood bark. On larger or commercial plantings, double-shredded hardwood bark mulch provides the best coverage, as it does not break down as fast as some of the others. Mulch should be applied in a two- to three-inch layer.

Beware overmulching around the bases or crowns of plants, particularly herbaceous materials, because the mulch will trap moisture and cause the crowns to rot. Take special care to use mulches that are sufficiently decomposed, since "green" mulches rob the soil and neighboring plants of necessary nitrogen during decomposition.

PRUNING AND TRAINING

The *American Horticultural Society Manual on Pruning and Training*, edited by Christopher Brickell (1996), states that, "At the simplest level, the purpose of pruning and training is to make sure that plants are as healthy and as vigorous as possible, free from structural weakness, and at the least risk of being infected by disease." Pruning, training, or cutting back can be reduced to a certain extent if the chosen plants are allowed to grow to the appropriate mature size for their position in the bed and are spaced correctly, based on their mature spread.

In the absence of this type of maintenance, vigorous, invasive, spreading, or especially colonizing plants can quickly overrun their intended space and demand immediate attention, putting to risk the design intent. Obviously, then, opting not to use plants that have these growth characteristics will help reduce maintenance. Even for those more intensively planted compositions, when plants with vigorous growth habits are feasible, their use should be a carefully considered decision, made only after the required level of maintenance has been ascertained.

Pruning and training are commonly accepted practices to assist in controlling these plantings. Not only can pruning improve the natural appearance of a plant, it can also enhance ornamental features such as flowers, foliage, and sculptural appearance. Pruning is also a management tool in that it can help to restrict a plant's size or maintain it within a desired size range. Training utilizes thinning and pruning techniques to "shape" or "mold" a plant to a desired shape, configuration, or size. That said, if you choose the right plant for the situation in the first place, you can minimize the need to prune, other than as needed for damage control due to frost, disease, or wind, or for structural maintenance and repair.

STAKING

Staking is generally necessary only for plants in the perennial and climber categories. If certain plants, such as delphinium, gladiolus, or hollyhocks, are not staked or do not have a supporting neighbor to lean on, they will collapse under their own weight, becoming useless—not to mention unattractive. For design purposes, it is wise, where possible, either to choose plants that are self-supporting—thereby reducing the need for labor-intensive staking practices—or to pair up plants that support one another.

Pea staking, hoop staking, brush staking, and ties are all alternative methods of this maintenance procedure, which helps to support plants in their upright form. The appropriateness of each method will be dependent on the particular growth habit of the plant needing support. If done correctly, staking is invisible, but this requires skill and time.

DEADHEADING

Deadheading, the act of removing spent flower heads, is required on many plants to extend their flowering periods and generally keep the plants looking "clean." After a plant has been deadheaded, the energy that would otherwise be used for seed production is redirected toward new flower production. Thus, deadheading extends the productive life of the plant from days to weeks, depending on the species.

For maintenance reasons, it is best to select and use plants that are self-deadheading or whose performance does not require this practice.

DIVISION

Plant division is generally associated with perennials and grasses. As these plant types grow from year to year they expand circumferentially around the base and root mass, dying out in the center as soil resources in the root mass become depleted and the active roots move outward. Slowly, the entire plant becomes weakened.

Division can counter this natural progression and rejuvenate the plant. After several years' growth, plants must be lifted so that their root masses can be divided. Depending on the species, certain plants require division more frequently than others in order to maintain their best appearance, so it is helpful to understand the plants that fall into this category. And when you include such plants in a composition, be sure to make note of this maintenance requirement and to ensure the long-term health of the plants.

Conclusion

A definitive and well-considered design process is the basis for developing successful mixed planting compositions. Of course, a wide range of variables come into play, some under the control of the designer, others not. Whether planning for a small "postage stamp" garden or a large campus or park landscape, designers who use the mixed approach can take advantage of a vast array of available plant types to extend the length of display across multiple seasons.

But simply assembling a wide range of plant types does not necessarily make a beautiful and harmonious composition. To achieve these goals requires, first and foremost, that the designer understand the *principles of art*, as this form of planting design, more than any other, is truly an art form. Second, as with any art form, the designer must develop the skills that will enable him or her to maximize the possible effects of combining the various forms, textures, and colors of plant life.

Nan Fairbrother in *The Nature of Landscape Design: As Art Form, A Craft, A Social Necessity* (1974) said that, "Form, color, texture, and shape are characteristic features of the material used, and indiscriminate mixtures cancel each other out like the music of a fairground, or two radios playing together. When the mixture is not indiscriminate, some of the subtlest and most satisfying effects are produced by combinations of plants with different growth patterns, which enhance each other like the superimposed themes of contrapuntal music." As Gertrude Jekyll said, it is like painting a living canvas.

But unlike a canvas, a planting composition is not something to just be looked at; it is a three-dimensional work of art that is meant to be *experienced*. The *architectural* component of planting design, whereby plants are installed to create a framework of spaces—requires in-depth knowledge of the structural characteristics of plants. A designer, therefore, must under-stand how to use plants in order to "give meaningful form to space and how their qualities can be used to enrich those spaces," as Nick Robinson described in *The Planting Design Handbook* (1992). Each plant "room" can be further developed to express a distinct character or mood.

As important to the designer as the planting design's architectural component is the need to fully comprehend the *horticultural* and *cultural* aspects of plants. Keeping in mind that the fundamental concept behind the success of the mixed planting composition is to ensure interest throughout the six seasonal periods defined earlier in Chapter 8 (page 218), the designer must be aware of how each and every plant grows and evolves throughout the year, including: what a plant's most prominent characteristics are, and when they are displayed; when its down period is; and how to complement, accent, and cover for any weaknesses. Equally important is to learn the existing soil, light, and moisture conditions; otherwise it will be impossible to select the specimens best suited to the environment under development.

In order to succeed, the designer must make a commitment to fine-tuning his or her observation skills—paying attention throughout the seasons, and noting how each plant responds to the environment and evolves over its life span. The designer must never forget that creating mixed compositions is as much about aesthetics as it is about horticulture, and as much about art as it is about architecture.

To design effectively takes the technical skill of the horticulturist, the ecological skill of the scientist, the building skills of the architect, and the creative vision of the artist (Robinson 1992). It's a tall order, but the rewards are just as great, in the form of unlimited opportunities for creative expression with plants.

Bibliography

Alexander, Christopher, 1979. *The Timeless Way of Building*. New York: Oxford University Press.

Austin, Sandra, 1998. *Color in Garden Design*. Newtown, CT: The Taunton Press.

Baige, Russell J. 1992. *The Herbaceous Perennial Garden*. College Park, MD: Maryland Cooperative Extension Service, Maryland Master Gardener Module.

Billington, Jill, 1997. *Planting Companions*. London: Ryland Peters & Small.

Bird, Richard, 2002. *Foliage Gardens: Instant Reference to More Than 250 Plants*. London: Cassell & Co.

Bisgrove, Richard, 1992. *The Gardens of Gertrude Jekyll*. London: Frances Lincoln Limited.

Booth, Norman K., 1983. *Basic Elements of Landscape Architectural Design*. Prospect Heights, IL: Waveland Press, Inc.

Booth, Norman K., and James Hiss, 1991. *Residential Landscape Architecture: Design Process for the Private Residence*. Englewood Cliffs, NJ: Prentice-Hall, Inc.

Brickell, Christopher Ed., 1996. *The American Horticultural Society Pruning and Training: A Fully Illustrated Plant-by-Plant Manual*. New York: Dorling Kindersley.

Brookes, John, 1991. *The Book of Garden Design*. New York: Macmillan Publishing Company.

Challis, Myles, 1992. *Large-Leaved Perennials*. London: Ward Lock Limited.

Clouston, Brian, ed. 1977. *Landscape Design with Plants*. London: William Heinemann Ltd.

Doyle, Michael E., 1981. *Color Drawing*. New York: Van Nostrand Reinhold Company.

Fairbrother, Nan, 1974. *The Nature of Landscape Design: As Art Form, A Craft, A Social Necessity*. New York: Alfred A. Knopf, Inc.

Fichner-Rathus, Lois, 1986. *Understanding Art*. Englewood Cliffs, NJ: Prentice-Hall.

Gent, Lucy, 1995. *Great Planting*. London: Ward Lock.

Grant, John A., and Carol L. Grant, 1954. *Planting Design Illustrated*. Seattle, WA: University of Washington Press.

Graves, Michael, ed. Nicholas, Karen; Burke, Lisa; Burke, Patrick; Abrams, Janet, 1995. *Michael Graves: Buildings and Projects 1990–1994*. New York: Rizzoli International Publications, Inc.

Grimm, William Carey, 1957. *The Book of Trees*. Harrisburg, PA: The Stackpole Company.

Hackett, Brian, 1979. *Planting Design*. New York: McGraw-Hill Company.

Harper, Pamela J., 1991. *Designing with Perennials*. New York: Macmillan Publishing Company.

Hightshoe, Gary L., 1988. *Native Trees, Shrubs, and Vines for Urban and Rural America*. New York: Van Nostrand Reinhold.

Hobhouse, Penelope, 1991. *Color in Your Garden*. Boston: Little, Brown and Company.

Jakobson, Preben, 1977. *Shrubs and Groundcover* in Clouston, B. (ed). *Landscape Design with Plants*. London: Heinemann.

Jekyll, Gertrude, 1908. *Colour in the Flower Garden*. London: Country Life LTD/George Newnes Ltd.

Johnson, Hugh, 1979. *The Principles of Gardening: The Classic Guide to the Gardener's Art*. New York: Simon & Schuster, Inc.

Joyce, David, 2001. *Foliage: Dramatic and Subtle Leaves for the Garden*. North Pomfret, VT: Trafalgar Square Publishing.

Kingsbury, Noel, 1997. *Design and Plant a Mixed Border*. London: Ward Lock.

Kingsbury, Noel, 2000. *Bold Plants: Using Architectural and Exotic Plants to Create Visual Impact in the Garden*. Singapore: Periplus Editions (HK) Ltd.

Lauer, David A., 1979. *Design Basics*, 2nd ed. New York: Holt, Rinehart and Winston.

Linn, Mike, 1993. *Drawing and Designing with Confidence.* New York: Van Nostrand Reinhold.

Lloyd, Christopher, 1986. *The Mixed Border—The Royal Horticultural Society: A Wisley Handbook.* London: Cassell Educational Limited.

Lloyd, Christopher, 1999. *Gardening Year.* London: Frances Lincoln Limited.

Lloyd, Christopher, 2001. *Colour for Adventurous Gardeners.* London: BBC Worldwide Ltd.

Lloyd, Christopher, 2005. *Succession Planting for Adventurous Gardeners.* London: BBC Worldwide Ltd.

Lynch, Kevin and Gary Hack, 1989. *Site Planning*, 3rd ed. Cambridge, MA: The MIT Press.

Martin, Edward C., 1983. *Landscape Plants in Design: A Photographic Guide.* Westport, CT: AVI Publishing Company, Inc.

Montero, Marta Iris, 2001. *Roberto Burle Marx: The Lyrical Landscape.* Berkeley, CA: University of California Press.

Nelson, William, R., 1985. *Planting Design: A Manual of Theory and Practice.* (2nd ed.) Champaign, IL: Stipes Publishing Company.

Ondra, Nancy J., 2002. *Grasses: Versatile Partners for Uncommon Garden Design.* North Adams, MA: Storey Books.

Ortloff, H. Stuart, and Henry B. Raymore, 1951. *Color and Design for Every Garden.* New York: M. Barrows and Company, Inc.

Ortloff, H. Stuart, and Henry B. Raymore, 1959. *The Book of Landscape Design.* New York: M. Barrows and Company, Inc.

Piper, David, ed. 1986. *The Illustrated Library of Art—History Appreciation and Tradition.* ed. Jack Tresidder. New York: Portland House.

Raven, Sara, 1999. *The Bold and Brilliant Garden.* London: Francis Lincoln Ltd.

Robinson, Florence Bell, 1940. *Planting Design.* Champaign, IL: The Garrard Press.

Robinson, Nick, 1992. *The Planting Design Handbook.* Aldershot, Hampshire, England: Ashgate Publishing Limited.

Robinson, William, 1933. *The English Flower Garden* (15th ed.). London: J. Murray.

Rutledge, Albert J., 1985. *A Visual Approach to Park Design.* New York: John Wiley and Sons, Inc.

Sert, Jose Luis, 1942. *Can Our Cities Survive?* Cambridge, MA: Harvard University Press.

Simonds, John Ormsbee, 1983. *Landscape Architecture: A Manual of Site Planning and Design*, 2nd ed. New York: McGraw-Hill Book Company.

Summerson, John, 1980. *The Classical Language of Architecture.* New York: Thames and Hudson, Inc.

Sutter, Anne Bernat, 1967. *New Approach to Design Principles: A Comprehensive Analysis of Design Elements and Principles in Floral Design.* St. Louis, MO: Allied Printing Co.

Verey, Rosemary, 1990. *The Art of Planting.* London: Little Brown and Company.

Walker, Theodore, D., 1985. *Planting Design.* Mesa, AZ: PDA Publishers Corporation.

Wyman, Donald, 1977. *Shrubs and Vines for American Gardens*, 5th ed. New York: Macmillan Publishing Co., Inc.

Index